ALLEN LANE

ANOTHER SORT OF FREEDOM

Gurcharan Das is a renowned author, commentator and thought leader. He is the author of two bestsellers, *India Unbound* and *The Difficulty of Being Good*, which are volumes one and two of a trilogy on life's goals, of which *Kama: The Riddle of Desire* is the third. His other literary works include a novel, *A Fine Family*, a collection of plays for the theatre, *Three Plays*, and a book of essays, *The Elephant Paradigm*. His book *India Grows at Night* was on the *Financial Times*' list of best books of 2013. He is general editor for Penguin's multivolume Story of Indian Business series. He studied philosophy at Harvard University and was awarded the Phi Beta Kappa for 'high attainment in liberal scholarship'. He was CEO, Procter & Gamble India, before he became a full-time writer. He writes a regular column for the *Times of India*, and occasional pieces for the *Financial Times*, *Foreign Affairs* and *New York Times*. He lives with his wife in Delhi.

PRAISE FOR THE BOOK

'Gurcharan Das is a man of many parts: business leader, author, playwright, traveller, student and modern-day gadfly. In this frank, funny, thoughtful—sometimes wistful—memoir, he struggles to come to terms with life. It begins with his early memories of Partition's horrors and takes us through an undergraduate life at Harvard, where he studied with the philosopher John Rawls, and his time as a victim of the Licence Raj in India; and it ends in a search for a natural moksha. Gurcharan's life is never dull, mirroring in many ways the story of independent India. Truly a life well lived!'— Raghuram Rajan

'It's a super book! An honest, riveting tale that will live long on bookshelves and in libraries. Thank you, Gurcharan Das, for a sheaf of whole grain in a market of chaff in an age of fakery'—Gopalkrishna Gandhi

'Combining candour, thoughtful introspection and wry humour, Gurcharan Das's *Another Sort of Freedom* is a memoir with a difference. Affecting, disarming and occasionally provocative—just like the man himself'—Shashi Tharoor

'A gracious invitation into the history-spanning, freewheeling inner life of an intellectual polymath and worldly entrepreneur, an admirer of life's pleasures and searcher into its spiritual mysteries'—Sunil Khilnani

'A great book, beautifully written! A story told with a lightness of touch and unflinching honesty, *Another Sort of Freedom* is an eventful memoir that takes us on an epic journey. We encounter historical landmarks, bustling cities of the East and West, and public figures, including politicians and corporate leaders. But at the centre is his rich, private sphere with its ups and downs, loves and losses, successes and failures'—Nandan Nilekani

'A lovely book! Here is a great account of the many-splendoured life of Gurcharan Das. A happy childhood in Punjab before Partition; then early years of hope in Nehru's India, and schooling in America and Harvard; next, up the corporate ladder in multinationals during Indira Gandhi's Licence Raj; returning home in the age of liberalization to become a commentator and bestselling author, when he plunges into the study of the ancient *purusharthas*—dharma, artha, kama. The narrative culminates in a restless search in his inner self towards a novel understanding of moksha. Read this book and be released from your cares and worries!'—Meghnad Desai

'*Another Sort of Freedom* is a revelation. It uncovers the person behind the CEO who quit at the acme of a business career to become a hugely successful writer and public intellectual. It shows a man who has struggled to live an examined, meaningful life on his own terms, but with admirable self-awareness of threats that might derail his project for "making a life", inspired by his father, alongside the perils of becoming a "dancing star" in his mother's eyes. All this endows the young boy with a lifelong self-confidence, but he is mindful how easily it can tip over into excessive self-regard, the *ahamkara* of vanity. A deeply moving, thoughtful and courageous book'—Sudhir Kakar

'*Another Sort of Freedom* is a delightful memoir, conjuring up lost worlds and sensibilities. It is an unassuming self-portrait of a wonderful writer, full of incidental insights'—Pratap Bhanu Mehta

'Just the right sort of memoir: even-handed, reflective, witty, irreverent and wholly entertaining. This is a life lived well, productively and enviably well. Gurcharan Das chronicles his personal journey, also tells the story of a generation finding its feet and character in a newborn nation. I expected to find it interesting, but I wasn't prepared to enjoy it as much as I did'—Manu S. Pillai

'Aside from his avatars as philosopher and commentator, Gurcharan Das is a wonderful storyteller. He's at his best here, telling his own story with both humour and acuity'—Arshia Sattar

ANOTHER SORT OF FREEDOM

A Memoir

GURCHARAN DAS

PENGUIN
ALLEN
LANE

An imprint of Penguin Random House

ALLEN LANE

USA | Canada | UK | Ireland | Australia
New Zealand | India | South Africa | China | Singapore

Allen Lane is part of the Penguin Random House group of companies
whose addresses can be found at global.penguinrandomhouse.com

Published by Penguin Random House India Pvt. Ltd
4th Floor, Capital Tower 1, MG Road,
Gurugram 122 002, Haryana, India

First published in Allen Lane by Penguin Random House India 2023

ISBN 9780143465775

Typeset in Adobe Garamond Pro by MAP Systems, Bengaluru, India

www.penguin.co.in

To the happy few who don't take themselves too seriously

Contents

Introduction

Live Lightly, Not like a Feather but like a Bird

'A book is the product of a different self from the one we manifest in our habits, in society, in our vices. If we mean to try to understand this self it is only in our inmost depths, by endeavouring to reconstruct it, that the quest can be achieved.'

—Marcel Proust

In writing a memoir, you depend on memory, which connects you to your former selves. Your imagination then sews these selves together with events, often unrelated, to create a pattern that makes some sort of sense to your present self. It is a natural process in the cultivation of your consciousness.

I have discovered that reliving one's life is even better than living it. The pattern, most persistent, in my relived life is of an unconscious struggle to break free from expectations. These expectations arose from my family, friends and colleagues, and tended to become oppressive. The most tyrannical ones did not originate from without. They sprang from the demons of my ego—from such things as vanity, wanting to be a somebody—resulting in a desire for premium treatment. Occasionally, I managed to liberate myself from these burdens, and when I did I experienced a certain kind of freedom, expressed by the ancient Sanskrit word *moksha*.

Moksha means liberation. Liberation from what? For the religious, it is freedom from desire, from the bondage of the cycle of birth and rebirth, to which my mystic father had aspired. Since I don't know if there is an afterlife, or a soul or God, I shied away from this word, until one morning. Leafing through my Monier-Williams Sanskrit–English dictionary, I discovered that moksha's original meaning was simply to be free. It offered many examples: a horse without a harness; a pearl emerging from an oyster shell; a prisoner released from jail. I could identify with this secular moksha. And if there is a theme in my life, it is of a struggle for this sort of freedom. I think of myself, however, not as a horse without a harness but a horse 'easy in its harness', as Robert Frost puts it. Civilized living entails, after all, limits to absolute freedom.

The best moments of my life have been defined by moksha, producing in me a spirit of lightness. Another nice Sanskrit word, *laghima*, connotes the experience of living lightly—not like a feather but like a bird. I have often experienced it when I take my work, not myself, seriously. The playful Hindu gods created the world in a spirit of lightness—it's called *leela*, divine play—reminding humans not to take themselves too seriously.

This book brings to a close a quarter of a century's search for a rich, flourishing life based on the classical Indian ideal of life's four goals, *purusharthas*. Prior to this book, I had explored the first three. *India Unbound* was the first—on the aim of *artha* or material well-being. In my second book, *The Difficulty of Being Good*, I examined the goal of dharma, moral well-being, via a contemporary meditation on the ancient epic the Mahabharata. My previous book, *The Riddle of Desire*, was a biography of kama, the third goal of desire and pleasure. And finally, this book, although a memoir, has turned out to be about the fourth aim, of moksha, offering an all-natural, non-religious, non-transcendental view of freedom.

Each volume in the quartet on the aims of life has investigated a different source of human happiness. I have concluded, much like Aristotle, that the pursuit of multiple goals is far better, more human and less dangerous than chasing a single, paramount goal. The goals are sometimes in conflict—dharma, for example, is a duty to another, while kama is a duty to oneself. A successful life needs to find a balance between them. We need to reach a state of equanimity in this regard, in order to live a harmonious life.

This book is thus a memoir, not an autobiography. A memoir is a collection of memories, reflecting on specific themes, touchstone moments, turning points in one's life, while providing an intimate narrative about private and public events that occurred along the way. An autobiography is simply the story of a life, presenting the facts in a chronological manner from the beginning to the end.

What do I have in common with the two-and-a-half-year-old child whose photograph my mother used to keep adoringly on her mantelpiece? Nothing, except that I happen to be the same person. I was born in Lyallpur, Punjab, during World War II, when Hitler, Churchill and Hirohito were bashing everyone about. How to remember the daft things I did at four when I can't even remember what I said yesterday? Fortunately, my mother kept a diary—a habit she'd picked up during her time in Kinnaird College, Lahore. The first reference to me occurs soon after I was born: 'this is a restless baby'; by age two, I have become 'a difficult child'; by four, she is calling me a 'troublemaker'. One day I discovered that I could run, and I have been running ever since. It was the happiest of childhoods, until the partition of India, when our world collapsed. The lunacy of Partition—people ready to kill cheerfully in the name of their God—initiated me early into the modern idea of the absurd.

Just as in living my life I had to choose which path to take, so in reliving it, I have had to select memories from my life, painfully aware of what I've left out. When you select, the result is a bit of invention, and it raises the question of truth. Hence they say, there's little difference between fiction and non-fiction—except that fiction has to make sense. Moreover, one's memory tends to flatter. One is inclined to choose the interesting rather than the boring bits. Since no one wants to write a boring book, this risks making your life more interesting than it was. So, it is best include the bad and the good. There is no such thing as clean, unalloyed truth—there are only unreliable memories. In the end, no can ever be sure about what really happened.

The other problem I struggled with was how much to focus on my family. Clearly, my parents were important influences, and they have got their due. So has my sister—whose tragic life has left me with scars. My wife, however, is a private person, who was extremely wary of this project. In deference to her, I have tried keep much of our conjugal life private. She appears, thus, to be a shadowy figure at times, except in the early scenes, when we met, got married and began our life together. I have adopted the same reticence when it comes to our children. Discretion has made me avoid using names in some cases. In other instances, I have actually changed the name to protect the person. Justice also demands that some things not be told.

Every generation is happy to celebrate its victories but glosses over its failures. A memoir can help make amends. The failures of my generation are many. We have still not come to terms with India's partition, failing to bring to closure the ghastliest event of our lives. Too many of us stepped unthinkingly into the shoes of the departing 'white sahibs' at Independence and didn't bother to reform colonial institutions or fashion a new modernity truer to the spirit of a free nation. We lost our economic freedom when we adopted Fabian socialism—it turned into an ugly 'licence, permit, inspector raj', which persisted for too long, thereby sacrificing two generations to lost opportunities. We also adopted a thoughtless form of secularism, refusing to have an honest conversation with tradition. This has paved the way for the regrettable rise of Hindu nationalism. Some of these failures could have been mitigated had we succeeded in giving a decent education to our children. It would have helped, for example, to integrate the English language in a natural, organic way into Indian life. This failure resulted in English speakers becoming an elite caste that has monopolized power, wealth and privilege over the past seventy-five years while condemning the vast majority to be deaf in their own land. These disappointments, in the end, do cast a shadow over an otherwise reasonably happy life.

A few years ago, an interviewer from the BBC asked me about the major influences that had formed me. I didn't give her a coherent answer, and the question lingered. This book has allowed me to reflect on this, but instead of answers there are more questions. How much do I owe to the wonder that was India? How much to the magnificent humanism of the modern West? I became a classical liberal not from reading works of the eighteenth-century Enlightenment but from the lacerating personal experiences of the Licence Raj. I'm not sure how the son of a deeply spiritual father ended up as an agnostic. Nor can I say how much of the globetrotting multinational manager remains in me. At the end of my travels, I find that I have a Western mind and an Indian heart—an odd mixture of a British empiricist's brain and an Indian Buddhist's soul.

Of one thing I'm sure: I cannot live anywhere else except in the chaotic, magical world of our subcontinent.

There are many reasons to write a memoir. Some people hope to appear considerable in the eyes of their friends. Others, to draw attention to their nicer side, so that friends will forget their embarrassing moments, including the practical jokes they played on them. Still others, to get even with their enemies—not by saying nasty things about them but by saying nicer things about oneself. In my case, the memoir has helped me to understand myself. It is only when I began to relive my life that I discovered the persistent leitmotif of moksha and laghima. This refrain has made me aware of the many demeaning human bondages in my life, mostly of my own making. The continuing struggle to be free of them remains a work in progress towards a certain sort of freedom. In the end, a memoir is a story, and what is the world, says the *Yoga Vasishtha*, but the impression left by a story.

1

Dancing Star

*'. . . all nature is perverse
and will not do as I wish it.'*

—Charles Darwin

I was born on 3 October 1942, although official documents claim it was a year later. The discrepancy is explained by a custom popular among Indian middle classes to lie about your age. On my uncle's advice, my reluctant parents perjured themselves on all official documents, hoping it would give their son a competitive advantage. As far as I can tell, it left me with a disadvantage—girls in school quickly lost interest in me, thinking I was too young.

World War II was raging when I was born. Hitler, Churchill, Stalin and Hirohito were bashing everyone, blowing up the world. But India was strangely quiet, addicted to peace. Throughout the murderous twentieth century, India managed to escape the world wars, and the bloody experiments of fascism and communism. When King George V laid the foundation stone for the imperial city of Delhi in 1911, the British plan was to be around for a thousand years, but Mahatma Gandhi came and busted that dream. So no one was surprised when, five years after my birth, weary Englishmen packed up and left without firing a shot, leaving

1

behind, absent-mindedly, the English language and a headache. Indians still can't make up their minds about their national language.

I was born in Lyallpur, named after the British lieutenant governor, Sir James Lyall, who insisted on adding 'B.A.' after his name. An orderly provincial town in the Punjab plains, Lyallpur came up along the Lower Chenab Canal in the last quarter of the nineteenth century. It was lined with trees and greener than other country towns, which were mostly dusty jumbles of anarchic flat-roofed brick houses. My maternal grandfather, Wazir Chand Varma, whom everyone called Bauji, had moved there a generation before my birth. In 1977, Lyallpur disappeared from history when Pakistanis changed its name to Faisalabad, after King Faisal of Saudi Arabia bribed them to embrace an extreme form of Islam.

My grandfather swore that we were 'pure'. We'd lived always in Lord Rama's land. Soon after he died, however, the science of genetics was born and broke his myth of purity. 65,000 years ago, a band of Homo sapiens had crossed over from Africa to Asia, walked along the southern Asian coast to Australia, stopping in India, where they had mixed with pre-modern humans to create the 'first Indians'. Our second ancestors came more recently, 7500 years ago, from Persia. They mixed with the locals to create the Harappans, who went on to fashion the amazing Indus Valley Civilization. A third migration came around 2000 BCE from China, but it confined itself to the north-east. A fourth lot arrived around the same time, Central Asian pastoralists from the Kazakh Steppe, who spoke an Indo–European language and mixed vigorously with the locals to create the Vedic civilization. Far from being uncontaminated, we are thoroughly mixed up, like the rest of humanity.

Surprisingly, the mixing stopped one day around the turn of the millennium, when the caste system became rigid. While the mixing continued in China, creating the homogeneous Han people, Indians went on to become so plural that an Indian village is more diverse, genetically, than entire Chinese empires. As for my caste, we are Aroras, one of two mercantile communities of Punjab. Since we lived in a border province much influenced by Islam and Sikhism, I grew up relaxed about caste. I even felt sorry for high-born Brahmins who never got the respect they deserved.

My mother acquired the habit of keeping a diary from a Christian nun who taught English literature at Kinnaird College in Lahore. I cried all the time, she wrote, and didn't let anyone sleep at night. I'd throw up as soon as I finished drinking milk and wouldn't put on weight. She was forever weighing me on the vegetable seller's scale. She would place me in a tin bowl on one side, and he'd put coloured stones in the other. Despite her urging, he refused to switch to iron weights. She'd hold her breath as he balanced the bowls with a string of jute. On the day an extra stone was added, she would reward him by buying extra quantity of vegetables and walk away with a light step. The vegetable seller now had a vested interest in my size.

Two years had gone by. My father hadn't yet found a house in Lahore. Hence, we were living at my grandfather's home in Lyallpur. She had moved here, pregnant with me, on the day news arrived confirming the mass murder of a million Jews by the Nazis at a slaughterhouse in Auschwitz. I was born on 3 October, between the first and second battles of El Alamein, when Indian soldiers helped the British to defeat Rommel and the Nazis, a major turning point in the war against the fascists.

While tragic wars raged outside, life in Punjab carried on as usual. My father had spent the early part of his career in the field, managing Punjab's canals. My parents had lived in canal colonies in the countryside. When he was finally transferred to Lahore, the capital city, my mother was delighted. She was going back to civilization. During her college days, she'd fallen in love with Lahore—its sophistication, its smartly dressed people and its intellectual conversations.

Even though it was her parents' home, my mother was frustrated in Lyallpur, longing to get away from that provincial town. There were several theories about my father's failure to find a house. Bauji claimed it was because my father was diligently absorbed in his work, busy building irrigation canals. Vade Mama, my mother's elder brother, believed that the demand for government housing in Lahore exceeded the supply. Satinder Mama, her youngest brother, declared that my father lacked influence, or 'pull', as he called it. The middle brother, Raj Mama, got it right. He called it sheer lack of common sense—my father hadn't bribed the officials and pushed his name up the waiting list. My mother's diary, however, notes that she didn't believe any of these theories. Her husband just hadn't bothered.

At age two and a half, I discovered I could run. At first it was to avoid falling, but soon running became a necessity, and I've been running ever since. To begin with, I had the run of the house. It was my kingdom.

I would survey its vast expanses and recesses daily. I would go past the jasmine and gardenia bushes in the open courtyard, into the covered veranda where the sun's rays danced as they filtered through the blinds in the afternoons while everyone slept. The rays would fall from one angle on to the wall, then enchantingly on to the carpet. I would climb up the three staircases with Vade Mama to go to the roof, and we would look down over the town spread below. Everyone in my kingdom was well disposed to me.

Before long, I could outrun my mother. As we went out, I'd run ahead of her. She'd try to keep up, but soon she'd be out of breath. To deter me, she'd give me a smack. Instead of stopping me, it had the opposite effect. Running and smacking got connected somehow in my mind, becoming a game. I would run, go whack someone, and I would laugh. My mother discovered this bizarre sport in the Company Bagh, where we went in the evenings. While she relaxed on a bench in the park, gossiping with friends, I'd be running about, smacking other kids and laughing my head off. She'd try to keep watch, but I managed to escape at times. Soon, she'd hear a cry. She would rush to the scene and apologize to the aggrieved mother with an embarrassed smile. From a 'restless baby', I had become a 'difficult child' in my mother's diary.

I must have been feeling invincible one evening, because I slapped a boy double my size. He shrieked, then reciprocated, hitting me back with impressive force. I howled. Both mothers rushed to protect their own and got into a mighty argument. There was much blaming and mayhem. A policeman joined the fray. He escorted me back home and narrated the events to my grandfather, who quickly realized their incendiary potential—my adversary was a judge's grandson at the sessions court. Raj Mama suggested that I be taken on a dog's leash henceforth; the policeman approved. Others felt I had to be disciplined. Finding that matters were getting out of hand, my mother rushed to grab me. 'Stop it! He's my dancing star!' Suddenly, the action stopped, the commotion ended, and the policeman left quietly.

No one knew quite what a 'dancing star' was, but the endearment stuck. 'At least, my grandson didn't cry,' Bauji said proudly. I showed Vade Mama where I'd been hurt; he advised me to confine my smacking to kids my size. The following evening, my mother asked if I wanted to go back to the Company Bagh. I nodded fearlessly. When we returned home, everyone looked up expectantly. Did I whack the VIP's kid? I had not. Raj Mama was disappointed. My mother confessed that I had done something worse. I had bit the bully and then laughed—it was an odd sort of laughter, she said, as though it had teeth. The bully had got scared and had run away. Satinder Mama declared that I was destined for greatness. I'd found the mantra: run a little, smack a bit, laugh a lot. After all, I was a dancing star!

We lived at 7 Kacheri Bazaar, on one of the eight roads emanating from the brick clock tower at the centre of our town. Poham Young CIE, a British colonial officer, had designed it to replicate the eight lines of the Union Jack. Our road led to the sprawling Company Bagh, named after the East India Company, where everyone went in the evenings to see, to be seen and to 'eat the air'. Our street was named after the courthouse, and not surprisingly, it was littered with houses belonging to lawyers like my grandfather. A lawyer's practice was highly competitive—to succeed, you had to board and lodge your out-of-town clients at home. And a client didn't come alone; half the village accompanied him and stayed for weeks. Villagers were happy to perjure in court in exchange for a junket to the city. In the summer, clients slept outdoors, and the number of charpoys outside a lawyer's house disclosed his status. Vade Mama would sneak out at night, count the beds before each lawyer's house and announce Bauji's market share the following morning.

Our life varied with the seasons. We'd spend the day in the open courtyard, where most of the business of the house was done. In the summers, we moved to the covered veranda. before the sun rose high. By midday, it was hot, and we went deeper inside, into the cooler rooms. Bamboo shades came down after lunch as the house prepared to sleep. We returned to the courtyard in the evening, after Mashkiya had cooled it, sprinkling water over it from his goatskin bag. We even slept in the courtyard on summer nights and watched the brilliant stars. The routine was reversed in the winter. We slept inside, came out gradually with the morning sun, spent the day moving our chairs along the sun's path and returned inside at sunset.

As he rose in the world, Bauji grew particular about his appearance. I'd watch the servant bring in his polished shoes, helping him to put them on. He then assisted him with his coat. When it was time for the turban, all conversation ceased. He made one, two and then three turns around his head with the starched white cloth, and it was done. The servant offered him a silk handkerchief and gold watch. He'd take a last look in the mirror, twirl his moustache. Feeling like a man of substance, he'd open the gate and strut off to his chambers. After he left, I'd go off to Bhabo, my grandmother. She'd be coming out of her puja room, where dozens of gods stared at me amid burning incense. Bhabo would then dress in a starched embroidered sari, ready for her morning rounds. Soon, we'd set off in our tonga, drawn by our horse, Bijli.

'Why do you have so many gods?' I asked Bhabo.

She thought for a while, and then replied, 'There are millions of gods, but there is only one God.' All the gods in her puja room, she explained, were symbols of the one God.

I was left confused.

Bhabo and I either went to celebrate a birth or cheer at an engagement or mourn a death. She always tied a band of jasmine on her wrist, and the tonga smelled of its fragrance. We'd go past Civil Lines, where our alien rulers had tried to create a bit of England but hadn't succeeded. The avenues were broader, bungalows more spacious. We passed Government House, a dazzling white building surrounded by colonnaded verandas amid acres of green lawn. It suggested the dignity of the district collector. Our carriage went along geometrically laid roads, passing the curving, gravel driveways of lesser officials of the Raj. The air here smelled different. Bhabo preferred the bustle and chaos in our part of town. She felt naked, she said, in these 'inside-out' houses where the verandas and gardens faced the outside.

To escape the bustle, my grandfather would go to the Company Bagh in the evenings. He'd sit quietly in the park, getting carried away by the fragrance of the magnolias. One evening, he smelled something different, nauseous and unpleasant. Near him, on a bed of marigold, lay a young Hindu's body. He informed the police, who explained that the boy had been killed in a fight with a Muslim gang. The boy must have come into the garden to die alone in peace. Everyone put it down as a one-off murder. They didn't realize that it was a premonition of an insanity that would soon envelop Punjab.

On our tonga journeys, Bhabo told me wondrous tales from the Mahabharata and Ramayana. She believed the heroes of the epics were her ancestors and wanted me to grow up to be like them. So, I'd be flying with Hanuman one day, readying for battle against the ten-headed Ravana; on another day, I'd be Krishna, stealing butter, stopping the flood, killing Kansa and dancing with a thousand *gopis*—all in a day's work! My mother tried to discourage Bhabo, complaining, 'He's already too restless.' But Bhabo replied, 'Heroes are supposed to be restless.' She wanted me to keep running—if I slowed, I might fall. Only once did she put the brakes on. When I was speaking too quickly, my words couldn't keep up with my thoughts, and it all came out sounding like gibberish. Since humans think twice as fast as they speak, she advised me to think twice before speaking. I must have taken her counsel, because a few months later, I went past the baby-talk stage and was speaking in complete sentences. She was sure she'd heard me say, 'Would you like a cup of tea? It will relax you.'

My grandmother was a believer in karma. I stepped on an ant one day, and it upset her. There'd be consequences, she feared. This was why, if she saw ants or spiders in her room, she'd pick them up and take them outside. She said that if I was good, I'd be rewarded; if I was bad, I'd be punished. She predicted that I would be a success in life, but I must remember that it wouldn't be my doing alone; it would be my good karma. Her crash course in karma stayed with me for years, till I became an agnostic.

As I try to make sense of my early days, I feel a certain unruliness was innate in me. It may have been an early sign of my life's script. My life would be an unending struggle for moksha, for 'liberation' from social fetters and expectations, like a horse without a harness. Perhaps, this was why I was drawn to Bijli, our horse. First thing in the morning, I'd go down and watch Suresh, the syce, grooming her. Bijli was beautiful without her harness. Suresh said that Bijli was a 'full-breed', not like the emasculated horses in the bazaar. Her ancestors came from the faraway Fergana Valley in Central Asia. He had got her from Multan, the old trading centre for horses from beyond the Hindu Kush. On special days, he'd let me feed her, lifting me up on her back and giving me a turn around the stable. I never forgot Bijli. When I went to America at age thirteen, my favourite TV serial was *The Lone Ranger*, whose brave horse, Silver, was the true hero of the show. Silver would remind me of Bijli.

My mother breathed a sigh of relief when my brother appeared in the world. He was the opposite of me: he was relaxed, slept most of the time and was content with the world. After two years of mayhem, there was the prospect of peace in the house. My youngest uncle, Satinder Mama, declared, 'After a storm, there is a calm.' But Bhabo was worried. My brother was too quiet. My eldest uncle, Vade Mama, suggested we call the doctor. But before that my middle uncle, Raj Mama, did an experiment. When no one was looking, he gave the baby a tight slap on its bum. When my brother howled, there were celebrations. Vade Mama wanted to name him Kumbhakarna, the powerful hero in the Ramayana who would sleep for six months at a time. My mother vetoed the idea. She preferred Manni, short for Mantosh.

Manni would fall asleep in unlikely places. There was panic one morning because he had disappeared. The entire family and staff were commandeered to look for him. Someone went to search in the courtyard; another was sent to the roof; the nurse combed the nursery. After an exhaustive quest, the cleaning maid found him sleeping peacefully under Raj Mama's bed. My mother believed that Raj Mama had put him there deliberately and didn't speak to him for a week.

Satinder Mama was my favourite because he had a cat. If anything went wrong in the house, everybody blamed the cat. Raj Mama grumbled that he couldn't sleep because of the 'damned Bil-li'. Bhabo murmured that it had finished the milk once again last night. Vade Mama was all for getting rid of the 'non-sleeper'. Bauji thought it unnatural for a grown man to be so fond of a cat. Raj Mama's verdict was to look for a wife for Satinder Mama—only those who couldn't get a wife ended up with a cat. Satinder Mama ignored everyone. He was deeply attached to his cat and told Bhabo if he died before his cat, she should sprinkle his eyes on her cat food—so that he'd live inside his cat. Returning from college one day, he announced he'd found a name for his cat. He was studying English literature and had come upon a new word, insomnia, 'not being able to sleep'. It was an apt name, everyone agreed, much better than the generic Bil-li. Bhabo objected, however. She couldn't pronounce 'Insomnia'. The new name was soon forgotten, and we continued with Bil-li.

One morning, Satinder Mama decided to take us to the clock tower in the main bazaar. My brother and I were thrilled. We wanted to take the cat. Satinder Mama hesitated. Suresh said, 'No cats allowed!' In the end,

Satinder Mama bribed the syce with a promise of Bengali sweets. After a search, we found a box for Bil-li, placed her in it and were off. As the carriage started, the cat grew suspicious, tried to jump out, but Satinder Mama held her firmly in the box. Then, she let out a deafening 'meow', which woke up the mongrels sleeping under the sun. They 'bow-wowed' in sympathy and began to follow us. Bi-li responded with another 'meow'. Other dogs joined the procession, cantering to the syncopated beat of 'meows' and 'bow-wows'. More dogs were roused on the way as Bil-li built up a regular fan following. Meanwhile, the horse got frightened. Bijli decided to gallop, the tonga picked up speed, and we were clip-clopping at an amazing pace. The canine procession was left in the dust.

Satinder Mama noticed that Suresh was getting nervous. He reminded him of Lyallpur's first rule of the road: anyone going slower than you is an idiot; anyone going faster is a maniac. You set the pace. When we reached the clock tower, Suresh declared that he'd never made it to the city centre in seventeen minutes. It must be some sort of a record. We went directly to the sweet shop, where Manni and I received lollies, Suresh got a box of sweets and Satinder Mama treated himself to ice cream. Bil-li got nothing. Next, we went to buy groceries. At each store, Satinder Mama rebuked the owner either for manipulating the scale or for overcharging. Having heard this refrain over the years, the shopkeepers smiled resignedly. Each commercial transaction was a challenge in our family. It was always *us*— educated, honest, tax-paying citizens—versus *them*—tax-dodging traders. Pure and simple caste prejudice. As Aroras, we were higher in the pecking order. Despite our low opinion of merchants, we loved money and were always looking to make more. Bauji was engaged secretly in moneylending, but no one was supposed to know.

Before long, it was time to return. On the way home, Bil-li was calmer. She had got used to the carriage and dozed most of the way. The return journey was uneventful until Satinder Mama spotted a familiar figure on a bicycle—a large, stout, moon-faced man, approaching on the horizon. It was Raj Mama. Without a care, he was whistling with reckless gaiety a tune from the latest Bombay talkies. As we passed, he raised his arm and gave a smile. Bil-li let out a warm meow of recognition, which roused the same pack of mongrels. Its injudicious leader did not recognize the friendly nature of the meow and connected with whoever was the closest—in this case, the bicyclist's ankle bone.

Raj Mama let out a cry. We turned around to look and saw his hands leave the handlebars as the bicycle swerved. Suresh stopped the tonga and jumped to the rescue. Raj Mama, all happy and bright a moment before, was now in the dust, a melange of arms and legs and wheels. The mongrels looked on calmly. Suresh helped to lift up our uncle, depositing him and his mangled bicycle on the tonga's front seat.

On reaching home, we recounted our adventure excitedly. Everyone came rushing down. After a few minutes, my mother noticed that something was wrong. My baby brother was missing. Satinder Mama had a look of horror on his face—we had left Manni behind in Chaura Bazaar. My mother howled and rushed to the bazaar with Satinder Mama. They found my brother asleep on the counter of the sweet shop. My mother took him in her arms, and he woke up without a fuss. My mother was happy and gave the Bania a handsome tip, telling him to distribute sweets to all the little rascals in the bazaar.

After we returned, Manni enjoyed being the centre of attention.

'You got lost?' Vade Mama asked.

'No, they got lost,' he replied.

'But you must have cried?'

'I didn't feel like it.'

'Nothing wrong in having a nice cry,' Vade Mama said. 'It scares everyone.'

The incident must have affected me, because I didn't let my brother out of my sight for the rest of the day. When we were alone in the evening, my mother overheard us talking.

'Today was a scary day?' I said.

'No, it wasn't,' my brother mumbled.

'Weren't you afraid, all alone in the bazaar?'

He shook his head.

'I'll never leave you again,' I told him.

Thus ended a memorable day in Lyallpur. My mother recorded it dutifully in her diary, which is why I'm able to reproduce it with some confidence. I mostly remember Bil-li, Bijli and my zany uncles. She wrote that I was a free, somersaulting, light-footed spirit, running and laughing a lot. 'Running is good,' Bhabo always told me. I found that no matter where you run, you just end up running into yourself. I was developing a talent for life. I didn't smack or bite anyone again, but my laughter scared my mother sometimes. She couldn't have known it then, but running and laughing would become the building blocks in nurturing laghima, 'the spirit of lightness', which would go on to define my attitude towards life.

My mother's innocent endearment, 'dancing star', was also a prognosis. I once asked my father if stars really danced. A man of science, he knew about these things. He said: as the light from a star billions of miles away races towards us, bouncing and bumping through layers of atmosphere, the light bends; the star appears to wobble before our eyes, to twinkle and to dance. I was satisfied with his explanation until I went to university. There I encountered Nietzsche, who gave an entirely different meaning to my mother's words. 'You must have chaos in your heart to give birth to a dancing star,' wrote Nietzsche. I didn't give much thought to my mother's heart, but I did wonder what sort of ups and downs life had in store for me, pushing me to take quirky, unconventional paths at different points in my life.

I had that rarest of childhoods: a happy one. While I was learning to live lightly in the cheerful cocoon at 7 Kacheri Bazaar among my wacky uncles, the world outside was turning heavy, burdened with war and tragedy. My birth in 1942 coincided with two other events that wouldn't be repeated: Gandhi's call to the British to 'Quit India' and the Great Bengal famine. The 'Quit India' movement spread like wildfire, surprising the British. They were not amused and threw the Indian nationalists in jail. They always thought Gandhi was a bit cracked. When he pulled this stunt in the middle of a world war, Churchill had to remind his fearful countrymen that Gandhi was merely a 'seditious Middle Temple lawyer posing as a half-naked fakir'. Gandhi replied that nobody could hurt him without his permission.

Although our middle-class family was not given to patriotic displays, my mother mentions in her diary that we were divided between those who hated and those who admired Churchill. Satpal Uncle's visit hardened the lines. Bhabo's firebrand nephew, a Marxist, had just returned from doing relief work in the Bengal famine, in which 3 million had died and whole villages had ceased to exist. He'd seen a man fall dead of starvation in front of his eyes. He blamed Churchill. It was a man-made tragedy, he said. Although he didn't create the famine, Churchill had diverted food meant for India's famine relief to feed the troops in Europe. British officials in India were horrified. Indians, in any case, were 'breeding like rabbits', said Churchill. Even pink-jowled Tories, sipping gin and tonic on their smug verandas, were shocked at these words. His adviser, Lord Cherwell called the famine a 'figment of the Bengali imagination'. I was, of course, too young to take sides, but the Anglophiles in our family were put to the test.

Churchill, the greatest Briton, hated Gandhi, the greatest Indian. He didn't release Gandhi from jail until he was almost dying from a fast. It would be good riddance to an enemy of his glorious empire, he felt. Churchill didn't hide his feelings: 'I hate Indians . . . they're a beastly people, with a beastly religion.' He thought Hindus were weak, superstitious and cunning; Muslims were manlier, though dimmer intellectually; and Sikhs were loyal but unstable. Much of this is forgotten. History only remembers the two leaders with a single stroke: Churchill for defying Hitler; Gandhi for winning India's freedom without shedding an ounce of blood. To us, Gandhi would always remain our flag of freedom, our 'liberator with clean hands'.

2

Blithe Spirits

'Hail to thee, blithe Spirit!'

—Percy Bysshe Shelley

Satinder Mama loved reading English novels. In one of them, he discovered 'bed tea' and decided it was high time to introduce it to 7 Kacheri Bazaar. My mother relates in her diary that he went to the kitchen one morning to instruct the cook. His instructions were meticulous: it should neither be too weak nor too strong; not too hot, not too cold; not too much milk, not too much sugar. Then, he taught him how to bring the tea to his room. He told him to enter his room gently exactly one minute before he woke up and place the cup softly on the table beside his bed without waking him up.

The cook was confused. How would he know when it would be one minute before the Sah'b woke up? Satinder Mama told him not to fear—he would know. There would be vibrations, even the birds would hear them. By now, Manni and I had joined in, and we watched them perform two 'dress rehearsals'. The cook was sceptical, but Satinder Mama reassured him that this was the practice in the best hotels. In that case, the cook felt that he should be earning the 'best hotel salary'. Eventually, his patience exhausted, the cook went to complain to my grandmother.

This wasn't a hotel, and this newfangled nonsense of the Laat Sah'b would not do. What if everyone decided to have bed tea? It would need an army of bearers. She could see a revolution brewing in the kitchen and decided to act. She went to my grandfather, even though he didn't want to be disturbed at that time.

Bauji had a cherished routine that began with a cup of tea and a copy of the *Tribune* as the sun's first rays entered the courtyard. He had quickly glanced at the headlines of the war. Rangoon had fallen in the east to the Japanese Army, but the allies were advancing in Italy. He was poring over page four for the progress of civil and criminal cases in the law courts when Bhabo arrived. He was in good spirits that morning and listened to her patiently. After a few minutes, he quietly and efficiently put the kibosh on Satinder Mama's plans for bed tea. Bauji had other things on his mind. Should he attend the Burra Sahib's 'At Home' the following day? An invitation to Government House was an honour, confirming his position in Lyallpur's society. In his younger days, he would have scrambled for an invitation. But these were unusual times. The British were in the middle of a world war and didn't want to be distracted by Gandhi's pesky, subversive campaigns. Although he was in jail, the country was all fired up by his Quit India movement. To make it worse, the American president Franklin D. Roosevelt was on India's side, needling Churchill to commit to India's independence. This put Churchill in a pickle. He couldn't easily dismiss Roosevelt—he needed America to win the war.

Bauji reasoned that to be seen consorting with the White district collector (DC) in these times would have been unpatriotic. But to be absent would be seditious in the eyes of the Raj. The DC's upcoming party was the most-talked-about subject around town. The bazaars hummed with the tittle-tattle about who was going and who wasn't. The Hindus were expected to boycott the party, and the Muslims, most likely, were to attend. The opinion in Varma Villa was also divided. The older set sided with Bauji, thinking it wrong not to support Britain against the evil Nazis. The younger lot was with Gandhi and considered it a betrayal of the freedom movement if Bauji attended. Either way, my grandfather was damned. There was no escaping it, and he got more and more irritated.

The weighty debate in Bauji's head came to an abrupt halt as a chorus of schoolboys passed by our gate. One by one, they read aloud at the top of their lungs the inscription on our newly installed letterbox: 'Barma Billa,

Bazir Chand Barma, BA, LLB, Advocate, Bunjab High Court, Lahore, Bunjab.' The letterbox had been Vade Mama's brainchild. To hang a letterbox with your name inscribed on it was the latest fashion in Kacheri Bazaar. He felt it would reinforce his father's rising status. This incident doesn't appear in my mother's diary, and I think my cousin Jeet must have narrated it many years later. Vade Mama had got a carpenter to make the box, and a sign painter with a limited knowledge of English to inscribe it. Everyone was encouraged to write letters to each other to 'try out' the new letterbox. A number of 'trial letters' were sent, but the mailman refused to use the box, preferring to deliver the mail personally. It made sense from his point of view—he got a fresh glass of buttermilk each time he delivered the post by hand.

Vade Mama did not anticipate that his chic statement would become an inspiration for every passing schoolboy to test his command of the English language and his lungs. Regrettably, the sign painter had also been partial to the letter 'B' and had written 'Billa' instead of 'Villa', 'Barma' in place of 'Varma', Bazir for Wazir, and Bunjab for Punjab. Vade Mama hadn't bothered to get the corrections made. Bauji tried to hold back his annoyance. It was bad enough to have his name bellowed out by every street urchin, but to have it mispronounced added to the insult. He tried to hold his anger all day and declared calmly over dinner that he was convinced Vade Mama was not his son. The midwife must have switched him, said Raj Mama.

But Bauji's mind was on more serious matters. The marriage of his fourth daughter was approaching, and it was a chance to show off his class-one sons-in-law to the world. He was secretly pleased with himself at having secured another coup—a high-ranking official in the Indian Army for his fourth daughter. A man of the world, he understood the importance of status and had wisely married off all his daughters to the new class of officials that emerged after the First World War. The traditional choice would have been to seek a landlord's son—wealth still resided with the landed. But his turned out to be a shrewd decision. Power and prestige did, indeed, shift from the landed gentry to the English-speaking professional classes; and besides, his choice had saved him from paying an expensive dowry.

Bauji had married his eldest daughter to a class-one officer in the Indian Railways, who impressed everyone with his luxurious saloon-on-wheels with its drawing room, dining room, bedrooms and staff quarters. The second girl married a professor of English in the prestigious government college in Lahore, who later went on to become a principal in Ludhiana. He was an accomplished tennis and bridge player, which gave him entry into a grand social circle in Lahore, and he flaunted it, casually dropping big names. The third daughter, my mother, married a civil engineer in the Punjab government's Department of Irrigation. Thus, my grandfather bought social status, and his family rose from the middle-middle to the upper-middle class within a generation.

A regular part of Bauji's routine was the barber's daily visit to give him a shave before he set out on his evening walk to the Company Bagh. The barber was his confidant, with whom he shared his ambitions, his status anxieties. As he sat in a fragrant corner of the courtyard, watching the gleaming razor wipe the lather cleanly from his chin in the barber's mirror, Bauji presented his dilemma. Should he go to the Burra Sahib's 'At Home'? The conservative barber's advice was to show up. Bauji agreed, and as he rose, he informed him that all his sons-in-law had confirmed that they'd be coming for the wedding.

'What a sight!' the barber proclaimed. 'Seeing three class-ones standing in line to welcome the guests!' It would surely bolster my grandfather's elevated standing in Lyallpur society. The barber had played an important role in certifying the background of his future sons-in-law and had almost derailed my mother's marriage. He'd gone to my father's village and returned with the news that my father's family were impoverished landlords; in fact, my father's father was a lowly schoolteacher—it was thus an unsuitable match. Vade Mama suspected the barber had neither been bribed nor plied with enough samosas by my father's family. In any case, Bauji had overruled the barber, pointing to my father's prospects as a class-one engineer. If the miserable barber had had his way, I may never have been born.

The day of the wedding arrived. Being a methodical man, Bauji had organized comfortable rooms in his neighbours' homes for dozens of relatives who had arrived weeks in advance. He had also assigned duties to his sons at the reception. Vade Mama had to stand at the door to welcome the guests and escort them in. He had a grown-up son, my cousin Jeet, who was assigned the job of ensuring the toilets were clean and to direct the guests to them. He handed Vade Mama a guest list, asking him to place a tick mark beside the name of each attending person. Jeet volunteered to help his father in this task. He took the initiative and added a couple of new columns. Beside each name, he made a provision for occupation and monthly income. He thought Bauji would appreciate his initiative to grade his guests, but it had the opposite effect.

There was commotion among the first guests as soon as Jeet began inquiring about their income. Bauji acted quickly, apologizing for his grandson. Vade Mama took charge of the guest list, deleting the offending columns. Amid the mayhem, a tall, grand lady in silk appeared before Jeet, asking him imperiously for directions to the bathroom. He inquired helpfully, 'Number one or number two?' She turned red. Jeet informed her that the numbers corresponded to the two calls of nature. 'You mean you have separate facilities for each?' No, they didn't. 'Then why . . .?'

Jeet began to explain his logic, but she was in no mood to listen. She swore and was about to give him a slap when he nimbly moved back. The incident would have gone unnoticed, but Jeet bragged about it to his friends. They, in turn, told their friends, and the story spread quickly and soon was on everyone's lips. Since her husband was an important official in the law courts, Bauji grew alarmed. He rushed to do damage control. He claimed that his grandson was showing symptoms of 'being cracked' and would have to be examined.

Trying to control his temper, Bauji asked Jeet the next day why he did those asinine things. Jeet replied with the assurance of a man who had rehearsed his reply: since there were 200 guests and only two bathrooms, he felt a system was needed. He'd made a study and discovered that it takes two to three minutes to do number one, five to six minutes to do number two, or eight minutes if someone was constipated. Bauji asked how he'd got to the exact numbers. Jeet replied that he had been recording with a stopwatch how much time each person spent in the lavatory. 'Here, I can show you the results,' he said, pulling a scruffy sheet from his pocket.

Bauji was stunned. Jeet said he was merely being helpful, letting the next person in the queue know how long they'd have to wait. As the news spread of his time-and-motion study, Jeet became an instant hero with the younger set. A few days later, the news hit the bazaar. Who was circulating it? Suspicion fell on Satinder Mama, who was sporting a fashionable, puffy hairstyle—he must be the culprit, showing off at the barber shop. Anyway,

Jeet became famous. Taking advantage of his celebrity status, he insisted on free tea and biscuits at every shop in the bazaar.

The wedding, however, went off smoothly. Except for the corpse. They found a body at the neighbour's door as the bride and bridegroom were going around the fire, and the pandit was intoning the Vedic 'swa-ha'. They said it was a Muslim boy. He'd been stabbed, then staggered along the street till he reached our neighbour's gate, where he just collapsed. They'd found him face down; his face was covered in blood and vomit, and his nails were clinging to the ground. It was a communal killing, the police declared the next day, revenge for a Hindu death from the previous week. Bauji could not understand the madness of the Hindus and Muslims killing each other after having lived together for hundreds of years.

These incidents were becoming a part of daily life in those days before Partition. The idea of a homeland for Indian Muslims had grown ever since Jinnah pulled it out of a hat a few years before I was born. Bauji thought it was foolish to break up India. But no one really believed it would break. Besides, our family was more interested in the gossip of Kacheri Bazaar than in politics, and the corpse was soon forgotten. Uncle Satpal tried to keep the incident alive. He kept ranting for days on the evils of religious fanaticism, trying everyone's patience. Jeet said that Satpal was equally fanatical—he'd neither change his mind nor change the subject.

Uncle Satpal was my mother's cousin, and she admired him hugely. He had dashed his bourgeois family's hopes of a solid professional career to become a Marxist, and he'd joined the Bombay Commune. He was underground until Hitler attacked the Soviet Union in December 1941. The Indian communists then switched sides and joined the allied war against fascism. This meant parting company with Gandhi's Quit India movement. Thinking the communist turnaround unpatriotic, Satpal left to work on famine relief in Bengal. Everyone was surprised when he emerged suddenly in Lyallpur during the wedding. He looked gaunt, like a man who had suffered. My mother rushed to the bazaar and had a wedding outfit stitched for him. She watched proudly as he stood up boldly to my middle aunt's overbearing, Anglophile husband, who persisted in calling Churchill a hero for saving mankind from Hitler. Satpal quietly said that Churchill was a brat, clutching on to India like it was a toy. Roosevelt, in his eyes, was the greater man, who was pushing for India's freedom.

Seated next to my mother at the wedding dinner, Satpal whispered, 'Bootlicker,' referring to my Anglophile uncle. He then gave my mother a tutorial in communist ideology. He asked her to imagine a world free from oppression—from the cruelties of capitalism, religion and colonialism. He wanted human beings to be free from deceit, from being false and unjust. She didn't think she'd ever see such a world. He confessed being torn by the communists' decision to support imperial Britain against Gandhi's Quit India movement. Of course, Gandhi's was the better cause, but he couldn't feel too enthusiastic because Gandhi, too, was a part of a reactionary bourgeoisie. He would only deliver us a false freedom—the Indian proletariat would remain enslaved. Earlier, we'd been exploited by the British bourgeoise; we would now be exploited by the Indian bourgeoise. My mother gave him a peculiar look, getting irritated by his bizarre views. She decided in the end that moral blindness was part of the human condition, and she went on to record this conversation dutifully in her notebook.

Conversation was the chief occupation in our house. If two people were together, they wouldn't read or play board games; they'd sit and chat over cups of tea. If there were three, so much the better. They would natter endlessly about people they'd never met, nor would ever meet. The wedding had provided much food for gossip. The corpse next door and 'number one or number two' had dominated our concerns for some time, as had Satpal, whose naive idealism everyone found unrealistic and impractical. Soon, another event pushed these to the background.

Jeet was romantically inclined, according to my mother's diary—and it mentions a reckless wager he'd made with Satinder Mama. Whoever announced 'I love you' to the first woman who passed by the house would win. The stakes were two annas. The two set up vigil on the first floor, from where they could watch people passing below. I remember them rehearsing their lines. Jeet spun a coin in the air, and since he lost he had to go first. After a short wait, he spotted a middle-aged lady with an umbrella coming their way. He rushed downstairs and uttered the magical words, 'Darling, I love you!' An umbrella can be a treacherous weapon, especially in the hands of a woman in fury. Jeet bit the dust under the offended woman's blows. She sensed victory. He screamed in pain. The house came rushing down, and Jeet was rushed to the doctor. The lady turned out to be the headmistress of a girls' school. She was an acquaintance of my grandfather's, and he went and offered her an apology. When she learnt who had accosted her she withdrew her police complaint. Jeet's injury was not serious, and he was back home in the evening. His first act on returning was to collect his reward from Satinder Mama.

A few days later, Vade Mama came home wildly excited from the bazaar. Japan had attacked India in the east. The Japanese were marching from Burma towards the Brahmaputra Valley through the towns of Kohima and Imphal. News of the war supplanted the 'I love you' incident. My uncles were thrilled at the prospect of another British defeat. Bauji got irritated. Didn't his sons realize that the Japanese posed a bigger threat? Vade Mama retorted that we were already under alien rule. And who was to say which foreigner was better? Satinder Mama confessed that he was secretly enjoying Britain's discomfort in the East. The speed of the Japanese advance showed that colonial empires were flimsy structures built on pillars of rotting clay.

We wondered who our real enemy was—Britain or Japan. The older generation was on Britain's side, the younger sided with the Japanese. Raj Mama said Japan was an Asian power and that we should support Asia over Europe. My uncles applauded the successive fall of Hong Kong, the Philippines, then Malaya and Indochina. The surrender of Singapore was a thrilling blow! My mother was neutral. Satpal was in a dilemma. As a communist, he had adopted the Soviet Union's neutral position against Japan, but when the Soviet Union invaded Japan, he had to follow the Communist International's directive and turn 180 degrees. Satinder Mama was counting on his hero, Subhas Chandra Bose, to help Japan against the allies. When Satpal called Bose a running dog of the Japanese, Satinder Mama was offended. But the real question was always the same: Would the British ever give up India?

After many pages on war and politics in my mother's notebook, I finally find mention of me. I am four now and she refers to me as 'Troublemaker' (with a capital T). She expresses her a concern about Jeet's dubious influence on me and then recounts the following incident. One rainy morning, my mother and I were in Chaura Bazaar. People were walking with umbrellas. There was a big puddle in the middle of the road, and they were all carefully going around it. While she was bargaining for mangoes, I ran and jumped into the puddle. It raised quite a splash, wetting the passers-by and soiling the mango seller's stall. Apologizing to everyone, my mother made an embarrassed exit. On the way home, she chewed me out. The next day, she told Jeet to take me back and offer an apology to the mango seller whose shop I had spoiled. After doing our duty, Jeet and I spotted a painting of the Taj Mahal in a shop window. I insisted on buying it. Jeet haggled and brought down the price. But the problem was cash. We didn't have any.

'Should we just take it?' Jeet whispered.

'What?'

'I was joking,' he said.

'Oh!'

Bauji refused to open his purse when we got home. I begged the others for a loan. My mother relented in the end, pawning a bracelet. There were oohs and aahs when the painting arrived. We wanted to put it up on the drawing room wall, but Bauji turned us down. He approved, however, the anteroom, where his clients waited sometimes. Jeet brought a ladder and a hammer. I was assigned to hold the pencil and box of nails. Jeet measured the wall, found the centre, marked the spot with a pencil. The he climbed the ladder; I handed him a nail; he struck a blow; the nail went clean through, but he missed the mark. Some plaster came off the wall. Jeet struck a second nail and missed again. More plaster came off. We moved to a different wall. When the picture went up finally, it was still off-centre. By now, the walls of the anteroom had many holes, and plaster covered the floor. When Bauji saw the mess he cleared his throat with a harsh, grating cry. We knew this sound well. He employed it in court, and it never failed to strike terror in the witness's heart.

The air was tense when we assembled in the dining room for lunch. Jeet decided sensibly to absent himself. Bauji scrutinized me and called me 'Troublemaker'. Everyone was a bit nervous, but nothing was said about the pockmarked antechamber. From a 'restless baby' of six months I'd become a 'difficult child' at two and a half; and now I was a four-year-old 'Troublemaker'. The epithet stuck. My mother managed to change the mood, announcing excitedly that my father had found a house and that he was coming to take us to Lahore.

When my father arrived, I felt I was meeting him for the first time. He couldn't have been more different. He was small, shy and quiet. With a serene face, he listened rather than talked. And he seemed to listen from far away, not with his ears but with his eyes. He smiled a lot, and it was a smile of such sweetness that it lit his whole face. When he was about to speak, he didn't say anything for an instant, making the others uncomfortable. He looked vacantly in the air, his face intent. When he spoke finally, it was as though he were continuing a conversation. The only time he could not be stopped was on the subject of water. His work life as a canal engineer was defined by water, and he was working untiringly to bring water to irrigate arid Punjab.

My mother blamed his guru for his eccentricities. When he had been a student at the Thomason College of Civil Engineering in Roorkee, my father had discovered a spiritual path and had turned away from the Arya Samaj traditions of his own and my mother's family. The mystical guru of the Radha Soami sect had initiated him into the egalitarian path of bhakti and Sufism, of direct union with God through love and meditation. It had appealed to my father's modern, scientific temper, because it sought the truth, not in faith alone but in evidence gained through meditation.

Even though I was very young, I could sense that my father was unusual. He walked lightly, as though he was moving in air, slightly above the ground. He seemed to do everything lightly—think lightly, act lightly, even feel lightly. He treated everyone in the same way, unlike the others in the Kacheri Bazaar house, whose relationships were defined by hierarchy. Bauji was always deferential to his clients in high positions but matter-of-fact in dealing with others. This sense of superior and inferior was absent in my father—he spoke to the servants as he did to the masters. He looked at the cook and Bauji with the same sincere eye, which made them feel comfortable.

Bauji wished his son-in-law had been taller. He looked at me with disappointment—he wanted tall grandsons. My mother wished my father wasn't so quiet and remote. Vade Mama found him detached, aloof and not particularly ambitious. Bauji agreed, observing that if he had been more worldly, he would have got a house by now. Bauji explained that the government was a person. If my father had grown close to the head of the housing department—flattered him, sent him sweets at Diwali—he'd have got a house earlier. My mother thought it was all unfair: her husband worked hard but others got the credit. Bauji advised her not to make the same mistake: 'Be sure to visit his boss in Lahore; get to know his wife; take her shopping.'

We left for Lahore on 7 August 1946, a day after America dropped the atomic bomb on Hiroshima, thus ending World War II. It had taken 50 million lives, a frightening statistic. It also ended my sojourn in the idyllic cocoon of Kacheri Bazaar. It had been fun with Jeet, my madcap uncles, Bil-li and Bijli. These blithe spirits introduced me to living life with laghima, 'lightly'. They played jokes, laughed and lived for the day. Life was a low-stakes game, not to be taken too seriously. By making life into play, they managed to shake off the dullness of their bourgeois world and shield themselves from the tragedy of the war outside. They might also have fired my ambition for moksha, which would become a lifelong struggle for another sort of freedom.

While I was acquiring a talent for life, there was another storm brewing outside which would turn our world upside down and wipe away forever my charmed existence in Lyallpur. The communal killing of the boys had been a premonition, an omen of Partition. Tragedy would soon engulf us.

3

Thuh Pencil Box

*'Insanity in individuals is something rare—
but in groups, parties, nations and epochs,
it is the rule.'*

—Friedrich Nietzsche

The year is 1947, and the British have begun to mark their departure from India. My mother, however, is more interested in my departure to school this cold January morning. I am four and a half and have recently been enrolled in kindergarten in a school in Model Town, a middle-class suburb of Lahore. The headmistress had wavered initially, saying she would place me on the waiting list. My mother was visibly disappointed, having fallen in love with the school's colourful walls and its resplendent green playing field. As she was leaving, the head asked perfunctorily about me.

'Frankly, he's a troublemaker,' my mother said with a sigh.

She told the head that I had received a present, a toy car, the previous day, and I promptly broke it. And then I had spent the rest of the day trying to put it together. My mother felt so embarrassed because it had been given by her husband's boss. The head was completely disarmed by my mother's lack of guile. She thought for a minute and then she said, 'We'll take him.' She'd had a change of heart, she said, because it was the

24

most original reason she had heard for schooling a child. She hoped they would be able to cope with her 'troublemaker'.

On my very first day, I lived up to my reputation. Pointing to an apple drawn on the blackboard, the teacher said, 'Thuh apple.' Each of my classmates, in turn, repeated after her until it was my turn. I said, 'Thee apple.' So, began our first skirmish. She repeated 'thuh apple', and I insisted on 'thee apple'. The battle of wits over the definite article went on for a few seconds until she threw up her hands. Trying to control herself, she asked why I insisted on saying it the wrong way.

'My mother says thee apple,' I said.

She wanted my mother to come and see her. Since it was my first day, she didn't punish me. My mother was furious when I told her what had happened. The next morning, she marched off to school with a grammar book, and so began another battle for the definite article. Happily, it came to an end quickly when my teacher realized that the pronunciation of 'the' does change before a vowel. It was 'thuh boy' but 'thee apple'. And before a consonant, thee apple would turn into thuh big apple. My teacher was also impressed with my mother's degree from Lahore's prestigious Kinnaird College. They quickly made up, blaming the mix-up on the defective English language.

My problems, however, did not end there. Initially, the teacher appreciated my asking questions. She called me 'curious'. Soon, the questions became tiresome, and she concluded that I was a troublemaker. Each time I'd raise my hand, she'd grow wary, and before I could ask anything, pat came her reply: *nahin*, 'no'. Nahin became an insistent refrain at school, and I began to believe they'd changed my name from Ashok Kumar to Nahin Kumar. One especially weary day, she confessed to the Head that she was feeling 'shattered' and looked forward to the end of the term when she would see my back.

They did, in fact, change my name. My father's mother suspected that my mother, her daughter-in-law, had given me my name because she was secretly in love with the Bollywood star Ashok Kumar. This wouldn't do, and so she took me to the Radha Soami ashram, placed me at the saint's feet and asked him to give me a name. He looked down and smiled; and I looked up, perplexed. Since she'd set me at his feet, he suggested why not call me 'Gurcharan Das'? And so, I was transformed at four and a half from a cheerful Ashok Kumar, 'prince of happiness', to Gurcharan Das, 'humble servant at the guru's feet'. He thought I could do with a bit of humility. As far as I can tell, though, the name change didn't help. I find too much humility borders on pride, and false humility is even more insulting than open pride.

The guru explained to my family that he was seeking not to make me think less of myself but to make me think of myself less. His definition of humility was to take one's work seriously, not oneself seriously. If I achieved that, I would get a feeling of weightlessness, which would be energizing. I was also introduced at the ashram to the word 'moksha', 'liberation'. Everyone kept parroting it, and it didn't make sense to me. My father explained years later that they were using the word in a spiritual sense, as release from the cycle of birth and rebirth. It left me cold. Since this life seemed to elude me, why would I want to worry about the next one?

I was adept not only at breaking toys but also at switching pencil boxes. All the kids in my class had the same blue pencil box—it cost two annas—except for a rich kid, who had two; and one of those was shiny red, imported from England. I felt sorry for Ayan, a poor Muslim kid, who didn't have any box. He sat next to me and was forever borrowing my pencils, and I didn't like it. At noon one day, the bell rang for recess. Everyone rushed out. Once the teacher left, I was alone. I picked up the second box of the rich kid—the shiny red one—and placed it on Ayan's desk. No one liked the rich kid anyway. He came to school in a car, while the rest of us walked to school. He was bigger than us, wore expensive clothes and bragged about his toys.

After recess, the class resumed. Ayan looked puzzled seeing the gleaming box on his desk. Suddenly, there was a cry; then there was commotion. The rich kid was screaming that someone had stolen his pencil box. The teacher made us all stand up as she went around the room, asking each one if they knew of the thief's identity. When it was Ayan's turn, he confessed that there was a red pencil box on his table, but he didn't know who had put it there. When my turn came, I was scared and confused. I looked at Ayan but didn't say anything. The poor kid was led to the front of the class to be punished. Just before the teacher's ruler hit his palm, he looked at me and he cried.

'You know I didn't do it. Tell them!'

I didn't know where to look and remained silent.

Even today, after all these years, I don't understand why I didn't speak up. It is easier to comprehend why I switched the boxes. I thought it unfair, perhaps, that Ayan did not have a box and the rich kid had two—an early socialist act of redistribution. But why did I remain silent, especially when Ayan was about to be punished wrongly? It must either be cowardice or temporary insanity, which sometimes grips human beings, especially when they are threatened. The truth is, I have been unable to forget this incident. Even now, I wake up with nightmares.

A few days later, the rich kid arrived in his swanky car at our middle-class doorstep. He and his mother had come to thank me for 'finding' his pencil box. With a superior air, he showed off an expensive train set imported from England. Both of us opened the box eagerly. Just as the steam engine and carriages were beginning to move smoothly on the rails, I felt the itch again. I grabbed the red engine, twisted it hard and banged it on the floor, breaking it. The rich kid screamed—the same bratty cry. It scared my mother. She was in tears, apologizing profusely. The boy was angry and began to pack off the rest of the train set. Mother and son left soon, shaken and confused. I spent the evening trying to put the broken engine back together. Again, I'm not sure why I did what I did. Was it revenge on Ayan's behalf? Or envy for his being wealthy? My mother wrote in her diary that I was in the habit of breaking toys and then trying to put them together again.

She complained to my father when he came home. He took the news calmly. It was probably envy, he felt.

'But envy is a bad thing!' she cried.

Yes, envy was destructive, he said, but it also had a positive side. Watching me trying to fix the toy, he said, it also created a desire to do better. It led to ambition, to emulate the successful. She was getting irritated with my father, but he wasn't taking my 'destructive instinct' seriously. He went on unperturbed, claiming that envy might also be an unconscious desire for equality—no one should excel. I might even grow up to be a communist, he teased her. My mother was not amused. There was already one Marxist in the family, and that was one too many. Although she liked Uncle Satpal, she didn't want his sort of life for me.

A few weeks later, I fell sick and didn't go to school. My mother was surprised when my teacher dropped in to see us. After a few minutes of polite chatter, she looked at me and reassured us that I'd soon be up and about. She then sprung a surprise, asking me baldly to bring her a glass of buttermilk each morning, as I lived so close to the school. My mother agreed readily, but I was embarrassed. After she left, my mother could see I was angry. I didn't want to be seen carrying buttermilk for my teacher. My father had the same reaction. My mother assured us that it was common practice—she, too, had provided her teacher with buttermilk when she was my age. It felt like a bribe to my father. And I, too, didn't think it was fair. My grasping teacher must have been aware of my discomfort, but she didn't let on, accepting the buttermilk as her entitlement. Eventually, she must have realized how resentful I felt, and told me to stop getting her buttermilk.

The other person who came to visit me at home was Ayan. He stood shyly behind his mother, looking unhappy. She coaxed her son to come forward and hand me a purple balloon. 'Get well soon!' he managed to say. Ever since the pencil box incident I had been extra nice to him—I would share my lunch with him, especially when I had something special in my lunchbox; this was my way of apologizing, I suppose. My mother welcomed them both and took them inside. She brought milk and biscuits for Ayan and tea for his mother. I was happy to see Ayan, but he was uncomfortable. Over tea, his mother told us that her husband worked in my father's office. He was an overseer, not an officer like my father, which immediately established our unequal status. I was grateful that no one brought up the pencil box that day, especially because my parents didn't know anything about it.

Soon, Ayan also relaxed. I brought out my toys, and we began to play. His mother complained that the boys in school made fun of her son—of his broken English, his clothes and his religion. My mother tried to comfort her, saying that boys could be cruel. When they got up to leave, I ran back to my room, brought out my pencil box and handed it to Ayan. 'You're my friend!' I said. But he refused to take it. Eventually, our families became good friends, visiting each other off and on. My parents never allowed our different religions or social status to come between us. Later that year, Ayan's family would play a crucial role in helping us during the Partition riots. Of the dozens of images stored in my memory, one reappears persistently. It is of Ayan, etched sharply and shadowless in my mind, giving me the same look from that ill-fated afternoon when I did him wrong.

One afternoon, as the school year drew to a close, I came running home, waving a mid-term report card. My mother asked eagerly if I'd stood first. It was the wrong question, my father told her. She should've asked if I was happy in school. What did I enjoy doing? The competitive pressure to stand first undid the purpose of schooling, he felt. Parents needed to help a child to discover his or her passion. We weren't all Mozarts (Mozart knew that he was a musical genius at four). Most of us stumbled through life, trying to find what we like. I must have listened to my father, because when school opened, our teacher asked us what we wanted to be when we grew up. 'Happy,' was my answer. She said that I didn't understand the assignment. My father said that she didn't understand life.

My mother ignored my father's advice. When we were alone, she would ask how the others had performed. I told her that Ayan had stood first, and the rich kid had come last. She smiled at that, and she kept asking the same question for the next fifteen years. There is a moment in childhood when the door opens and lets in the future. My mother's competitive instincts made me realize the world judges you for your successes. If I became a soldier, she would want me to be a general; if I went into politics, she would want me to be prime minister. My mother wanted me to be 'somebody', not a 'nobody'. It had been different when I was a baby; she had adored me whether I burped or screamed or broke my toys. But as time went on, she was more affectionate when I achieved something. My father didn't care. For him, success was not the key to happiness; it was the other way around—happiness was the key to success.

One monsoon evening in mid-August 1947, the weary British got up and left India. They thought they'd be returning to rows of gorgeous Georgian houses, glistening white, built with slave sugar and glorious, imperial wealth. But they returned to a bombed and impoverished country, devastated by the war. What they left behind in India was not the Viceroy's House or Victoria Memorial or even Lutyens's bungalows. It was an intangible sense of freedom, which was in their blood but which they ironically denied us, as our colonial masters. Nevertheless, it got transmitted through education and the institutions they left behind. It became woven into our lives and has stayed. I would grow up in a free country with the kind of self-confidence that my parents could not have imagined.

A few months earlier, my father had come home early. He had surprised us and took us to Anarkali Bazaar. We went past Lawrence Gardens and

Faletti's Hotel, where my mother's upper-class friends met in their best chiffon saris for tea and cucumber sandwiches. My mother believed all the romantic things they used to say about Anarkali Bazaar—that it was a 'paradise on earth'; all its women were beautiful and its men handsome; if you couldn't find it here, it wasn't worth having. Not surprisingly, the bazaar swept her away that afternoon with its bustle, gaiety and laughter . . . until we heard the news.

As she was testing a jasmine scent in Bhagwan Lal's perfume shop, the shopkeeper's radio announced that Britain had decided to chop India into two and create a new Muslim nation of Pakistan. The bitter Hindu shopkeeper said that it was Britain's spiteful parting shot. His partner was not surprised—it was the outcome of years of 'divide and rule'. My mother sighed, saying it was the price of our freedom.

There had been speculation for weeks if Viceroy Mountbatten would actually cut up our country. When the decision was announced, it sent shockwaves. Muslims were pleased; Hindus were devastated. Anarkali Bazaar lost all interest in commerce that evening. There was a buzz, and a cry rose. Windows sprang open above shops, and people rushed out. There was a single question on everyone's minds: Would Lahore remain in India or be given to Pakistan? A London barrister, Sir Cyril Radcliffe, who had never been to India, would do the actual carving in five weeks on a map he'd never seen.

A train of half-alive Muslim refugees arrived on 9 August with harrowing tales of murder, arson and rape. The next morning, Muslim clergy in Lahore's main mosque vowed revenge, calling upon a jihad to kill non-Muslims. They singled out Sikhs for their alleged crimes against Muslims in East Punjab. Thus occurred the great massacre of the Hindus and Sikhs of Lahore. It was terrifying! We saw columns of black smoke rising from the bazaars; there were sounds of gunfire and women wailing. Two thousand people were killed in twenty-four hours.

At midnight on 14 August 1947, the British Raj came to an end. There were celebrations across the country but not in Lahore, where killing and looting continued. It seemed unreal to my mother. She had felt Britain's empire would continue forever, but suddenly it was no more. On 17 August we learnt that Radcliffe had awarded Lahore to Pakistan, and we had become refugees. It was no longer safe to be a Hindu in Pakistan. There was a smell of fear on Lahore's streets as Muslim mobs began a serious hunt for Hindus and Sikhs. The following day, the barbers of Lahore did brisk business as Sikhs cut off their hair and shaved their beards, hoping that anonymity would save them. Prices betrayed the state of affairs. Panic-selling of Hindu homes, furniture, clothing and kitchen utensils brought a crash in their prices, while panic-buying by the departing Hindus sent the prices of gold, weapons, horses and tongas skyrocketing.

Ayan's parents came to fetch us in the evening and hid us in their house. Ayan and I invented a game. We concealed ourselves under his parents' bed and held secret discussions on how we should escape to safety from our hiding spot. He surprised me, asking suddenly if my father beat me. I shook my head. He said his father beat him regularly to make him conform to the will of God. 'Every morning, I wake up thinking if I will be beaten today.' I felt lucky that my father had never laid a finger on me. But my heart went out to Ayan. I told him that I would protect him from his father. 'But how? You are leaving.' I told my mother I didn't want to go. She said that she, too, wanted to stay on. Ever since college, she'd been in love with elegant, literary and cosmopolitan Lahore. She loved the city, and she didn't want to move.

But it was an impossible wish. At ten o'clock, Ayan's father reported that we had been discovered by guards of the Muslim League and would have to flee. My mother was frightened. My father made desperate phone calls. In the end, the enterprising husband of my mother's younger sister came to our rescue. An officer in the army, he requisitioned a truck and showed up in the early hours of the morning. My mother wanted to stop at home to collect our valuables, but she was told that doing so wouldn't be safe. Before leaving, my parents went to Ayan's father and mother and handed them the keys to our house. My father said that he was gifting all his worldly belongings to them. I told Ayan that all my toys would now be his. We then piled into the army truck and left with only the clothes on our back.

On the way to the Wagah border, we saw tens of thousands of Hindu refugees walking to India. My mother began to cry. She wondered if her family in Lyallpur was among them. She had not heard from them. In his last letter, Bauji had insisted stubbornly on staying back. Just as we crossed the border, my father, my military uncle and the driver gave a cheer. We were safe! My mother smiled for the first time. An hour later, the truck deposited us at my father's guru's ashram on the banks of the Beas.

We looked down at the rushing water and were happy to be alive. We walked through the gate to find amazing calm inside.

Our journey was not over. The next day we took a bus to the railway station in Jalandhar. There was chaos at the station. No one knew when our train would arrive. Refugees were huddled on both sides of the platform. On the east platform sat Hindus and Sikhs waiting to go to Delhi. On the west, scared Muslims were expecting a train to Lahore. They crowded, snuggled together, believing that they were safe in a group. As each train approached, the refugees would get up. Pushing and shoving, they would rush towards it, but the last four trains had not stopped. Finally, our train arrived. Everyone made a dash, but my father held on to us, making us wait. My mother was anxious that we wouldn't get a seat. After a few minutes, he took us in calmly and found our compartment, and we waited for the train to move. We must have waited for four or five hours. Finally, my father got up to check with the station master. My mother implored him to be careful. She held on to us, clutching my younger brothers to her chest. I went to the window to watch my father. I tried to lean out, but the safety bars stopped me.

I watched a tall, handsome police officer standing still on the platform. A train was coming from the opposite side—from Delhi, going to Lahore. Activity on the platform increased. The policeman continued to stare ahead with determination. All of a sudden, two Sikh teenage boys emerged from nowhere. They came from behind, shouted 'Musalman' and thrust their kirpan through the policeman from behind. He did not cry. He just fell and died. My mother pulled me away. She tried to shut the window; it wouldn't close.

There were shrieks as the incoming train slowed to the sound of bullets. My mother pushed us down, beneath our seats, and we lay there on the carriage floor. Instead of stopping, the train began to speed up again. It wasn't going to stop. There was more shooting, then more cries and screaming. The train full of half-dead bodies passed. My mother cried silently. I asked her insistently when my father would come back. The same question haunted her.

It was quiet after some time. We came out of hiding. An elderly Sikh forced his way into our compartment. Clutching my baby brother, my mother screeched, 'We are Hindus! Please don't . . .' She then saw my father behind him and stopped mid-sentence. We rushed towards him.

The Sikh sat down with a sigh. My father introduced the melancholic stranger. He was a landlord from Kasur, my father's home, and he knew our family. My father had found him standing at the ticket window when the shooting began. He looked vaguely familiar. My father took him by the hand, and both had found shelter in the toilet. The stranger did not say a word and continued to stare mournfully.

Our train began to move. After a while, the gloomy Sikh spoke. He'd lost everything. His whole family had been killed in a massacre, led by a Muslim sub-inspector of the police. Fortunately, my father's family had left the previous day, but my aunt—my father's sister—had stayed behind with her husband. They, too, were killed in the butchery. Hearing about my aunt's murder, my mother began to cry. He wanted to continue, but my mother asked him to stop. She couldn't bear it; besides, there were children around, she said.

There was a long silence. My mother asked my father if the train to Shimla would be running. The Sikh gave her a peculiar look. My father explained that we were not out on holiday. He had been posted by the government to the hill station because it had become the new capital of Punjab after the loss of Lahore to Pakistan. We would transfer at Kalka for the train to Shimla. There was another long silence. Just before we reached Kalka, the Sikh couldn't contain himself. He began to cry as he told his story fitfully, which I have reconstructed from my mother's diary.

'They rushed into my house with swords, screaming jihad,' he said. 'My seventy-year-old father was closest to the door. In an instant, they cut off his head. Then they cut my son's legs. Before he fell, my poor brave boy, he hurled an axe at them and got one of them. They struck him again, but he refused to die. And I, a coward, concealed behind the cupboard, was watching it all.'

He broke down. Gradually and incoherently, he described what happened. My mother's diary describes that the Muslim intruders broke the door to the inner rooms, where his wife and daughter were hiding. They dragged out the screaming women. One of them lopped off his wife's breasts while the others cheered. Then he cut her throat. At this moment, the Sikh lost consciousness; he then saw a man carry off his fifteen-year-old daughter on his shoulders. When he came to, it was morning and deathly silent. He stole out of the house and did not find a single living person. Inhaling the smell of decomposing corpses, he ran. On the main road to Lahore, a kindly Gurkha stopped his military truck and hid him until they reached the railway station, where my father found him.

'Here I am now, shamelessly alive, with nothing to call my own and nowhere to go.'

Soon, we reached Kalka, and from there took the miniature train to Shimla. The view from the window of the snow-tipped crests of the Himalayas brought relief, a soothing balm to our weary emotions. Our eyes feasted on resplendent carpets of ferns, soaring pines and deodars. The stench of death had been left far behind. What was extraordinary was not the wounds that Partition left behind but how quickly we recovered our spirits. Every time she stepped on the Mall in Shimla, my mother felt like shouting, 'We are free!' She couldn't believe it. She had to pinch herself every morning to remind herself that India was finally rid of the British.

Partition was my moment of political awakening. Although I was very young, it left an indelible scar. In later years, I did try to establish some reliable numbers in relation to this putrid stink of history but found that no one is quite sure. The consensus is that it rendered around 10 million homeless; 20 million Hindus left West Punjab and East Bengal, while 18 million Muslims went the other way to Pakistan. Over half a million lost their lives; 2,20,000 people were declared missing; 75,000 women were abducted and raped.

Who was responsible for this vile series of events? It depends on whom you ask. Hindus blame the Muslims for breaking up 'Mother India'. Muslims feared that the British Raj would turn into a Hindu Raj after the British left, and they would be persecuted. Both blame the British, not only for botching up the split but for creating the problem in the first place by their divide-and-rule policy that solidified separate religious identities. Mountbatten failed in his duty to provide security for the millions who were displaced by Partition. I also blame religion—I'm convinced that it is not a sound basis for nationhood. Nor is race, language or culture.

The irony is that Partition did not achieve anything. The Muslims who killed Hindus thought they were exterminating a beastly Hindu religion. The Hindus who killed Muslims were cleansing India of Islam. The fact is that both religions are well and alive today.

The futility of Partition introduced me early to the modern idea of the absurd. Even a five-year-old, who couldn't make sense of the policeman's murder, could intuit the absurdity of some things. I had experienced it before in the incident of Ayan and the pencil box. Whose fault? Some blame the evil inside us. I believe it was temporary insanity. If I had been defending myself in court, I would have taken that plea. Insanity is intoxicating. Flirting with madness is one thing, but madness soon starts flirting with you, and by then it's too late.

Many years later, I read Saadat Hasan Manto's story 'Toba Tek Singh', and it reawakened the theme of insanity for me. Set in a lunatic asylum, its characters are actual lunatics, but they seem to be the only sane people, who can see through the absurdity of Partition. 'If we are in India, where on earth is Pakistan?' they ask. 'And if we are in Pakistan, then how come it was India the other day?' The ordinary person, the refugee, suddenly lost his mind when he could not call 'home' what he'd always called home, and so he was temporarily unhinged. Isn't there a bit of lunacy in all of us, helping us to cope with a world that thinks it is sane?

Such madness is also contagious. Ever since Partition, I have been wary of crowds. In groups, especially religious ones, people easily go mad. In 1947, people joined mobs, setting houses and villages on fire. Packs became bigger. Soon, the subcontinent went insane. Partition may have been the trigger, but madness is always lurking in crowds. The madness of crowds is usually mean and petty, like the two cowardly boys on the railway platform who killed the policeman.

My life had taken such a bizarre turn, and so early. Till the age of five, I had had the cheeriest of childhoods imaginable. Lyallpur had been a carnival of delights, filled with aromas of Bijlee and Bil-li amid incomparable humans. How quickly the happy remembrances of those blithe spirits were replaced with dark, repulsive memories of Lahore. I sometimes wish that my mother hadn't kept a diary. It was through this that I first bumped into Ayan, then into Partition—both without warning.

If you think someone is sane, you just don't know enough about them. Those who escape into madness experience a new freedom, a different sort of moksha, as they try to make sense of another order. Sometimes, their madness may be kinder, saner than our usual idea of sanity. The pencil box was my own temporary descent into insanity, when I ran over poor Ayan. Luckily, I never ran over anyone again.

4

The Awkward Age

*'Appear weak when you are strong,
and strong when you are weak.'*

—Sun Tzu

After surviving Partition, we settled in Shimla. I was enrolled in St Edward's, a Christian missionary school run by the Irish Brothers. On the first day, I surprised myself—I broke into tears when my mother left me in the headmaster's office. When he took me to Class 1, I stood behind the door, refusing to go in. The teacher was half asleep, and the kids were targeting her with paper airplanes. One flew past, landing at the head's feet. Everyone jumped up when they saw us. I was shorter than the others, my hair cut square, parted in the middle. I was ill at ease in my new, ill-fitting khaki shorts, which braced tight around the thighs, and new Bata shoes, a marker of our middle-class status. When the bell rang in the afternoon, the class cleared, but I stayed at my desk, wondering what was next. I would have stayed there had the teacher not come back to pick up her bag. She told me to go home.

There was nothing striking about my school days. I played during recess, worked in the study periods, enjoyed sports and managed to stay comfortably in the top half of my class. Between five and seven in the evening, everyone in Shimla got dressed up to go strolling on the Mall, to see and be seen. It was a ritual from colonial days when Shimla was 'Simla', the grand summer capital of imperial India from where the viceroy ruled the Indian empire, stretching from Burma to the Red Sea. After we returned home, we'd gather around our spanking new Murphy radio and listen to the news at night. There'd be a hush as the authoritative voice of Melville de Mello filled the room. There was freedom in the air, and the news was mostly about Jawaharlal Nehru and Mahatma Gandhi. Nehru inspired in us the ideals of democracy, socialism and secularism. Saints had founded our nation, and they could do no wrong.

One evening, after coming back from the Mall, my mother began to howl. We were huddled around the radio, and Nehru had just announced that Mahatma Gandhi had been assassinated. After his short speech ended, she repeated his poetic words: 'the light has gone out of our lives'. And she kept repeating them over the next few days. My father was relieved that the assassin had been a Hindu, not a Muslim. Gandhi, the greatest apostle of non-violence, had a violent death. Sickened by Partition's brutality, Gandhi had gone on a fast unto death two weeks earlier to shame the bloodthirsty mob. Defenders of the violence (on our side of the border) called themselves Hindu patriots and claimed that they were trying to save Hinduism. At five in the afternoon on 30 January 1948, the fanatical assassin, Nathuram Godse, armed with a Beretta automatic, shot the seventy-eight-year-old Gandhi, much weakened from the fasting. Gandhi uttered 'He Ram' and slumped. Godse tried to shoot himself but failed and was seized. He was tried for murder in May and hanged in November the following year. My father wanted to know: How did killing Gandhi save the Hindu religion?

There are pages missing here in my mother's diary, and my own memory is unclear. The next thing I remember is from three years later. We were living in the wilds of Bhakra Nangal, where my engineer father had been transferred to design the powerhouses of the dam on the Sutlej River. His job was to harness the energy released from dropping an awesome volume of water from a 200-meter-high concrete wall stretched half a kilometre across a jagged Himalayan gorge. They planned to raise half a million cubic metres of concrete from the ground to create the great dam, which inspired feelings bordering on ecstasy among the men working on it.

My father seemed to work untiringly, caught up with the magnitude of the challenge. It was dusty work. He'd come home covered in mud, his files laden with dust. He didn't usually talk about his work, but in those days he'd go on excitedly about the scale of the challenge. Ninety thousand men, who'd never built a dam, were working together. While blasting a tunnel into a rock one morning to divert the river, nine workers got caught in a landslide. His team tried everything but without success. When they'd given up hope of saving the men, a junior engineer came up with a desperate plan. They worked all night. By the morning they had rescued the men. When my father came home, he was crying, and his team was following him. They embraced the junior engineer as all of them wept with happiness. I will never forget the scene.

After the nightmare of Partition, the dam was like a great waking-up dream, becoming real by the day. Looking towards the future can make up for the most dreadful past. It was clear to me, even at age nine, that this was the age of hope. Its chief purveyor was our prime minister. Jawaharlal Nehru was our hero, and we never stopped talking about him. He was a handsome man; all the women were secretly in love with him. You can imagine the excitement when we learnt that he was coming to visit the Bhakra Nangal Dam. Preparations went on for days, and on one fine morning in 1952, I found myself sitting proudly beside my father amid thousands of workers. We listened with reverence to Nehru's words. Nehru said that there was probably no such dam as high, where men worked tirelessly for the good of mankind. He spoke about his vision of India—to build a just, casteless, socialist society without the inequalities of wealth. But he wanted to do it with democratic freedoms, unlike communist Russia and China. As he neared the end of his speech, a junior engineer got up to go to the toilet. Nehru got distracted and stopped. Annoyed, he went off on a tangent, ranting about discipline and courtesy. My father asked my mother a few days later why such a great man, making history every day, would get diverted by something so trivial.

After the speech, the prime minister's party went on a tour of the dam. Arriving at the powerhouse, they found my father standing with his boss. Nehru looked at my father and asked him if anything needed improving. Before my father could answer, the boss replied obsequiously, 'Nothing, sir, thanks to your grace.' Nehru turned again to my father and repeated his question. My father admitted readily that the load-bearing walls could be wider. Nehru did not pursue the matter, but news of my father's 'insubordination' spread quickly. He had broken the cardinal rule of hierarchy, disagreeing with his boss in public. My mother heard about it in the market and got worried. The boss was a popular man, who had carefully cultivated his image. But he was also the sort of person who wanted his ego massaged by juniors. My father had not joined his coterie of sycophants. Sure enough, the following day, my father was punished by being reassigned to an insignificant role. A few months later, the design office of the powerhouse, along with my father, was moved to Delhi. The 'load-bearing walls' were widened quietly.

I was now eleven and growing up in the nation's capital, whose seven cities had been the graves of empires. On this dusty plain, each conqueror, sultan and emperor had dreamt of immortality, building a new capital to last a thousand years. Each ended up as a tomb. We settled in a spanking new flat in a white-washed colony called Kaka Nagar. The flat was on the ground floor, with a pocket garden that became our outdoor bedroom on sizzling nights in the summer (those were the days before air-conditioning). Our neighbours were mostly engineers, my father's colleagues. We were not more than a mile from India Gate, which belonged to the seventh empire, the British. On the other side, we were under the shadow of Purana Qila, a fort of the sixth, the Mughal Empire. While digging, archaeologists had discovered artifacts and memories of the ancient Indraprastha, the legendary city of the Pandavas from 2000 years earlier.

My mother's first objective was to get us into school. Both my parents felt that we needed a corrective to our lopsided schooling in Shimla, where we had lost touch with Indian ways. We had learnt to parrot 'Twinkle, Twinkle, Little Star' and 'Baa, Baa, Black Sheep' but nothing about our own civilization. After checking around, my mother decided it was going to be Modern School. It was supposed to provide the sort of education that synthesized tradition and modernity, and had reasonably high standards. But how to get us into the coveted Modern School? She had faced the same challenge a decade ago when she had tried to enrol me in kindergarten in Lahore. There were four of us now, three boys and a girl, ages six to twelve. I was the eldest, followed by two brothers, Manni and Tutu. My sister, Meera, was the youngest. We didn't have money or connections, but my mother had determination.

Early one Monday morning, she went to Modern School on Barakhamba Road. The principal wouldn't see her. She waited till lunch. She returned on Tuesday and the same thing happened. She came back feeling lost, friendless, and she cried all afternoon. On Wednesday, she tried again, but without luck. She was feeling totally defeated when the phone rang. It was an old friend. They'd been classmates in Lahore and hadn't seen each other since Partition. After catching up on family news, my mother couldn't contain herself and poured out her misery. Her friend happened to be married to a high official in the Ministry of Education. The official made a thirty-second phone call, and we got into Modern School. My mother remembered her father's instruction from Lyallpur: the government is a person. Life in Delhi would quickly confirm the magic performed by two Urdu words—*sifarish*, influence; and *rishwat*, bribe—opening the doors to one's innermost desires.

On the following day, the principal was all charm and smiles, and offered my mother tea in a cup of bone china with a silver spoon, reserved only for VIPs. From a disagreeable worm sitting on the bench outside his office, my mother had turned into a princess. Taking recourse to politeness, the best form of hypocrisy, he couldn't apologize enough. He tried to ferret out her background or information on the source of her power, but she didn't give him the satisfaction. Then, he tried a different tack. He questioned if her children would be able to cope with the high standards of his school. My mother suggested naively that he ought to test us. Suddenly, he smiled, thinking she had fallen into his trap. That afternoon, all four of us went dutifully into the exam room and came out a few hours later with flying colours. The principal was vanquished.

So began my daily journey on a bicycle to Modern School, to learn writing, reading, arithmetic and a hundred useless facts that go under the name of education. Teachers forced me to buy a dozen books that strained my mother's budget and my bicycle carrier. The books had been prescribed by soulless bureaucrats, and their main objective seemed to be to take the fun out of my life. But they didn't know who they were dealing with. I did not rebel, nor ask, 'Why do I have to do algebra?' I had seen through their game, and I was going to play to win.

I was always waiting for something to happen. In that hope, I accompanied my mother one evening on her daily round of Connaught Place. Named after the Duke of Connaught, the third son of Queen

Victoria, Connaught Place, or CP, formed two concentric circles, creating an inner, middle and outer promenade, with seven lanes radiating from a circular park. Everyone in Delhi converged on CP in the evening, no matter what the season. Between six and eight, the thing to do was to get dressed and stroll along the wide, circular Georgian-style colonnade with its glamorous shops and smart cafés. My mother went there to be seen and to see others, and it reminded her of the Mall in Shimla. We'd wander, stopping before glittering shops, hoping to run into someone. Since we didn't have money to buy much of anything, we were content at looking at the beautiful displays in the shopwindows. My mother had a great, unrequited desire to be a part of Delhi's fashionable society, and she would watch with yearning the parade of young men and women that went past, dressed in the latest fashion.

One day, while waiting for my father to join us in CP, we heard a familiar voice. My mother turned around but couldn't place it. She hesitated, then she exclaimed with a cry of surprise. It was the same friend who had got her children into Modern School. The two were thrilled to see each other. As they plied each other with a thousand questions, my eyes fell on a girl standing beside us. She was tall, slim and utterly beautiful. There was playful gaiety in her eyes, which attracted me like a magnet. Under a mass of raven hair, she was vaguely familiar. I was introduced to her: she was Alisha, a friend of their family. Soon, I remembered—she was in my school. I smiled, but she looked through me.

My favourite teacher in Modern School was Mrs Sahai, who did many fun things with us. One afternoon, she showed us a film—Walt Disney's animated feature *Bambi*. Bambi was a deer, whose best friend was a rabbit, Thumper. I loved the film, and I was sad to see it end. After the film, Mrs Sahai asked, 'What did Thumper's father say?' I raised my hand. 'If you can't say something good about someone, don't say anything at all.' She was all smiles with my answer. Then we spoke about Partition, the reasons for the violence. 'What was Thumper's advice to stop people fighting?' No one was sure. I took a stab. 'You must not be nosy; stop prying into their affairs.' I must have been right, because she gave me another smile. She was starting a club, Thumper's School of Happiness. 'Who wants to be a member?' she asked. All of us raised our hands.

I ran into Alisha a few days later. She was eating at the same long table at lunchtime. I was in a daze seeing her, my breath taken away. I smiled at her, but she looked the other way and continued talking to her friends. The following day, I thought I would catch her attention with a clever remark, but it fell flat. She pretended to be interested, but the conversation didn't flow. I didn't have much to say. She listened carelessly, her gaze wandering towards the others. The only time I got her attention was when I fell off a chair. I'm often clumsy. I was showing off, clowning around after finishing lunch. Before I realized I was on the floor. I had a bloody lip and had to get stitches. I hoped she'd show sympathy, maybe even walk me to the infirmary. But she got up and left with her friends. An older boy in senior school came to my aid.

'Alisha is a snob,' he explained. She was from a wealthy family that owned a textile business in Surat. You had to be rich or powerful to get her attention. Since I wasn't either I didn't stand a chance. While bicycling home that evening, I remembered reading somewhere that you could impress a girl by giving her flowers. When I reached home, I asked my mother for money. 'What do you need it for?' she asked. I refused to answer, and she refused to give me the money. So I decided I had to earn it. I had to get rich in order to catch Alisha. I woke up the next morning thinking about how to make a fortune. I thought of different ways, but none of them seemed up to scratch. All of a sudden, it came to me. I would perform a play. I would collect money by selling tickets in advance. Even if they didn't like the play, I couldn't lose—they'd have already paid for it.

The first decision: which play to perform? After school, I went around Kaka Nagar, asking people what play they'd like to see. Mostly, they didn't have a clue. Some thought I was testing them—they lied to impress me. Others tried to flatter themselves and tossed in Shakespeare's name, which made them sound literary. In the end, I decided on *Hamlet*. It had a sword fight. The next day, I went to the school library and found a copy. I tried to read it but didn't understand a single sentence. I must have looked bewildered, sad. The librarian came up to me. I explained my problem, and she returned a few minutes later with a copy of Charles and Mary Lamb's *Tales from Shakespeare*. I opened it to the chapter on Hamlet, and I smiled. I could read it. As I was leaving, the librarian offered to help me write the play.

I accepted her offer promptly. She said she would adapt it, so that it could be performed in forty-five minutes. The next item on my agenda was to form a theatre company. I bullied everyone younger than me in

Kaka Nagar to join our company; a few older kids also agreed. Soon, we were a ragbag of a dozen cast and crew, ranging from ages four to fifteen. The librarian gave us the script in a week. She said she'd help us learn our lines. I wanted to play Hamlet, but another kid objected. I convinced him, saying that Laertes was the better part because he kills Hamlet with a poisoned sword. Soon, we were in rehearsals. The librarian would drop by regularly, helping us with our lines. Her cousin, who had a shop in Daryaganj, loaned us props and costumes. The swords were a big hit; we wasted a lot of time because the kids only wanted to do sword fighting. I delegated the job of making the tickets to two kids with the best handwriting.

'Admission: 50 paise. Doors open at half past six. The fun begins at seven.' It was my cousin Jeet's idea to raise the ticket price from 25 to 50 paise. He also added the word 'fun' on the ticket. On a visit to Delhi, he had stopped by to see us. He reasoned that if they could pay 25 paise, they would also pay 50 paise. Besides, they'd value the play more if they paid more. He advised me to give a target to each member of the company. They had to sell tickets first to their families, then go around and sell them to their neighbours. When I protested that some members of our company were only four years old, he corrected himself.

'Make it, all members over six.'

I was full of enthusiasm. I made a special ticket for Alisha, hoping desperately that she would come. On her ticket, I crossed out 50 paise and wrote 'free'. Jeet asked me how the project began. I told him I wanted to get rich in order to impress Alisha. He listened and then gave me advice. 'Alisha won't come,' he said. She was a snoot, not worthy of my obsession. Life was a game, he said, and I must play to win. I must put Alisha out of my mind. Instead, get some hot shots. 'Who is the biggest shot in Kaka Nagar?' My father's boss, perhaps. 'Well, make him chief guest.' He told me I could be anything I wanted to be. Teachers, parents, politicians and Alishas—they only instilled fear. I had to stick to my own game.

Jeet announced to my parents that I'd never go hungry in life. Because one, I had ideas; two, I could get things done. These were the two keys to be an 'entrepreneur'. I was hearing that word for the first time. 'Who knows, he might even become a spiritual entrepreneur!' Jeet said. My father was puzzled. Jeet explained that a guru, after all, was someone with an idea and a talent for organizing. And wasn't spirituality our biggest industry? He felt I might even challenge the Radha Soami Guru one day. 'He is royalty born mistakenly in a common family,' Jeet said about me. My father was not amused.

The fun began at seven on the opening night. I looked around for Alisha, but she didn't show up. Then, I forgot my lines. Freezing before the audience, I stood paralyzed on the stage for what felt like an eternity, suffering a thousand deaths. Finally, the lines came back to me. But there was another glitch. The lights were facing the audience, not the actors. Ophelia's father got up and quietly turned their direction. The rest of the evening went off smoothly. I enjoyed taking revenge on Claudius. Laertes was happy to get the better of me in the sword fight. But at one point, things took a dodgy turn. I misjudged the distance between Laertes and me in the fencing scene and gave him a heavy blow with my sword. The poor fellow fell off the stage. The result was a crash and subsequent yell of pain. It was an accident, of course, but he got inflamed, determined to kill me. The stage became the scene of a real-life sword fight, both of us locked in mortal combat. He struck a blow, and I was thrown into the audience. There was wild cheering. When it was over, someone remarked, 'How amazingly realistic!'

But I didn't become rich after the play. Instead of making money, I was in debt. We still had to pay for hiring the lights and the curtain. So I went around the next evening collecting donations to pay our bills. To my surprise, people came forward, happy to rescue me. One of them commented that my play had brought the Kaka Nagar neighbourhood together. After the bills were paid, I was left with a little money. On my way to school the next morning, I stopped at Bengali Market, where I bought red roses. At lunchtime, I waited for Alisha. She didn't appear, and I'd almost given up hope when she burst in giggling with her friends. They placed their books on an empty table near mine to 'reserve' their space and went to collect their lunch boxes. I got up quietly and placed the roses on Alisha's book. Then, I panicked. How would she know they were from me? I quickly tore a page from my notebook, wrote my name and placed it under the flowers.

Her friends spotted the roses immediately and turned to look at Alisha. My heart was racing. She sniggered as she read my name out loud. They looked around, laughing and jeering, and spotted me. I felt ridiculous. I didn't know where to hide. Mortified, I slunk away. I had hit the wall of the absurd. More than humiliation, I was struck by the illogical nature of the snob's choices. Even a twelve-year-old could spot the falsity of her worldview. Since I still had money left, I bicycled to Bengali Market the next day. I saw a bouquet of white carnations in the flower shop. I spent all the money I had on the bouquet, and I went and presented it to the school librarian. The look on her face was my deliverance. I had sought recognition from Alisha but had got redemption from the librarian. God had made a saint out of a sinner.

The winter break began a few weeks later. I had little to do except observe the pretensions of my mother's friends. An essential part of mother's morning was to get dressed and meet her friends over coffee at eleven. They were the wives of my father's colleagues in the irrigation and power department, and lived in Kaka Nagar. It was my mother's turn one morning to host the coffee group. She asked me to help, warning me not to show-off—it wasn't polite. 'Maybe just a bit,' I said. The robin does it, and people find the bird adorable.

'Quick, it's Sheila Dewan,' my mother said as she saw Sheila from the window. 'And I'm not ready!' I protested that she had not paid for her tickets to my play. 'She's tight-fisted,' my mother said, combing her hair as quickly as she could. The bell rang, and I rushed to the door. A lively, round woman in a pink sari walked in. She leaned perilously close to me, exposing her ample bosom through her low-cut blouse. 'Come, give Aunty a hug.' I was tempted to collect my debt, but my mother arrived before I could open my mouth.

Soon the others joined in, and they quickly became absorbed in talk about those who were absent. 'Poor Shanti, she's still looking for a boy for Veena.' Sheila had suggested her own nephew, but Shanti had such airs, playing hard to get. Well, it now seemed that she would get her comeuppance—someone had seen Veena with a man in Lodi Gardens. 'Who, who . . .?' asked the chorus. Sheila wouldn't tell except to say that he was older, charming but penniless. It was a scandal, they agreed.

A few minutes later Shanti arrived. 'Shame on you, gossiping behind my back!' Their elevenses would have ended if they couldn't gossip. Sheila remarked that if you're not talked about, you might as well be dead. Shanti looked around. 'But where is the modern girl?' Indeed, their husbands' boss's second wife was missing. They called her the 'modern girl' because she smoked, drank and danced with men at the 'tea dance' at Ambassador Hotel. But before they could get started, the modern girl walked in, her nose in the air, wearing a mask that concealed slow-boiling malevolence.

Just then, the phone rang. It was my father; he wanted me to rush over on my bicycle with papers he'd left behind. I didn't want to leave when things were getting interesting. The lies of my mother's friends were so elegant, revealing more about themselves than about those they talked about. I was beginning to learn, not about what they were saying but about what they were hiding. But duty called, and I pulled away reluctantly.

In the end, Veena would have the last laugh. I learnt later that she and her Lodi Gardens man had been genuinely in love. Although scandal would dog her for years, she didn't give him up, rebuffing all her mother's offers. Eventually, the couple eloped. Her husband turned out to be not only a fine human being but amazingly successful as an entrepreneur. Of all the marriages in the Kaka Nagar coffee group, Veena's would be the best, by far.

Soon after the winter break, our class began to prepare for UN Day. Just as we believed in socialism, we believed in a new moral world order based on the United Nations. We marched single file, learning to salute, turn about face and stand at ease. Our class had been selected to stand along Rajpath, the old Kingsway, to cheer as the prime minister's motorcade went by from India Gate towards Raisina Hill. There was great excitement, and our teachers were in a state of hysteria. India Gate wore a festive look, with thousands of students and a continuous stream of flags around—the blue UN flag alternating with the Indian tricolour. Nehru's open car arrived on time, preceded by motorcycles and a pilot car with a siren. He looked unbelievably handsome in a cap and a long white coat, with a red rose in the lapel. All of a sudden, he threw a garland of marigold flowers. It came towards me, but I failed to catch it. Brushing my arm, it landed on my neighbour, who became an instant celebrity. I was sad, disappointed.

It is hard to imagine the spirit of hope and idealism that pervaded my parents' generation. As I think about it, the garland symbolized all the fine things that Nehru gave us. He united the most frustratingly diverse people on earth into one nation. We owed him our love for democracy. He taught us to respect minorities, and he nurtured secularism. He injected in us the modernist ideals of liberty and equality, giving us a youthful sense of optimism. He strove relentlessly for Hindu–Muslim brotherhood, his way, perhaps, to obliterate the stain of Partition. And yet, in our personal lives, it did not erase our prejudice against Muslims. Come to think of it, I can't remember having a close Muslim friend, not since Ayan. I don't think it was deliberate—I'm as secular as they come. It's just that the two communities lived separate lives.

My failure to catch the garland that day was an omen of a different sort—a prophesy that I would turn one day against Nehru's command socialism, which sacrificed two generations to missed opportunities. We'd have to wait forty years, till 1991, to regain our economic independence. It's a ghastly thought, but I wonder sometimes: What if Japan had defeated the British–Indian forces in the battles of Kohima and Imphal in 1944, and what if we'd won our independence a few years later from the Japanese, not the British? Who knows, India too might have adopted Japan's successful growth model, becoming an Asian tiger and a middle-class nation. Instead, we latched on to Nehru's failed Fabian socialist dream and have still not created an industrial revolution.

Adolescence is an awkward age; it is when you begin to see through life's half-truths. Alisha's rejection of the roses helped me to grow up. As did the serene, insincere lives of my mother's eleven o'clock coffee group. The spontaneity of my childhood was long gone, and I'd begun to think of myself as someone in disguise. Beneath the obedient, agreeable, well-brought-up boy, who did reasonably well at studies and sports, lay a mocking, derisive and shadowy under-self. I was learning to play the game, pretending to know more than I did, appearing to be stronger than I was. Uncovering life's little deceptions was liberating, although I was unaware at the time that it was another phase in my secret journey to a certain kind of moksha.

Good old Kaka Nagar remains the neighbourhood of my mind. Years later, when I returned to live in Delhi, I was drawn to Kaka Nagar magnetically, somewhat in the way I had been pulled to Alisha the day we met in CP. I have chosen to live near that neighbourhood, revisiting sometimes the lanes etched in my memory, deliberately taking the longer route when I go shopping in CP. Going past my old school, I'm still filled with unrequited yearnings. Alisha was my first love, but I wasn't good enough for her. I thank her, however, for giving me my first entrepreneurial shot. I learnt from performing *Hamlet* that I could make things happen. The dreadful experience of forgetting my lines also inoculated me forever against stage fright; I lost my fear of audiences. Even today, when I have to speak in public, I'm a little nervous before I go on. But as soon as I hit the podium, I'm right at home. There are other memories as I drive past Modern School. How can I forget the image of my mother waiting outside the principal's office? Although three generations have since gone by, the typical Indian mother still experiences the same humiliating ignominy in getting her child into a decent school. The great Indian middle-class struggle goes on. If sifarish doesn't work, there's always rishwat.

My awkward age was, in fact, an age of hope. The Bhakra Nangal Dam, one of Nehru's 'temples of modern India', made me aware of an optimistic spirit in the air. People like my father were inspired by Nehru and his irresistible vision of a modern India. Anything was possible, they felt. My own memory, however, is blighted by my father's insecure boss, who could not tolerate the light shining on a subordinate. The memory of Nehru is also stained by his excessive sense of self-importance, which distracted him from completing his speech that day, diminishing him in my eyes. The other dark cloud in my adolescent memory is the tragic, pointless murder of Mahatma Gandhi, possibly the greatest Indian who ever lived, apart from the Buddha.

5

Slippery Bananas

'. . . and then the fun began.'

—Napoleon Bonaparte

I was no longer a child, nor a grown up. Somewhere in between, I was shuffling from who I had been to who I would become—young enough to dream of being somebody, yet old enough to be cynical about everybody. Since my parents could not afford to take us to Kashmir during the holidays, I told my friends I was going to meet God. Each year my father would buy two adult and four children's tickets by the Frontier Mail to a tiny village station situated on the banks of the Beas River. From there, it was a fifteen-minute ride by tonga to the Radha Soami ashram of a mystical sect where our souls would connect with God (Radha means soul; Soami means God). Because of the Guru, I figured we had a direct line to God and could get an out-of-turn appointment. I had planned to tell God that he hadn't done such a good job in creating people, especially me.

Once, on the Frontier Mail, I hit my kid sister, Meera. Then I felt bad and apologized. My father did not interfere—he kept reading a book. He said he was reading about two birds on a tree, one eating its fruit, the other watching it. He said that the two birds were symbolic of the two voices inside each of us. The one who'd slapped Meera was the eating bird; the one who'd apologized was the godly bird.

'You mean, there's God inside me?'

He nodded.

'In that case, we don't need the Guru.' I could make a direct appointment with God.

The main event at the ashram was the Guru's satsang. It was in an open space covered with a cloth canopy. In a gathering of thousands, the Guru gave his daily discourse to 'truth seekers'. After listening for a while, my middle brother, Manni, and I would get bored—the Guru never seemed to come to the point. So, I'd give Manni a nudge, and we'd sneak out to play cricket nearby. One day, Manni hit a sizzling cover drive. The ball went past the boundary and landed at the Guru's feet. I ran after it, entered the satsang, unmindful of the thousands of eyes on me. Then I picked up the ball and ran out. The Guru continued his discourse, ignoring the interruption.

We expected to be punished, but my father seemed more amused than angry. He advised us, however, to play farther away. Then he went into a cobra position on his yoga mat. Meera asked him what he was doing.

'Trying to make my body lighter,' he said.

'Why?' she asked.

'I feel freer, less burdened.'

Just then, the couple staying next door arrived. Trying to ignore my father's yoga position, they began to complain to my mother about kids playing cricket in a holy ashram. They were recent converts. They didn't think it proper to bring kids to an ashram—it wasn't a holiday resort. My mother apologized, reassuring them that the boys would be shifting their cricket to another spot.

'We have not come on a holiday,' Meera corrected them. 'We have come to meet God.'

The visitors looked at each other. Meera advised them to watch her father doing yoga. 'It will make your bodies lighter. Yours are heavy and burdened.'

They didn't appreciate being lectured by a six-year-old, and my mother had to apologize again. The water was coming to a boil in the kitchen, and my mother rose, asking if they'd like some tea. No, they did not. Tea was unhealthy, they said.

While she was gone, the husband gave us some advice. 'Children, karma is always watching us,' he said. 'It knows when you're bad, when you're good. So, it is best to be on good behaviour.'

I told him that karma worked slowly in my case—the results would only be seen in my next life, and by then I'd be dead in this one. He gave me a look and decided to change the subject. Trying to be friendly, he asked me what I wanted to grow up to be. 'A cricketer?' he asked condescendingly.

'No, 'I'd prefer to be a guru.' Cousin Jeet had put the idea in my head. 'I would like to have a big, sprawling place like this, people bowing to me all the time and a private line to God.'

When my mother returned, the neighbours told her that her children said the most peculiar things. At lunch that day, we gathered that they had recounted their conversation to all who were present. The news about our doings spread quickly. By late afternoon we were famous. My mother was embarrassed when someone stopped her on the street and asked, 'What do you feed your kids, sister-ji?'

In the following day's satsang, the Guru had a different take on the matter. Yesterday's cricket ball, he told the devotees, offered some lessons. One was how to live. 'Don't take on the burdens of the world. Live as though you are playing a game.' Another lesson was that satsang is a means to an end, like the cricket ball. The end objective of a satsang was to motivate us to meditate and achieve moksha, liberation from the cycle of birth and rebirth. 'Think of ourselves as railway passengers,' he said, explaining that the satsang was like a railway station. We could wait on the station platform all our lives, but we would not reach God unless we got on the train.

He had a third lesson. 'You have come to this ashram to get away from the walls that divide people. Here, we try and pull down those walls, and we build bridges. So, don't get annoyed at a cricket ball. Don't judge others; focus on your own meditation, on God and your moksha.' My mother felt relieved after the Guru's message.

Ever since we had arrived, there had been incessant talk of God, and it prompted Meera to express scepticism about His efficacy. She reminded us about our neighbour's dog in Delhi who had been very sick. All four of us had prayed for the Lhasa Apso. Either God did not hear her prayers or he wasn't powerful enough, because the dog died. I don't think my father gave her an acceptable explanation. He was more interested in teaching us about moksha that morning. He told us the story about a moksha tree that provided shade, a refuge for travellers lost in the jungle. It also taught them how to climb its branches to escape from the frightening jungle animals. Finally, it gave them its fruit, which freed them from their fears and sufferings. Meera approved of the tree and wanted to eat its fruit right away.

The Guru's satsang did not have the desired effect on our neighbours. They continued to complain and had even gone to the security office to file our names. My mother was wary when one of the security staff had smilingly referred to us as 'troublemakers'. Since we were under watch, we had curtailed our cricket. The next day, my parents went early to the satsang, and I was left in charge of my siblings. The four of us were sitting around spiritless, waiting for something to happen. We were on the first floor and had a clear view of the devotees going past below. There was a tray of bananas staring at me in our room; one of the bananas was half peeled. This was when the idea came to me. What if we flung a banana peel out of the window and it landed near our neighbour? Nothing quite relieves boredom like a stirring thought. Manni did not think it a good idea. He said karma was slipping yourself on the banana peel you'd thrown for someone else. But I felt karma didn't work like that. It waited to strike the one who most deserved it—i.e., our neighbour.

Suddenly, life was full of banana peels. Manni and I began to remove the peel and give the bananas to our younger siblings to eat. I explained that success lay in the slipperiness of the peel's underside. The key was to ensure that the peel landed properly and at the right time—it had to hit the ground just before the prospect got there. My youngest brother, Tutu, said he'd never seen anyone slip on a banana peel. I assured him that it worked; I'd seen it in a Laurel and Hardy movie. 'Monkeys like bananas,' Meera observed. 'But monkeys don't slip on banana peels,' Tutu corrected her.

It was a delicate operation, and I felt we had to rehearse. I'd learnt about the importance of rehearsing during our performance of *Hamlet*. So, trial runs began. Tutu would hand me a peel, I'd glance below to check if anyone was looking, and then I'd drop it. It took three trials before I got the hang of it. The next thing was to find out when the target was leaving the building. I asked Manni to go and check if our neighbours were in their room. Yes, they were, he reported; but they would be leaving soon. I told him to hide behind a pillar and report instantly when he saw them exit. Meanwhile, I rushed downstairs and collected the trial peels—they could be used as evidence.

'The target is leaving,' Manni announced. We took our positions. Tutu handed me a peel. I located the target—he was walking with a complacent smile. His wife was following him. I then released the missile. A few seconds later, the victim's left foot stepped on the peel. He performed a pirouette, trying to regain balance. He landed with one foot in heaven the other on the banana peel. The next moment he was sitting on the ground, shaken but not hurt.

As I think back, the whole operation seems improbable. It was a difficult task, and I still don't know how we pulled it off. It was beginner's luck, perhaps. We made several mistakes, though. We looked down from above—the temptation to see our victim slip was too great. Sure enough, he looked up, and he saw us grinning. He was breathing fire. Instead of going to the satsang, our neighbour marched off to the security office. Another mistake we made was to assume that they would join in the fun. No one likes to be the fool—even Oliver Hardy didn't laugh when he bit the dust. Years later, I would learn that it takes a wise man to laugh at himself.

Our incensed neighbour recounted his tale at the security office, demanding that the guilty be evicted from the ashram. Luckily, a hard-nosed person was manning the office, and he insisted on hard evidence. So the neighbour returned to the crime scene to collect the evidence. But he was out of luck. No one had seen us throw the banana peel. He came to our rooms looking for proof, but I had thrown all the peels in a rubbish bin down the street.

When my parents returned from the satsang, we could not contain ourselves and gave them a full, blow-by-blow account. We were laughing, but my father didn't even smile. He grew serious and unhappy. He said that it's wrong to seek revenge; karma would have taken care of it. And those who hurt others, eventually face their own karma. He then explained the difference between deliberate and undeliberate acts. We had no way of knowing if the ball would enter the satsang—it was an undeliberate act. But the banana peel was a deliberate act of revenge. He declared us guilty, and made us go to the man and apologize. Instead of getting placated by the apology, our neighbours were on the warpath. But gradually they grew calm, realizing they now had their evidence.

Again, they marched off to the security office, where the same pitiless man asked them to repeat their story. Our apology was the confession of our guilt, they insisted. After listening calmly, he grew quiet. Then he smiled and announced that action had been taken. Since they had got their apology, nothing more was to be done. The matter was closed. The neighbours returned disappointed. My mother, however, felt contrite and took a basket of fruit to them as a sign of repentance. She was also upset with me. 'You have a perverse streak, just like Jeet!' she yelled. She thought up different punishments, but my father vetoed her. He felt I had learnt my lesson.

I don't know what I learnt from this episode. I don't think it was the spirit of revenge alone that had been driving me. I just wanted to have fun. I might have also wanted to loosen up our uptight neighbours. What I did not realize was that new converts tend to be fanatics, and fanatics are determined to be offended. Nevertheless, over time, I did sober up and got out of the habit of playing such pranks. For example, I rejected Tutu's idea of throwing a bucket of water on the target the following week.

There was relief all around when it was time for us to leave. I looked up from the tonga at our rooms above. Our neighbour stood at the window, pleased to see the back of us. As we went past the security office, they waved to us and wrote 'Departed' after our names in the register of 'Troublemakers'. I'm not sure if God was equally pleased with our departure from the ashram, because we never got a chance to meet Him.

We rode along the Beas River for three miles, passing a line of buffaloes going towards the water, flicking flies with their tails. At the railway station, we took a train that delivered us in a couple of hours to Ludhiana. Once again, I was united with my maternal grandparents, uncles and cousins.

As we were finishing dinner on our first night in Ludhiana, my grandmother, seeing my empty plate, asked, 'Do you want some more?' I hesitated. 'Don't you like it?' Of course, I did. 'You didn't like it, I bet.' I insisted I did. In that case, I had to have some more. She poured a generous helping, and I groaned. After a while, Bhabo said, 'Shukar hai!' I asked her why she kept repeating those words. She was thanking God, she said, for still being alive. Meera tried to correct her, saying that God wasn't a good listener—our neighbour's dog had died, despite our prayers. Ignoring her, Bhabo continued. So many had suffered, so many had died in Partition—she was grateful to be alive.

After dinner, Bhabo brought out a luxurious tray in red velvet with a display of fifty-one keys tied in a gold-coloured cord. With a sad laugh, she told us that she had fully expected to return to Lyallpur. On her return, she would have opened with these keys the safe, the chests, the cupboards and the drawers. She had given a month's salary to the staff, telling them to clean the house daily while she was on 'holiday'. She would telegram ahead, so that they would have dinner ready.

'Be sure to water the plants!' she had hollered from the carriage as she was leaving.

'Stop living in the past, Bhabo-ji,' Raj Mama interrupted his mother impatiently. His own take on Partition was that it was like a few bad days you get in Punjab's winter. The good days were back again, and life was now normal.

'Normal?' Bhabo asked, wondering if it was normal to be living in some Muslim's house, someone they would never know, who had to flee to the other side of the border and who might even have died on the way to Pakistan.

Bauji had lost everything. From a man of substance at the height of his career, he had sunk to a refugee's life of struggle and hardship. His tired eyes seemed to ask where the prime years of his manhood and strength had gone. He had slowly restarted his law practice by documenting the properties that the refugees had left behind. Then, he fought for their claims with the newly created Refugee Rehabilitation Department, succeeding eventually in recovering 10 per cent of his client's lost assets. The quaint Muslim house in which Bauji's family was now living had come, in fact, from his struggle to get 10 per cent of what he had left behind.

Bhabo had planted jasmine and gardenia bushes in the courtyard, and hung identical blinds in the narrow veranda to give her a mild illusion of the place she had left behind. The *guchcha* of keys was her only tangible possession of the past. It never ceased to bring back memories of happier days, helping her to bear the pain of all that she'd lost.

There were many refugee families like Bauji's in Ludhiana. Partition may have dampened their spirits, but it could not hold them back for long. They pulled themselves out of the abyss gradually and, with restless energy, began to change the sleepy provincial town into an industrial hub. My uncles, too, regained their spirits and soon were back in form. Bade Mama set up a moderate law practice. Raj Mama became reader in economics at the government college. Satinder Mama completed a master's degree in English literature and became lecturer at the same college. Bauji's redoubtable son-in-law, Harish Kathpalia, was now principal of the government college in Ludhiana. Jeet joined the elite cadre of the Indian Railways, where he became a highflyer, popular on and off the tennis court, especially among women. I had hoped to ride one day in his saloon, but alas, he got caught in a scandal and returned to Ludhiana to become an entrepreneur.

A few days after our arrival, Satinder Mama got the idea that we should not waste our holidays. He proposed to introduce us to English literature. Claiming to make me and my brothers into 'perfect English gentlemen', he drew up a list of books, including *Gulliver's Travels, Alice's Adventures in Wonderland, Huckleberry Finn, Great Expectations* and *Animal Farm*. When my mother objected that the books were too difficult for children, he reassured her that a 'perfect gentleman' read a few good books early, and they stayed in his head all his life. She also protested the idea of turning us into 'English' gentlemen when the English were gone.

Cousin Jeet dropped in on our 'home school' one morning. We rose to say 'good morning'. Jeet asked if the morning was *really* good. Or, perhaps, the morning would *become* good? Or maybe we were *feeling* good this morning? Satinder Mama was not amused. As he was leaving, Jeet suggested that an essential part of being an English gentleman was to learn cricket and tennis from a professional. Principal Harish had professional teachers in his college, Jeet said. We should meet him.

That evening, we were taken by my mother to meet Harish Uncle, who lived in a sprawling colonial bungalow, which came with being principal of the government college. It was surrounded by vast green playing fields, watered daily and cared for meticulously by an army of gardeners. We were in awe as our eyes fell on an impressive display of silver cups and trophies on the marble mantlepiece. He casually mentioned that they were prizes that he and his sons had won in tournaments. While we were having tea, three elegant young men in whites walked in. Two were holding tennis racquets, one had a cricket bat under his arm. They looked grand.

Harish Uncle told his sons to take us to the playing fields, introduce us to the sports staff and initiate our training. I was invited to join tennis and cricket lessons, but my siblings were considered too young. My mother bought me a sports shirt, shorts and tennis shoes—all white. So began an 'essential' part of making me a perfect English gentleman.

Jeet insisted on getting me a bicycle that I could ride to the playfield. Off we went the next day to Chaura Bazaar. Just as we arrived at the store, Jeet realized his mistake. From the door, he spotted his bank manager examining a new bicycle. Since Jeet had fallen behind on his loan, the manager was the was the last person he wanted to meet.

'Ah, Jeet Varma! Just the man I wanted to see,' hailed the man.

'Just a minute, sir. I'll be right with you,' replied my cousin.

Jeet did some quick thinking. He knew the bank manager's office was around the corner; he was also aware that the manager had not seen me. He whispered to me that I should wait outside the store, count to twenty and then come in and give the following message to the bank manager: 'Sir, there's smoke in your office. They're asking for you.'

I did as I was told. Just as the manager began to reprimand my cousin, I entered and gave the message. The man jumped and ran instantly. We made a quiet and dignified exit. Jeet took me to a far corner of the bazaar and treated me to an ice cream; after a decent interval, we returned to the bicycle shop. Just before we entered, Jeet advised me not to sound too enthusiastic—he had planned to bargain. I spotted a gleaming Raleigh in English racing green and fell in love instantly. Looking bored, Jeet went up to the shopkeeper and began to bargain. With resignation, he looked at me and said casually, 'We might as well take a trial.' The shopkeeper said that they did not normally allow trials. 'These are not normal times, brother,' Jeet replied. Before the shopkeeper could say anything, Jeet took charge of the object of my desire. As we came out of the door, he picked a second bicycle for himself from a stack leaning against the wall. The shopkeeper stood in a state of mild panic.

'I'll race you,' Jeet said to me.

I jumped on the bike and sounded the bell. Jeet was soon waving to the shop owner while we rode into the wind. We passed the clock tower, went over the railway bridge, past the women's college, and finally reached home. Jeet got busy with paperwork related to his factory; I waited to return the bicycle. I kept waiting all day, but he didn't seem to be bothered.

Bauji noticed the two bicycles in the evening. Over dinner, he turned to me with affectionate irony that old age accords to youth and said, 'I see you have a lovely new Raleigh!' I confessed that we had not paid for it yet.

Bauji turned to Jeet. 'Do you steal bicycles, sir?'

Jeet shook his head.

'You have nice manners for a thief, sir,' Bauji said.

'If I wanted to be a thief,' Jeet retorted, 'I would run for election, go to Delhi and steal the country, sir.'

Bauji turned to me. 'A thief steals from his peace of mind, son. There's no such thing as a rich thief.' Before I could reply, Jeet informed him that our jails were full of bicycle thieves while the real crooks were looting the country.

The next day, Jeet and I returned the bicycles to the relieved store owner. He'd lost all hope, and so he welcomed us with a smile. Jeet had a proposal for him. Since I was visiting only for a month, would he rent the Raleigh? But they didn't rent bicycles. Jeet asked, 'Then what do you do, my good man?' The shopkeeper said they sold bicycles. 'What a silly idea!' Jeet said. 'You'll make far more money if you rent it out.' He asked for a paper and pencil and demonstrated that his profit from the bicycle trade would double under his proposal. The shopkeeper looked at the numbers and then, dubiously, at us. Finally, he agreed. I walked out proudly with a new bicycle, ready to become the perfect English gentleman.

I had several attractive female cousins. One was Jeet's sister, and a couple of older daughters of my aunt had come on a holiday. They were given a room next to ours, and one day I walked in by mistake. The older one had just come out of the bath, and her naked buttocks were exposed to the world. I stood transfixed. My senses were inflamed, filled with sensual emotions of raw desire. She saw me and screamed. I was frozen on the spot. She quickly covered herself and accused me of voyeurism. I denied it. But she didn't believe me and informed my mother, who insisted that I be punished. Bauji interrogated me and was satisfied that it was not a deliberate act. The matter soon died, but the memory of a gentle light falling on her beautiful, light-brown, naked bottom persisted for years.

It was at this time when Raj Mama's gas problem flared. He'd go around farting from room to room. The only thing that helped was someone to listen to him narrate the state of his stomach. Hourly bulletins on his digestive tract began early in the morning and went on till evening. He moved from room to room mournfully, groaning, gasping and doubling up in agony. Bhabo moaned that she'd given him everything possible—Western medicines plus the Ayurvedic, homeopathic and Unani remedies. What fixed the flatulence in the end was the annual economics debate in his college.

As Raj Mama was climbing the steps to his office, Raju, the diligent secretary of the economics department, sprang on him. The debate was only ten days away, and they had yet to decide on the subject. Raj Mama looked queasy. The secretary guessed it was the old problem—the entire department knew of it. The debate gave Raj Mama a sense of self- importance. The thought energized him. Raju suggested 'Capitalism versus Socialism' as the subject. It was sure to pull a crowd, thought Raj Mama, but it had already been the subject of earlier debates. 'How about "Central Planning"?' Raju asked. Raj Mama thought it too boring and too Russian. In the end, they settled on a spicier version, 'Abolish the Planning Commission!' Raj Mama managed to land a bigwig from Delhi as chief guest and proudly sent out gold-embossed invitations to everyone important in town. And thus, his flatulence went away.

On the evening of the debate, there was much excitement in the house. All of us attended, of course, including my baby sister. The audience soon began to fill the lecture hall. Bauji sat in the VIP rows in front, along with Principal Harish. Raj Mama spread a rich velvet cloth on the dais, which gave a gorgeous touch to the occasion. As VIPs began to arrive, Raj Mama ran to and fro, conducting them to their seats. Soon, the hall was full; late-coming students hung on to the banisters.

'What a crowd!' Bade Mama said.

There was cheering and stamping of feet as Raj Mama went up to the podium and began, 'Ladies and gentlemen, welcome! I am going to briefly introduce the subject of our debate.' He promised 'not to stand between the audience and the attractions to come', but that was exactly what he did. He filled the hall with his sonorous voice for a full fifteen minutes. The audience began to fidget. Finally, he introduced the chief guest. Tarlok Singh, member of the Planning Commission, confessed that he had not bargained for such a large crowd at a debate about a complex, technical subject. He began to trace the intricate history of central planning, and before long he had put us all to sleep. The audience woke up momentarily when he mentioned Partition, Nehru and Gandhi. At dinner that night, Raj Mama was beaming like a hero as we all dissected the minutest details of the event.

The next episode about Raj Mama needs a caveat. It seems improbable, but I have included it because it's in the family lore. It took place apparently about six months before our visit. The family is divided on this. Some insist that it happened; others deny it, including Raj Mama himself. My mother's diary is silent. It had to do with an invitation that he received from his colleague to attend his wedding in Delhi. Raj Mama seldom travelled out of Ludhiana, and he was excited for this opp. He arrived at the station much too early. He placed his luggage in the retiring room and began to pace the platform. During the first hour, he synchronized his watch with the railway clock and went to check twice with the assistant station master if his train was on time. When he heard an engine whistle or the sound of a goods train being shunted, he looked up and wondered if it was time.

In the second hour, he ascertained the exact spot on the platform where his compartment would halt. He moved his luggage there and found a bench to sit on nearby. While he was killing time, he spotted a friend who happened to be taking the same train. They went over to the railway stall, and while relaxing over tea and biscuits, they began to quarrel. It was over something that had happened many years ago. The argument became heated. Both forgot the time, and both missed the train. Raj Mama returned home quietly; and he left equally quietly the next day.

Our holiday in Ludhiana was a great success. Yes, it brought back sad memories of Partition, a nagging reminder that I was the offspring of a country that had to pay the price of independence by getting mutilated. The borders of the new nation were scratched by a scornful British bureaucratic pen, and it tore the hearts of millions like my grandfather. In his eyes, the birth of a spoiled theocracy in Pakistan was a monstrous act of treason. The historic blunder not only deprived him of his home, but it was conceived falsely, born of religious hatred, surely not a sound basis for nationhood. As if to prove the bungle, Pakistan went on to become a nation where a crooked few would rule the impotent many, where corrupt politicians and unscrupulous generals would be allies one day and execute each other the next.

What hurt Bauji the most was the British betrayal—he'd trusted and admired them, learnt so much from them. Then, one day in August, they simply tossed away their jewel in the crown, like some cheap trinket. They bolted without providing any sort of protection to 20 million refugees, undermining their greatest legacy—the rule of law and order. Oh, yes, Mountbatten said some tender things. But in a separation, it is the one who is not really in love who says the more tender things. Bhabo's guchcha would remain forever a symbol of Britain's perfidy. And yet, most Indians did not feel bitterness or any resentment towards the British. It might have been due to Gandhi's ethic of forgiveness.

When I went to university, I discovered that all nations had been invented. The political scientist Benedict Andersen would teach me that they are 'imagined communities'. A nation state based on common descent, language and shared culture is a European fiction of the nineteenth century. Because our colonial rulers referred to India contemptuously as a 'geographic expression', our nationalists also got busy creating a sense of oneness based on the 'wonder that was India'. Some Muslims protested; they did not share a fellow feeling for Hindus and wanted a nation based on Islam. Well, they got 'imaginary' Pakistan! Born in two parts, it was torn apart twenty-four years later, proving that religion is not a sound basis for nationhood. Nor is race or language. Since all criteria of identity fail, let's face the inconvenient truth: there is no glue that naturally unites human beings. The only reason I 'consent' to live in a place is because I want to live in it. It provides what I want: the rule of law to make my life predictable, gives me health and education, and creates opportunities for work and prosperity.

I was happy, even ecstatic, to see in Ludhiana that the same laghima, the absence of weight, still governed the existence of some of my family. 'Can't you ever be serious?' was my grandmother's perpetual lament. I have attended many schools, but in none did I experience the fun, the warmth of the home schooling in Ludhiana. Bauji, who turned bitter against the Raj, was amused by Satinder Mama's project to make us 'perfect English gentlemen'. I would go on to read some of the books on my uncle's list, but I wish he had focused on a gentleman's genuine qualities. While learning to say 'good morning' and playing cricket and tennis in the evenings, I wish we had been taught to be calm, considerate, self-effacing; to listen more, talk less. To be honest and kind, above all. Oddly enough, Mahatma Gandhi had also wished to become a 'perfect English gentleman' when he was in England as a youngster. He got a new wardrobe, stood in front of the mirror, arranging his tie and parting his hair. He took lessons in dancing, elocution, violin and French. But he, too, realized that there was something more to being a 'perfect English gentleman'.

The memory of Ayan's unhappy face kept returning. I remembered him again that day when I was in a panic over the 'borrowed' Raleigh cycle, wondering if Jeet ever meant to return it. No one reveals the complete truth—it comes disguised as a half-truth and is darker than a plain lie. Of all the people who have written about Partition, Saadat Hasan Manto came closest in capturing its futility, its insanity. Salman Rushdie's ironic gaze in *Midnight's Children* was a good effort. The wounds of Partition, however, will not heal until we have our own Tolstoy, who will write for us our own *War and Peace*, proving that the real losers in Partition were ordinary Hindus and Muslims, who practised their faith quietly, believing that religion was a private matter. He will hold a mirror to today's India and Pakistan, where Muslim terrorists and Hindu nationalists are well and alive, and ordinary people know in their hearts that borders created by bureaucrats deserve to be treated with contempt.

6

America, O America

*'Americans will put up with anything
provided it doesn't block the traffic.'*

—Dan Rather

We returned from our holidays to find Kaka Nagar boiling with envy. The news had got out: we were going to America. My father had been transferred to Washington, DC, as part of a team of engineers to negotiate with Pakistan the division of the water of the Punjab rivers. Since the World Bank was funding the development of the river basins, it was the mediator. My mother was delighted, but her coffee group were in depression, resentful that their husbands hadn't been selected. Sheila announced that Americans had people with whitewashed faces and pigeons dropped poop on your head there. She'd read in *Reader's Digest* that Irving Park in Chicago was called 'Pigeon Poop Park' because pigeons pooped on politicians there. 'Who wants to live in a nation of gangsters!' said Shanti. Alisha advised me to take American history in school—it would be a breeze, since they had so little of it. My father put these comments down to envy—people cannot tolerate the good fortune of others. Envy is a kind of praise, he said; it is better to be envied than pitied.

Our tickets arrived soon, and we left on the evening of 5-5-55 on an unbelievably luxurious Air India Super Constellation plane. (Air India was then the world's most admired airline, but it would soon be nationalized and go into terminal decline.) I felt like Hanuman, prancing above the clouds, soaring over the Himalayas. We broke our journey in London, where we were shocked to see white people cleaning the streets and serving us at the hotel. The waitress offered us a cup of tea. She came from the north and had to repeat herself several times before we realized that she was speaking English.

We arrived in the United States in the heyday of Eisenhower's America. 'I Like Ike' buttons were still around, leftovers from the campaign. There were cars everywhere with huge tailfins, in which people went to drive-in restaurants and drive-in movies. They were building highways to fit all those cars. I fancied myself in a Ford convertible with the roof down but instead found myself in an American high school. My mother was delighted that she didn't have to beg anyone to get me into school. Soon, however, she discovered that I was ahead of my class. She went and pleaded with the vice principal to allow me into the 'college prep' section. He refused. Looking at my brown skin, he offered me some advice. 'Coloured boys not s'posed to get too big for their boots,' he said in a southern drawl. Leaning back in his swivel chair, he told me that if I worked hard and stayed out of trouble, I would graduate with a vocational certificate. With it, I'd be sure to get a factory job. 'Welcome to the American dream, son!'

Each morning, I would rush to catch the bus at the 16th Street corner, and after a twenty-minute ride I'd find myself singing 'America the Beautiful!' in the school assembly. At lunch, I went down to the cafeteria. On my first day, the lady behind the counter wanted to know what I planned to eat. Looking at the vegetables, I said, 'Cabbage.' She said cabbage was a 'side' dish. 'What about potatoes?' I asked. 'Also a side.' I was confused. She said I needed a main dish. 'How 'bout meat? You'll grow up strong!' I was holding up the line, and kids behind me were getting fidgety. I said I was vegetarian.

'This is America—you want a bowl of raw, red meat,' the kid behind me quipped. The lady at the counter added that eating meat was natural. A kind, older boy jumped the line, came up from behind and explained, 'No ma'am, eating meat is a decision.' He took me to another counter, where he ordered a grilled American cheese sandwich and an 8-ounce carton of milk. It was delicious. I liked it so much that I had the same meal every day. On special occasions, I would give myself a treat and order cherry pie. Thus began my life as a vegetarian in America.

After school, I would walk back to the bus stand, put 10 cents in the slot and take the bus home. At our apartment hotel, a Black woman in bright-red uniform and wearing bright-red lipstick would greet me. She would turn the shiny brass handle in the elevator. When we reached my floor, I would say, 'Thank you.'

'Wackam, hun!' she would reply. It took me a few weeks to figure out that she was saying, 'Welcome, honey!'

Rushing into our apartment, I would be drawn to a humongous, magical wooden cabinet in the living room. Inside it was a tiny black-and-white TV. Each day at four thirty, my brothers and sister would be glued to *The Lone Ranger* on ABC. His horse, Silver, reminded me of Bijli. I loved the way they rode together and caught the bad guys. At the end of the show, the Lone Ranger would yell, 'Hi-ho, Silver, away!' Those words, spoken triumphantly, became my rallying cry. I ignored our neighbour, who often reminded my mother that TV had a deadly effect on kids: it would shrink my attention span and empty my mind. When her warnings went unheeded, she said with resignation, 'Welcome to America, the only country where parents obey their children.'

Because I did not get into college prep, I was way ahead of the others in the vocational section. I would raise my hand as soon as the teacher asked a question. It got so bad that one of the teachers asked me to stop doing that. 'Give the others a chance!' she said. But I couldn't help it— my hand would go up automatically. My classmates were cold towards me, and I could sense their resentment. One of them called me 'teacher's pet'. Another said, 'Just cause you ain't white, you don't need to suck up.' Eventually, I managed to control my natural exuberance, keeping my learning to myself. This modesty was new for someone used to swanking about.

I also had to attend a class called 'Shop'. The 'Shop Room' was filled with lathes, tools and machines, where we learnt to work with our hands. We were taught how to make a table, how to unclog a sink, how to fix a radio, and the best in our class could even repair a car. I wasn't good at all. Only the lower castes in India worked with their hands. My engineer father, however, applauded 'Shop', and he wished we had it back home. It would teach us to respect manual work, making us shed our high-caste prejudice.

A new American friend of ours, Joe Leeming, came for dinner a few nights later. My father told him about my problems with 'Shop'. Introducing me to a new a new word, he suggested I become a 'tinkerer'. A tinkerer combined knowledge with working with hands; he innovated and became an entrepreneur. 'We could do with more tinkerers in India,' my father said. I took to Mr Leeming. A bald bachelor, he was always entertaining, quoting from great books without showing off. I never knew quite what he did, but he began to spend hours discussing mystical ideas with my father on the weekends.

One day at school, I realized I was losing a rich White classmate every day and gaining a poor Black one. A lot was changing in Eisenhower's America. Everyone was becoming richer. The middle class was pursuing bigger cars, bigger TVs for their bigger homes in the new suburbs. The Whites were abandoning the cities for a big home in suburbia, leaving the cities to the Blacks. Eighty per cent of my school was White when I arrived in 1955, and 80 per cent was Black when I left in 1959.

America was preaching integration but practising segregation. The best thing about turning into a Black school was that we got a stunning Black history teacher, Miss Allen. The boys called her 'Sexy' because of her hour-glass figure. She replaced our grouchy White teacher, who had left for the suburban comfort of McLean, Virginia. Miss Allen used to bring a copy of the *Washington Post* and comment on history in the making. One morning in December 1955, she was reading excitedly about a forty-two-year-old Black seamstress who had refused to get up for a White woman in a bus in Montgomery, Alabama. The driver summoned the police, who arrested her for violating the city's segregation rules. The Blacks boycotted the bus service. There was a trial, and the Supreme Court declared segregation unconstitutional. Thanks to Miss Allen, we followed the story month after month. The woman was Rosa Parks. It was the beginning of Martin Luther King's civil rights movement, and it changed America before my eyes.

Miss Allen taught us that race was not a biological term. It was invented by White men who wrote books showing that Whites were superior. Whites were supposed to 'think'; Blacks were meant to 'labour'. It turned out to be a lie. Schoolbooks were rewritten, but people continued to believe the lie. 'And why?' she asked. Because peoples' minds were not free. America declared 'all men are created equal', but Blacks were not men for them. Americans spoke of 'manifest destiny' and killed Red Indians. I had a scary thought. What if Christopher Columbus had found us in India? Real Indians, not Red Indians. We, too, might have been the meat of 'manifest destiny'.

I told my father about Miss Allen's words. He agreed with her, saying that prejudice was universal—it was the common enemy of humanity. He reminded me about the 'Bhangi', a member of the lowest untouchable caste, in Bauji's home, carrying shit away in a basket. They had not yet put in a flush system, and only Bhangis were willing to clean latrines. Race in America was caste in India, both deciding your destiny at birth. It was ironic that I had come to America to learn about caste in India.

By the term's end, I decided Miss Allen was my best teacher. I think I was also in love with her. She had given another meaning to my moksha journey: 'You are not free until everyone around you is free.' In her final class, she got emotional. 'Learn to respect yourself, and this comes from knowing that your behaviour is based on truth, not on lies. When you disrespect someone, you disrespect yourself.' I got an 'A' in American history. It was not because there was so little American history, as Alisha had said. It was because I began to love history.

My mother used to take us shopping on weekends. Dragging a small cart, we would walk to Safeway with a bunch of discount coupons that she had clipped from our newspaper. Sometimes we would drop in at a competitor store, Giant, to check their prices and cash in our coupons. At the checkout counters in the supermarket, we would witness the American competitive spirit as everyone rushed to join a new line as soon as a new cashier came on. Next to Safeway there was a drugstore, where we were rewarded sometimes with an ice cream cone. Meera, my sister, always ordered strawberry flavour, and she licked it slowly. We'd gobble ours and then watch her longingly as she ate hers. The object of my desire was a banana split, but it was beyond our budget.

In the spring, we were taken to see *Oklahoma*. It was the first movie in 70 mm, and everyone was talking about it. I was in a trance as we came out of the theatre on 14th Street. All of us burst into 'Oh, What a Beautiful Mornin''. I begged my mother to take us to another movie, but she always made excuses. It was either 'not suitable for kids' or 'the movies—they'll ruin you'. Feeling frustrated, I stole 50 cents from her purse and went to watch *The Red Shoes*. The matinee ticket was 35 cents, but I also treated myself to popcorn and coke, and still had 5 cents left. It is the story of a ballet dancer who falls in love with an orchestra conductor. She has to choose, in the end, between her dance and her man. I fell in love both with the heroine and the hero. Except at the end, the film turned sad. I wanted to talk about it with my family but could not—I had stolen the money.

This led to a decision: I got a paper route to make some money. My parents agreed reluctantly. Early each morning I'd go house to house, pulling a wagon full of the *Washington Post,* delivering it to readers in my neighbourhood on 16th Street. It used to be beastly cold in the winter, and I had to be up at 5 a.m. If it rained or snowed, I would put a plastic cover on the wagon; people didn't like wet newspapers. I had to hold my tongue when they didn't pay me at the end of the month. When I complained to my boss, he advised me to swallow my pride—it wouldn't give me indigestion. They would eventually pay up, but only after repeated reminders. Some thought my British–Indian accent odd, but I didn't change to talking American. I was comfortable in my own voice. It was the Americans, I thought, who needed help with their accent.

I didn't much go for small talk. I'd lose interest as soon as people began to make polite conversation. It was meaningless yak-yak, filling the air stupidly. I wanted to talk about ideas. So I was a bit of a loner. But my mother was not. She loved meeting people and looked forward to the regular get-togethers of parents and teachers. She listened intently as they talked about how to improve the school. Soon, they would begin to talk about our neighbourhood—about garbage on the streets, local bus service, condition of the roads, etc. My mother was amazed that Americans belonged to so many local groups—Little League baseball, Girl Scouts, bowling leagues, book clubs, you name it. 'Americans are joiners!' Miss Allen told her. Later, I would discover that this was called 'social capital'.

I didn't mix much either with Whites or Blacks, except with Roy Hawkins. He was a tall, burly Black boy who looked at me with sad eyes. He was always quiet and sat at the back of the class. Roy invited me home one day. He lived close to the school, and we walked over to his greyish house in the middle of a Black neighbourhood. His mother had made a cake and was nice to me. She told me how Roy was so fond of me. The three of us were sitting chatting away when there was a knock. It was the police. They were suddenly barking orders, shining flashlights, even though it was daytime. They were looking for Roy's father. Roy's mother broke into tears. She was crying, telling them he wasn't there. They left after a while, but I was too shy to ask Roy why they were looking for his father.

My mother reported seeing a different face of the American police. Thinking she'd lost her purse on 14th Street, she was in a panic, looking everywhere. She spotted a cop, 'this nice man in blue', who joined her in the search. Soon, he found the purse, lying on a bench at a street corner. She must have dropped it. Nothing was missing, and she was relieved. When the policeman walked her home, she couldn't stop thanking him. She had witnessed a comforting aspect of the police, while Roy's mother had seen its scary face. My mother was left with a warm sense of safety; Roy's family was left with a feeling of terror.

A White girl from school invited me one day to her birthday party. I wasn't often invited, and so I was delighted at the opportunity. Most of the kids there were from school. Soon, we sat down to eat, and then, having stuffed ourselves, we played a popular game called Spin the Bottle. You sat in a circle on the floor with a bottle at the centre. A player would spin the bottle, and when it stopped spinning, you had to kiss the person of the opposite sex sitting where the bottle was pointing. An unwritten rule at this party was that Black boys kissed only Black girls, and White boys kissed only White girls. When it was my turn, there was confusion. No one was sure what I would do. I solved the problem by kissing every girl, Black or White. I kissed them so often, I kept getting bonus turns. I had found my mantra: 'If you are kissed, kiss back.'

On 15 August each year, we would receive an invitation to the Indian embassy for the Independence Day flag ceremony. It was always a grand event, with glamorously dressed men and women of the Indian community and Washington's diplomatic corps. We were low in the pecking order, children of a mid-level official, and were told to sit on the side and behave. The best part was the food after the flag ceremony. As we mingled in the crowd, my parents would introduce us to their friends and acquaintances. People invariably asked, 'And what will you grow up to be?' I wished I knew. I'd grin stupidly and give a stupid reply. It was boring to be asked the same question year after year. So, I decided to be creative. The following year, I said, 'Lion tamer.' This made an impression. A couple

from Eastern Europe decided to play along. They asked if I'd brought a
pet lion from India. I made up a story: US customs had seized my lion. It
grew homesick, but I wasn't allowed to keep him. So I donated him to the
zoo. Yes, I did visit my lion regularly.

'Indian children are remarkable,' the wife said.

To an elderly lady, I gave a different answer. I wanted to be an 'actuary'.
It was a word I had recently learnt in school. She raised her eyebrows and
asked why I had chosen that profession.

'Because I am interested in death.'

'How odd!' she said and went off.

I was now getting into the swing of it, inventing new future personas.
The next year, when the same question came up, I replied, 'Capitalist.'
Miss Allen had just introduced us to Karl Marx. My questioner asked why
I had hit upon that profession. I told her that I'd exploit labour, buy up
my competition, become rich and powerful. She grew quiet, and then left.
She told my mother that I was either over-smart or in need of therapy. I
got a mouthful when we got home. I replied, 'How am I to know what I
will be until I become it?'

Capitalist America was paranoid over the communist threat in those
days, building a nuclear arsenal and all. At school, they warned us to be
prepared. We were trained to hide, take cover under our desks when the air-
raid sirens went off. During the drills we lay down, not a muscle quivering,
and didn't make any noise. It was odd to be afraid of something that
didn't seem real. Some of my classmates took the threat seriously but Miss
Allen did not. She said that America would not be destroyed by bombs.
You had to crush the 'Idea of America' in order to destroy America. She
hated the drills, creating war mania. To her, all wars were absurd.

Three and a half years later, in late 1958, my family returned to
India. The river dispute had been settled peacefully. It is hard to imagine
anything getting settled today between India and Pakistan without a war,
or at least a war of words. Since I was in my final year in school, my parents
agreed to let me stay on. My mother worried about leaving me behind
in America. I was only sixteen and might go off to Chicago, become a
gangster. The problem of where I would stay was solved by a kind-hearted
Quaker. He ran International House, a hostel for university students.
They made an exception in my case, and I found myself suddenly among
graduate students of Georgetown and American University.

Instead of flying home, my father decided to give the family a treat. They boarded the *Queen Mary* to sail back to India. The night before leaving, my mother was in tears. As we walked past Meridian Hill Park, she said she was proud of me. Scanning the dark evening air and the empty street, she worried about leaving me alone. What if something happened, who'd help me? Her diary says that she cried the whole first day on the ship. My father agreed to let her call me, even though it was expensive. The connection was bad. It was a bit weird: she declaring 'I miss you', and I shouting, 'What? What?'

I liked I-House. The students there were older and a lot more interesting. I felt like a grown-up. They let me join a group learning ballroom dancing on Saturday afternoons, which became the highlight of my week. I can't explain the thrill I felt dancing. A dancer doesn't need wings to fly. Come Saturday and I'd be ready to fly like Hanuman, a shortcut to a certain sort of freedom—another milestone in my moksha journey. I especially liked to dance with Maria, a Brazilian girl, at the I-House. But she was older and went off with a dashing German from Georgetown University. Nor would I get the chance to use the fancy dance steps I'd learnt. Just as I acquired all this elegance, ballroom dancing gave way to rock and roll.

The school year was drawing to a close. As a senior, I had mastered the ropes and I felt lighter and wiser. I got straight A's in my final term, but I didn't know whom to tell the good news. I wrote to my parents, but they would only get the letter after a week. I told Roy, and he wasn't surprised. Then I remembered Mr Leeming, and I phoned him. 'Let's celebrate!' he said. He invited me to dinner at an expensive restaurant downtown. Did I have a tie and a jacket? No, but I could borrow one. Since he was also vegetarian, he chose a posh Swedish restaurant, famous for its mind-boggling veg smorgasbord.

As soon as we sat down, he gave me a copy of *Nonsense Rhymes* by Lewis Carroll. 'Nonsense wakes up the mind,' he said, 'and develops a sense of humour.' I would need humour to navigate the grubby world, he felt. We ordered sparkling grape juice, which they served in high fluted wine glasses. He looked me in the eye and raised his glass for a toast.

'Here's to bringing home straight A's!'

He wanted to know what I had learnt in America. I told him that I'd begun to love history, thanks to Miss Allen. And dancing, thanks to Maria at the I-House. Dancing made me forget myself, I said.

'Ah, the fine art of self-forgetting!' he mused.

'So, do you have a girlfriend?' he asked.

'Not really.' I blushed. I told him I liked both Miss Allen and Maria. Both were too old, he said. He wanted me find someone closer to my age. 'Ask them to teach you to make love.' I went red. Sex was an obsession in America, he said, but it was a normal part of life in the rest of the world. He asked if I read comic books. They were one of America's best creations, he felt. As we were leaving the restaurant, he quietly slipped me a check for a thousand dollars—it was to be my graduation present—a lot of money in those days!

The following week, I received letters from Harvard, Princeton and Yale. I had got into all three universities with full scholarships. On 3 June 1959, the *Washington Post* carried a story on page three titled 'Boy on Visit from India Stays to Excel at School'. It was about how a middle-class Indian boy—no big bucks, no rich WASP family—made good in America, graduating at the top of his class in school and making his way into the top universities. Later that morning, the vice principal of our school summoned me to his office.

I found him staring at my photo in the *Washington Post*. His lips were moving as he read the story. He looked up in shock. No one from his school had achieved this feat during his tenure. Putting on a fake smile, he told me that I had brought honour to the school and realized the American dream. I wanted to remind him that four years ago he had a different dream in mind. I had made a secret vow on that day of my humiliation: that I'd make a splash! Well, I'd got my revenge. I thanked him and left, and then I went to give Miss Allen the news. She gave me a smile and a hug, reminding me, 'Race is a social construct, not a biological fact.' She then presented me with an old, worn copy of Strunk and White's *Elements of Style*, which was sitting on her desk. 'It will help you to write well.' Her grandmother had presented it to her when she had graduated from high school.

The next week I got the cheeriest letter from my mother. By choosing Harvard, I had fulfilled *her* most cherished dream. She had spent enough time in America to know what Harvard meant. It was also *her* prize, she wrote, making up for the sacrifice, tedium and weariness of the years of raising me. Suddenly, it all seemed to have been worthwhile. Without guile, she wrote that I would now be able to rise from the dreariness of her middle-class existence to the glamorous life of the upper middle class. I cannot recall a more complete feeling of unalloyed joy in anything I ever read.

A dark cloud, however, hung over the American Dream of my friend. Roy Hawkins's mother had tears in her eyes when she hugged me at the graduation ceremony. My parents were not there—the journey was too expensive—and she and Joe Leeming took their place. I looked into her eyes, and I knew that Roy would be working in a factory next year, confirming the vice principal's shrunken idea of the American Dream. And not because his mom had not tried. She had worked hard all her life, leaving home at five in the morning, coming back late in the evening. When you're stuck in a menial job all your life, it is not easy to climb out.

I had seen both sides of the American dream. The promise of America was real for everyone, except if you were Black. Miss Allen cheered wildly at my graduation. America was a nation with flaws, but the dream was so big that you would be foolish not to go after it. Perhaps, this is why socialism never took root in America. Even the poor didn't see themselves as an 'exploited proletariat'—they were 'temporarily embarrassed millionaires'.

I had been a novelty in the complacent America of the 1950s. But it wouldn't be long before a hurricane of middle-class Indians would sweep America, after John F. Kennedy liberalized immigration in the '60s, changing entry criteria from quotas to merit. As America lost some of its self-contentment with the civil rights movement and the Vietnam war, Dr Patels became ubiquitous, techies from India became millionaires, taking over Silicon Valley, and others went on to become CEOs of giant multinational American companies. Indian immigrants became a 'model minority' with the highest per capita incomes in the land. The glow of their success was so bright that it could be seen back home, firing local ambitions, creating an IT revolution in Bangalore, Pune and Hyderabad.

7

Harvard

'But human excellence grows like a vine tree, fed by the green grass, among men wise and just, raised up to the liquid sky.'

—Pindar

On my first day at Harvard, a new spirit of moksha was in the air. At the master's reception for incoming freshmen, everyone seemed to be into a fashionable phrase: 'existential freedom'. It was a strange, exciting world, where the individual was paramount, not the nation, nor religion; where a person was free, determining their own future. People were speaking about being 'authentic', condemning the inauthentic middle-class life and its fake world view. It reminded me of the charming deceptions of my mother's middle-class friends in Kaka Nagar. At Harvard, the heroes of the day were Sartre, Camus, Heidegger, Nietzsche and Kierkegaard. It was heady stuff. The next day, I rushed to Lamont, the undergraduate library, and borrowed Camus's novel *The Stranger*. It moved me so deeply that I could not sleep for two nights. It even aroused an incipient, bashful literary ambition, and must have had something to do with my majoring in philosophy at Harvard.

But my mother got worried. Every Friday evening, I used to write her a 10-cent blue aerogramme about my doings of the week. It was a promise

74

I had made when she was leaving me in America. In my excitement with new ideas, I went on and on, quite thoughtlessly, about how life was absurd. There was no point looking for any meaning in it because a meaning did not exist. It was false to believe that bad things did not happen to good people. What happened could just happen to anyone. The answer was to learn to live without meaning. I mentioned Camus's line about suicide being the only true philosophical problem.

This frightened my mother. She replied instantly, demanding that I stop reading such rubbish. She asked, 'Did I make a mistake leaving you alone in America at a young age?' She advised me to learn a useful trade, like engineering, so I could get a job when I came back. 'Remember, you have to make a living!' My father had the opposite reaction. He was delighted that I was discovering new ideas, even though he did not believe in them. He felt the purpose of a university education was to 'make a life'. He advised me, however, not to write such letters—my mother was a worrier, best not to upset her.

From that day I began to keep a diary in order to write what I couldn't in my letters. Ironically, diary keeping was a habit I had inherited from my mother. I have found that a diary is a way to observe events and distort them to suit your temper, your inclinations. It is the distortion that is interesting, because it reveals something about you. Some people learn by taking copious notes. I have found that I learn by writing things down in my diary. Diary writing, besides, is good exercise, a bit like tillana steps, which are a good warm-up for a Bharatnatyam dancer. Anyhow, my mother kept my letters dutifully all her life and gave them to me before she died.

Although I am embarrassed to read my letters and diaries now, they have helped me to understand who I am—a useful thing for any human being. My diary records that I was drawn to the existentialist 'authentic life' because it built upon what I had learnt from my cousin Jeet, Miss Allen, Joe Leeming and my own moksha-seeking nature. My father believed in 'finding' himself (through meditation), but the existentialists said there was nothing to find. I'd have to 'create' myself—give myself values to live by. This freedom is scary, even to someone who'd always yearned to act freely, not mimic others.

I was torn between my mother's advice to 'make a living' and my father's to 'make a life'. I tried diligently to become an engineer, like my father, but the project got derailed. My tutor mentioned casually one day that I might be at the wrong school—there was another one down the river called MIT, and it did a better job of making engineers. My roommate added to my doubts. I envied him. He read *Anna Karenina* in his Russian Lit. class, while I was cramming Bernoulli's equation in fluid mechanics. Over dinner one evening, he suggested that if one were to have an affair with a married woman, it ought to be with someone like Anna. And what was I doing? While he dreamt of sleeping with Anna Karenina, I was calculating pipe friction at the wrong university.

James Watson, the molecular biologist, came to speak in our common room one evening. He was a hero at the time, having recently discovered 'the secret of life' by cracking the double-helix structure of the DNA molecule. Someone asked him about his own secret of success.

'Avoid boring people!' he said.

Boring people got in the way of the search for truth. Was he speaking of engineers? Watson would go on to win the Nobel Prize, but that evening he inspired me so much that I promptly switched my major to molecular biology. My love affair with biology, however, lasted only briefly. I went home that summer and discovered, for the first time, India's grinding poverty. One must be away from India to 'see' its poverty. It was a moment of political awakening—my second one after Partition. I was tormented for nights and wanted quick answers. So I switched to economics. John Kenneth Galbraith taught Economics 1 with Paul Samuelson, who taught as a guest professor from MIT. Both were famous names, although Galbraith sometimes used to fall asleep on his notes. I wanted to know how to make a poor country rich, but economists tied me up in mathematical equations. It was only after I discovered that economics was common sense that I figured out the answers for myself, and I began to enjoy economics. Most economists believed that it needed state intervention to bring prosperity quickly to a poor country. Socialism was the answer, they said, and it reinforced my faith in Nehru's socialism.

Meanwhile, I was being enticed by the romance of the humanities. I enrolled in an elementary course in philosophy. The humanities constitute the core of a university, teaching you that every sentence you utter is not a statement but a question. It was unbelievably exciting to debate with Socrates about the good life; interrogate Kant about what is moral and right; argue with Marx about equality; cross-examine Freud about desire.

I began to ask myself: Who am I? What is a flourishing life and how should one live it? I was following unconsciously my father's dictum of 'making a life'. The liberal arts, I realized, is not about mastering content but about learning how to reason and judge for yourself, as befits a free human being.

After a starvation diet in high school, I was hungry and wanted to consume everything. In the middle of my second year, I switched to a combined major of history and literature. I was now taking courses in Greek tragedy, Renaissance painting, the Russian novel, economic history and even Sanskrit. Harvard was a dream come true: a beautiful campus with professors who were titans and students who were philosopher–kings in the making. I felt I was merely a leaf on a gigantic tree of the human past, and I was carrying further Miss Allen's history project from high school. When I stumbled on someone's thought or feeling in the past, it felt as though a hand had come by and taken mine. Miss Allen had taught me to be sceptical of historians who filled the past with imaginary brightness or those who merely told the stories of tyrants, murderers and bad governments. When it came to India's history, I began to appreciate what Muslim conquerors had created rather than destroyed, and I stopped hurling abuses at them like my grandfather.

By now I had settled into a day-to-day routine at Harvard, not too different from that of my classmates. All our classes were in Harvard Yard, a bunch of red-brick buildings around Widener Library. In the lecture halls, I chose sometimes to sit near a window to feast my eyes on an elm tree or listen to the chirping of chickadees and goldfinches, reducing the professor's voice to a meaningless drone. I bought a bicycle from the money Joe Leeming had gifted me, and I loved zipping around Cambridge from Harvard Square to the Brattle Theatre, down to the neo-Georgian houses along the Charles River. Then I'd circle back past Café Pamplona, which had just opened with the first expresso machine in town. After crossing Massachusetts Avenue, I would turn into Quincy Street to face the shockingly modern Carpenter Center for the Visual Arts, designed by Le Corbusier, which never failed to remind me of magical Chandigarh, which I had seen during that summer.

One of my tutors in literature was the Palestinian scholar Edward Said, who taught me that the most effective way to destroy a people is to obliterate their sense of their own history. His scathing critique of my essay on Cervantes's *Don Quixote* brought us close. He would go on to write a provocative book, *Orientalism*, which created a new field of postcolonial studies. Both of us, he used to say, were deracinated exiles trying to cope with our postcolonial identity. I was a Hindu from a Punjabi middle-class family that had risen professionally in British colonial society; he came from a rich Christian business family in Egypt, which was so uncertain about the future that it sent their son to a privileged school in America. From there, Said had gone to Princeton, where he got his undergraduate degree in English, and was now writing his doctoral thesis on another uprooted exile, Joseph Conrad.

Said carried a chip on his shoulder, and our conversations invariably returned to the Western prejudice against Arabs and Muslims based on false, romantic images of the Orient. Although I didn't share his grudges, I sympathized with his thesis that political elites in both our postcolonial societies had bought a false, inferior view of themselves created by the colonial masters. He insisted that I must return to India after Harvard and free my countrymen from the mental fetters of colonialism. 'Was I really an uprooted exile?' I asked myself. Couldn't one be multi-rooted, like a banyan tree? I decided I was more confident in my skin, comfortable with both my Indian and Western roots. Said's advice, nevertheless, would stay with me in the future.

Besides Le Corbusier, I discovered other works of modernist and minimalist beauty at Harvard. On my bicycle rounds, I was thrilled at encountering the exquisite Law School buildings designed by the master of the Bauhaus school, Walter Gropius. I became a devotee of Bauhaus artists—Paul Klee, Lyonel Feininger, Wassily Kandinsky, Marcel Breuer, Joan Miró, Josef Albers, Jean Arp and especially the architect Ludwig Mies van der Rohe (I even considered becoming an architect). The search for beauty extended to music. My first encounter with classical music had been with Beethoven's *Eroica*. The National Symphony Orchestra had once played it in my high school. I had felt exhilarated and had instantly fallen in love. To learn more about Western classical music, I took Music 1 at Harvard, where our teacher, G. Wallace Woodworth ('Woody'), taught me how to listen to music.

I began to attend the Boston Symphony with student tickets donated by an alumnus. Once, an attractive girl from Radcliffe accompanied me. She was also an accomplished pianist. That evening we listened to Glenn Gould perform Beethoven's *Emperor Concerto*. After the performance,

I felt I was walking a few centimetres above the ground. Seeing me excited, she took me the next day to the music library in Quincy House, where we listened to a long-playing record of Gould's interpretation of Bach's *The Goldberg Variations*. I still remember the original Columbia Masterworks LP cover with thirty photos of Gould analogous to the thirty Bach variations. After that, she played one of the variations on the piano in the Common Room. 'This is genius!' I exclaimed and kissed her. I decided I was in love. But the matter didn't go much further because she already had a boyfriend. Over the years, however, I would listen to Gould's recording again and again, and would always be reminded of her.

By now my mother had begun to sink into despair at home. Her friends would ask politely what I was studying at Harvard. She didn't know what to reply. They consoled her, thinking that I must have failed in engineering, which was why I was flitting around the liberal arts. She worried about how I'd make a living in India—at best, I'd end up an impoverished lecturer in a provincial town. But my father understood: I was making a life! When she learnt that I was taking a course in Sanskrit, she groaned, 'A dead language . . . only the dead will give him a job!'

Meanwhile, even tolerant and liberal Harvard was running out of patience. Seeing me flit from flower to flower like a honeybee, the dean insisted I choose a single field of concentration and stick to it till graduation. It was a difficult decision, but I chose to get my degree in philosophy. I decided I wanted to learn to live an honourable, flourishing life, and so I'd focus on ethics. Professor John Rawls was the new god of moral and political philosophy at Harvard, and I enrolled in his course. He was lanky, bashful, and he stuttered—a terrible handicap, I thought, for someone who made a living by speaking.

One morning, we played a thought game in his class. He asked us to imagine that we were a group of self-interested persons trying to decide our principles of justice. He placed two constraints: we knew neither our class and status, nor our abilities and talents. Rawls cleverly navigated the discussion till we agreed on a principle of liberty and another of equality. The first guaranteed the greatest liberty compatible with same liberty for all—this appealed to my moksha inclinations. Although the second principle had a strong bias for equality, it conceded the fairness of an inequality that made the worst-off member in society better off. To understand the latter, I pictured the CEO of a company who'd just delivered huge profits. As a result, his salary had doubled. But the salary of everyone else, too, had risen significantly. The point being that the lowest-paid employee did not grudge the CEO earning far more because his lot had also improved. Here was an idea, I felt, that truly challenged my unthinking belief in the absolute equality of socialism. This game became the centrepiece in Rawls's famous book, *A Theory of Justice*. I went on to write my senior thesis under Rawls, and during the year and a half that I knew him, I grew to admire him for his modest, saintly manners. I had also learnt something from him about being a good human being.

Before confining myself to the study of philosophy, I had taken two detours in my intellectual journey. China invaded India in 1962, and I wondered if political theory might teach me how to think about it. I took Government 180, taught by Henry Kissinger, who was not yet a celebrity but was still an éminence grise. His message was that a nation has no enemies or friends, only interests. A leader's duty was not to pursue moral ends but only the nation's interest. When all nations did that, it brought predictability, a balance of power and peace. Because I couldn't follow Kissinger's heavy German accent, I used to sit in the front row of his class, and, to my dismay, he'd look at me and talk about Nehru as a model of how not to conduct foreign policy. Why did Nehru, he asked, naively support China's cause? Because in Nehru's eyes China was a kindred nation that had also suffered from the West's imperialism. As a result, Kissinger felt that India was undermining its own relationship with the West and compromising its national interest. China, in contrast, only pursued its own interest, and its invasion of India proved it. Although I did not particularly like Kissinger, I had to admit he was right.

My second detour led me to Sanskrit. One afternoon, I was wandering among the stacks of books at the Widener Library when I stumbled into the Oriental section. Instead of making a U-turn, I was drawn mysteriously towards Sanskrit. I picked up a slim volume on the Hindu concept of *leela*, divine play. I knew about the concept from Bhabo's stories of the gods. Soon, I found myself sitting on the floor, absorbed in the exploits of playful gods. At some point I fell asleep and woke up with a start when a distinguished-looking man in tweeds tripped over me. He lurched forward, swayed, but caught himself. I jumped to attention. It was Professor Daniel H.H. Ingalls, the greatest Sanskrit scholar alive. Seeing the book in my hand, he commented that it was written by one of his students.

The following week, I knocked on his door. 'Leela!' he smiled. 'Man suffers because he takes seriously what the gods take in fun.' I was charmed. Soon, I enrolled in his elementary Sanskrit class, not realizing that Ingalls was an old-fashioned schoolmaster who insisted on ramming Panini's rules of grammar into you. The rules were elegant, akin to mathematics, but learning Sanskrit was hard work. On a typical morning, I would arrive early at Widener, pull out Lanman's *A Sanskrit Reader* from the shelf and turn to Nala and Damayanti's story from the Mahabharata. I would then translate a passage for our afternoon class with the help of Whitney's *Sanskrit Grammar* on my left and Apte's dictionary on my right. It was tough going, but Ingalls reassured us that reading Sanskrit was good for the soul.

One spring day, I was captivated by Ingalls's discussion on the *siddhis*, perfections, imparted by yoga. I was drawn especially to laghima, the ability to make the body light, almost weightless, like a ball of cotton. Although Ingalls didn't dwell on it, the idea stayed with me. I began to think of laghima as a spirit of lightness, an attitude to life. I asked Bimal Matilal about my interpretation. He was a tall, thin graduate student from Bengal with curly hair flying all over. He was assisting Ingalls and knew about these things. He liked my version of laghima and added that Lord Krishna had a similar attitude—he stole butter, defeated demons, played the flute and flirted with married women, all in a day's work. Hearing his flute, women of Vrindavan sneaked out of their homes, went to the forest and danced the *raas leela* with their lover–god for an entire Brahma night.

'How long is a Brahma night?' I asked.

'4.5 billion human years,' said Matilal.

'That's a lot of dancing!' I said. -

'Krishna multiplies himself a hundred thousand times, making each woman believe she alone is dancing with him,' he explained.

'What a lot of fun!' I said. Krishna possessed the light-footedness of laghima, and it fired in me the ambition to live lightly in the same way.

I did not have much of a conventional social life at Harvard. I neither came from a privileged, old Harvard family nor was I new money, desperate to climb socially to join the smart, WASP eating clubs. Anyway, I found club members to be hideous, arrogant snobs, constantly playing power games. I was there, of course, before the 1960s revolution that changed social life forever at Harvard. Like the next boy, I did want to sleep with girls, but I was too shy, unable to break away from my austere, middle-class, Indian upbringing. There were also fewer girls around as Harvard was not yet integrated with Radcliffe, and they too were more careful with their favours. All this changed a decade later, when Harvard men were surrounded by sexually advanced females.

Summer was soon upon us. I wanted to go home but couldn't afford it. I'd gone back only once, and that too thanks to Joe Leeming's present. During the other summers, I had worked to earn my keep: one summer, I was counsellor for kids at a camp in Maine; on another, a waiter in a New Hampshire resort. This summer, I faced a dilemma. I could either earn a modest, steady salary as counsellor in the same kids' camp in Maine or take a risky job at Arthur Murray's dance studios in downtown Boston. In the latter, my earnings would vary from zero to big bucks, depending on how many female customers I enticed to the dance floor. Since I happened to be having dinner with Matilal and his friend Donald J., I asked them for advice. Donald J. answered promptly, 'No question. Be a dancer.' Matilal smiled quietly in agreement. It was in line with my ambition for 'living lightly', he said.

The next day, I went to the dance studio, where there was a poster at the entrance: 'Do you want to be a wall flower?' read the heading. The answer came in the next line: 'Or be Eleanor Roosevelt, Duke of Windsor and John D. Rockefeller Jr?'—all of whom supposedly had been pupils at the dance studio. But when I entered, I found that the pupils were mostly lonely, middle-aged men and women seeking company. Since I'd learnt dancing at the I-House, I confidently performed a few steps in the interview and promptly got the job.

Donald J. was seeking a roommate, and I agreed to share rooms with him in a flophouse near Central Square. He was a perpetual graduate student who hung around Harvard's Sanskrit department. He had grown up in a repressive Christian home that had 'denied him life'. He'd come home one evening and announced, 'God is dead!' His parents were horrified. Reading Nietzsche was a turning point in his life. From that day, he learnt to laugh at himself.

'If I didn't laugh, I would have cried.'

Laughter became his attitude to the world. 'I can only believe in a God who laughs and dances,' he once said. And this led him to the Hindu gods, 'whose style is dancing'. Dance and laughter were a form of liberation. Donald and I were kindred spirits in search for laghima and moksha.

My first week at the job was a disaster. None of the customers wanted to dance with me. I felt like a fool, like someone who had jumped off a cliff and was now in free fall. 'Dostoevsky, too, felt like a fool once a month,' Donald J. consoled me. I complained to him that the women who came to dance were lonely, and they wanted a tall white Nordic hulk, not a short brown man from India.

'You could be their Latin lover?' he said and smiled. He explained that just as shirts came in many sizes and colours, so did men. He advised me not to sound too intellectual on the dance floor. People went there to dance and have fun, not to discuss Nietzsche. Best to underplay my Harvard identity—it was intimidating for many people. 'Throw in something profound occasionally,' he said. 'Then laugh apologetically for having said it.'

We rehearsed his formula over the weekend. I stood before the bathroom mirror, put on a fake smile and learnt to make small talk. It was a Zen practice, he said, to laugh looking at the mirror. He taught me funny jokes. By Monday afternoon, I was ready to go on stage. The formula worked like magic. The women began to ask for me, initially out of curiosity and later because my stock had gone up from word of mouth. They discovered I was a good dancer, and they picked up the steps quickly. A few worked as salesgirls at Filene's and Jordon Marsh department stores, and were looking for dates. As I got into the swing of things, my fake smile became real. I learnt jokes and began to speak their language. Soon, I was enjoying myself and raking in the cash.

The company had a strict policy against getting involved romantically with customers. A few female customers did invite me for a drink, hinting at a longer-term relationship, but I stuck to the company policy. Instead, I fell for an instructor. She was tall, blonde and attractive. Although the daughter of a Presbyterian minister, she did yoga, read about Hinduism and was attracted to Indian spirituality. I let it slip that my father was a mystic. From that day, we started meeting after work, when she would ask me about my father's spiritual beliefs. I had gone out with the girls nearby at Radcliffe, but she was the one I had fallen for. She didn't have a romantic interest in me, however, and soon dumped me for a macho

Greek lover. I was hurt. I had been rehearsing for life, but the rehearsal had turned out to be life itself.

Other than that, it was a nice summer. I spent it reading in the mornings. Reading for pleasure confirmed literature's power, with its astonishing ability to liberate a human being. It became another marker in my moksha journey. My father would have called it 'making a life'. In late afternoon, I would get dressed, ready to go into the real world wearing the only suit I possessed. I had bought it on sale for $16.99, thanks to one of my female customer–admirers who worked at Filene's. After getting dressed, I would go down, buy a copy of the *Boston Globe* and read it on the subway like a seasoned commuter.

Photos of the glamorous Jackie Kennedy would stare at me from the pages of the *Globe*. She had been photographed going in and out of the revolving doors of the Carlyle Hotel in uptown Manhattan. There was the usual news of the Cold War and lately of the Cuban missile crisis, when President Kennedy almost brought the world to a brink. Another item reported that Bertrand Russell, the pacifist philosopher, had been jeered at the night before for saying, 'Better Red than dead.' Protesters had screamed back, 'Better dead than Red.' There was some baseball news of the Red Sox, and the rest were ads: announcing that you had to wear a Brooks Brothers suit to be a leader; with Ray-Ban sunglasses, you could be a sensational hero; you could be whatever you wanted to be.

Donald J. and I used to watch two films a week. Matilal joined us sometimes. We'd head off to the Brattle Theatre, an art movie house near Harvard Square, which showed the latest foreign movies of the 'New Wave'. We loved Fellini's movies, especially *La Strada*. Another, *La Dolce Vita*, was about a guy who sells his soul and becomes a gossip hound. Watching it, I felt I was in a circus, although it was about ordinary people who behaved like clowns. My all-time favourite was Marcel Carné's *Les Enfants du Paradis*. Set in the theatre world of the 1830s, it was about a courtesan and four men—a clown, a thief, an actor and an aristocrat. All loved her, each in his own, different way. But what made the greatest impression on both of us was the Apu trilogy by Satyajit Ray. We saw all the three films of the Bengali master twice.

Donald J. used to dance alone in his room. Nietzsche, too, had always danced in solitude, I later learnt. When his landlady peeped in through the keyhole, she found Nietzsche dancing naked; she summoned a doctor, who found him healthy but insane. Nietzsche said, 'Those who were seen dancing were thought to be insane by those who could not hear the music.' To Donald J., dancing was training in levity. 'Lightens your legs, so you're not weighed down by emotions or burdens of the ego.' He traced my romantic problems with the dance instructor to the problem that I took myself too seriously. He invited me to meet two of his friends, Richard Alpert and Timothy Leary, both professors of psychology at Harvard, who gave me a charming lesson in 'self-forgetting'.

Alpert claimed that a new-born baby had no awareness of its 'self'—it was not able to separate itself from the world. Soon it acquired its sense of 'I', its ego; as it grew up, it believed it was identical with this 'I'. But the 'I' also became oppressive, filled with anxiety over its worth and status. Thus, from time immemorial, human beings have tried to find ways of escaping from the chatter of the 'I'. The Greeks called it ekstasis, meaning 'standing outside of oneself'. Hindus and Buddhists tried to escape from the bondage of the 'I' through meditation. Tim Leary claimed he had achieved this state through psychedelic drugs, which relaxed him and connected him with others. Neuroscience, too, had confirmed, he said, that 'self-forgetting' involved transient reduction of prefrontal brain activity, making us feel connected with the world.

Walking home that evening, Donald J. exclaimed, 'No self, no ego!' His goal, too, was to liberate himself from the bondage of the 'I', to learn to forget himself. He reminded me of the therapeutic value of dancing, of laughing and of living lightly—they helped one to 'lose oneself'. Thus, our quiet conversations helped me to get over the dance instructor. One evening towards the end of the summer, I came home from the dance studio to find a note from Donald: 'Sorry to miss you. Gone to Nepal, mostly on foot.' Beneath the note was a present—a heavily marked copy of Nietzsche's *Thus Spake Zarathustra*.

Meanwhile, I learnt that Leary and Alpert had become an embarrassment to Harvard with their notorious experiments with consciousness-expanding drugs. The university fired both professors. Leary went on to become the 'LSD guru', whom Richard Nixon called 'the most dangerous man in America'. Leary retorted, 'I've lived one of the most interesting lives in the twentieth century.' In 1967, Alpert went to India and became a disciple of a guru, Neem Karoli Baba, who gave him the name Ram Das. He wrote a hugely popular spiritual book called

Be Here Now, which went through forty-three editions, and influenced Steve Jobs and many famous people.

The summer came to an end. From the money I had earned, I bought a tweed jacket, several Oxford blue button-down shirts and a pipe. I began to look like a Harvard man. Visiting Harvard during my final year was Isaiah Berlin, a liberal theorist, historian of ideas, an Oxford don and a gadfly. I took his course on Marx, which turned out to be charming and funny—non-stop string of anecdotes—and yet deadly serious. His starting point was Kant's dictum: 'Out of the crooked timber of humanity, nothing straight was ever made.' He called romantics dangerous because they had a single great idea for a perfect society and no price was too high. Those who got in the way were eggs to be broken while making an omelette. It was one of history's ironies, he said, that the Soviet Union—Marx's utopia of a classless society—was breeding a monstrous feudal class.

All this was sobering, and it turned me into a disillusioned socialist. You cannot aspire to complete liberty and complete equality, Berlin taught us. If people were wholly free, they'd be like wolves, free to eat the sheep. He preferred the fox, who knew many things, unlike the hedgehog, who knows only one big thing. He reminded us of the violence unleashed by the one big idea of religion—the Crusades, interminable wars between Catholics and Protestants, the Spanish Inquisition. I remembered India's partition and tried to imagine a world without religion. Berlin taught me to be wary of ideology, which created unattainable aspirations. By the end of the semester, Berlin and I had hit it off—he invited me to do a PhD in philosophy at Oxford. He had been a sensible corrective to my idealistic dreams, placing a cautionary sign on my road to moksha. It said that I was not meant to be a horse without a harness, tossing its head and running free. A better image of moksha was a horse 'easy in his harness', as the American poet Robert Frost suggested. For liberty to be real, there had to be rules.

I graduated eventually with a degree in philosophy and was now being pushed to become a 'dusty philosopher'. But I was ambivalent. Academic philosophy seemed to me too abstract—knowledge for its own sake—far from my practical desire to learn to be a good person and live a happy, flourishing life. Overall, Harvard had been a luxurious afternoon. There are the liberal arts and useful arts; I had chosen the former, and I'm convinced that Harvard did prepare me for 'making a life'. (I'm still not sure exactly what my father meant by this phrase, what it entailed in nuts and bolts, but I have an instinctive feel for it, and it has served me well throughout my life.)

The liberal arts helped to liberate me—freeing me to some extent from my obsession with my 'self'. I became interested in all aspects of human life. In my early fascination with Existentialism, I stumbled on a line by Nietzsche: 'You must have chaos inside you to give birth to a dancing star.' Those words reminded me of my mother's epithet. Her innocent endearment uttered when I was three was a portent, that I would turn at each crossroads to follow my own, unpredictable path.

By name-dropping shamelessly—Watson, Galbraith, Kissinger, Rawls, Said, Tillich, Ingalls, Berlin and others—I have conveyed, I hope, something of the headiness that we felt in the intoxicating, intellectual ferment of the early '60s at Harvard. In five years, this would be transformed into a different, more revolutionary atmosphere of 1968, when another sort of intoxication would replace it. But having dropped the names, I must confess that those grandees at Harvard did not necessarily respect undergraduates. Their deepest commitment was to research, and undergraduates were often in the way. There were, however, a few great teachers: Woody, in music, and Raphael Demos, in philosophy, who showed us quietly where to look and what to see.

Harvard had nourished a spirit of inquiry, making me question at each turn how real the heavens and the stars were. When I arrived there, I believed in God and in socialism. By the time I left I had rejected both. Losing socialism did not cause so much distress as losing God. In the latter, I'd let my father down. For years after that, I would genuinely try to believe in God; and each time I would fail. It was easier to give up socialism because of periodic news of horrors in the Communist world. Eventually, I would settle down to become an agnostic, a classical liberal, sceptical of all ideologies, both political and religious.

Although Harvard taught me to believe in my ability to reason, it did not turn me into a cynic. I would keep a free mind, open to the possibility of finding modest truths to give meaning to my life and a political system that would combine the right amount of liberty with equality. Overall, I came out confident, dependent on myself to make my own future. Harvard had been truly a liberating step in my moksha journey.

8

The Mouse Merchant

'Right now, this is just a job. If I advance any higher, then this would be my career. And, well, if this were my career? I'd have to throw myself under a train.'

—Jim Halpert in the American sitcom *The Office*

By a twist of fate I metamorphosed from a high-thinking Brahmin to a money-making Bania in the summer of 1963. I was back at home. My father had become chief engineer to the Punjab government, and we were living in Chandigarh, which had replaced Lahore, left behind in Pakistan, as the new capital of the state. After graduating from Harvard, I was waiting to go on for further studies to Oxford. There were many oohs and aahs as my mother showed me off to her friends—'a Harvard graduate!' I enjoyed being made much of, putting on suitable airs of a philosopher-in-the-making, speaking gravely about the meaning of life.

I am a natural show-off. While I tried to curb my instinct, I also wondered what life would be without a bit of showing off.

'And what is a Harvard graduate?' asked one of my mother's friends.

I fumbled, muttered something clever, silly. But she got me thinking. I tried to picture my classmates. What did we have in common? After some searching in my head, I concluded that what we all shared an open, liberal outlook. We were quietly perceptive and free from meanness. Our best quality was a calm self-possession, allowing us to stand alone. Our weakness: we were too self-critical, too self-conscious.

Thus the lazy summer rolled on until I discovered that I had developed cold feet. Lounging on the grass outside our veranda one evening, I looked up at the sky with an uncomfortable thought. Did I really want to spend the rest of my life in that stratosphere of abstract thought? Academic philosophy seemed so arid; it was no longer a search for the good life.

What had drawn me to philosophy were questions: How to live a life? How to be a good person? How to cope with a friend's death? This was how Socrates and the Upanishads had conceived of philosophy—a way of life, not just systems and propositions. To Aristotle, it had been the search for a flourishing life. But academic philosophers had forgotten all this and converted it into a theoretical discipline—at times, almost linguistic analysis. I was confused and nervous, and by the end of the week I decided I didn't want a PhD in philosophy. Nor did I want an academic career. I felt like a chicken-livered coward—quite a feat for a vegetarian. I had always been frightened of the dark. Veg or no-veg, my motto was: when in doubt, chicken out. But wait, wasn't mine an act of conscience, not cowardice? Conscience and cowardice have a funny way of ending in the same place. I decided I'd rather be an honest coward and save myself from wasting years of precious life.

What to do now? I was sure about one thing—I wanted a life of action rather than of thought. Even an idea in action is more vital than a mere idea. But what is a life of action? Two hundred years ago, I would have been a warrior in war and a farmer in peace. It was now a commercial age. After the Industrial Revolution and the rise of the middle classes, there were many possibilities. I went to my parents for advice.

'Do you want to achieve something or to make money?' asked my father.

'Does it have to be either/or?'

We both stood in silence, looking at each other, lost in thought. Making money wasn't so hard, he believed. What was tough was making it while doing something you loved.

'What you love won't pay the bills,' my mother warned.

I was torn once again between the old dilemma: 'making a living' versus 'making a life'. I didn't seem to be in a hurry to find an answer,

however. I was settling nicely into a routine of idleness, in line with the
French aristocracy's belief that idleness is the natural state of human beings.
Work is unnatural, they had felt, while leisure enlarged one. After a week
or so of patrician French living, I was asked by my father one evening,
'How was your day?' I told him I had taken a power nap in the afternoon.

'His power nap lasted all day,' my mother corrected me.

'Doing nothing is hard work,' I said in my defence. 'Being jobless is a
test of character.'

'No,' my mother retorted, 'being jobless is the result of too much
philosophy.' She told me bluntly to stop killing time and get a job.

As news of my idleness spread, suggestions poured in. Vade Mama
wanted me to become a lawyer—I wouldn't lack for money, as Indians
were always quarrelling. Satinder Mama was emphatic about medicine—
half the country was sick, he said. My mother thought Raj Mama had the
best idea—he wanted me to sit for the civil service exam. 'Nothing quite
like having a heaven-born brown sahib in the family,' he wrote in a letter.
My mother agreed. In her eyes, the Indian Administrative Service (IAS)
was the biggest prize in the job market. It meant power, prestige, lifelong
security, regular promotions whether you worked or not. But I felt uneasy
about becoming a bureaucrat.

My father's boss had other ideas. He came by for a visit. 'Look at me!'
he said grandly. 'If I had not discovered, embraced and lived my calling,
I'd have been lost to the world.' He wanted me to listen to my intuition
and discover my calling. He'd found his passion, engineering, in college,
and ever since he had felt 'joy in my heart, fire in my body'. He was
just warming up, a high Brahmin delivering a majestic speech, when my
mother interrupted. She had brought in tea, hot samosas and tamarind
chutney. Apologizing for the second-class crockery, she informed our
guest that she'd got an Ainsley bone China set in her dowry, but it had
been left behind in Lahore during Partition.

While he waited to pick up his train of thought, I confessed to the
puffed-up man that I couldn't find my intuition. I had tried but it seemed
to be lost. There were too many inner voices, too many possibilities. So,
I'd given up on the intuition business. Worse, I didn't know if there was a
'self' inside me. No matter how hard I tried, like Hume, I couldn't locate it.

'What? What?' he uttered, confused.

I told him what I'd learnt at university. There was a thinker of my thoughts in my consciousness, a feeler of my feelings, a dreamer of my dreams. But it kept changing from moment to moment. Yesterday's self was different from today's. Since there was no unchanging self within me, I had decided that I'd have to create my 'self' rather than look for it. I had no idea what that would be. Since I was going to fashion it, it ought to be a self with style.

My talk stopped the poor man in his tracks. He looked at my father.

'He's a philosopher,' my father said helplessly. After tea, the important man got up and left.

A few days later I got help from another quarter. My mother had set up an appointment with a retired judge of the Punjab High Court. She sent me off to him saying, 'He's a bit eccentric, but he's wise and a good family friend.' When I arrived, the barber had finished cutting his hair on the veranda and was beginning to give him an energetic head massage. He blinked a few times to make out who I was. Oil dripped over his eyes, blurring his vision. He looked bewildered. I explained my mission to the éminence grise but it didn't seem to register. His mind must be muddled, I thought, from all the friction on his head. His head was swaying back and forth.

'How old are you?' he asked suddenly.

'Twenty-one, sir.'

He began to say something but then changed his mind. He asked if I had a clue about what I wanted. Did I want something out of life, or was I typical of my useless generation, wanting only a good time?

'Does it have to be either/or?' I asked. 'Couldn't one want something out of life and still have a good time?' Since he didn't reply, I told him that I wanted a life of action, not of thought, and that this had prompted me to drop my plan for a PhD in philosophy.

His half-closed eyes opened, and he waved to the barber to stop. He understood, he said. I wasn't a Brahmin. So why would I want to confine my life to thought? Besides, there was too much thought in our country, not enough action. He was fully awake now. He got up abruptly, saying that I must stay away from a government job.

'What's wrong with a government job?' I asked.

'Officials!' he replied. Officials suffocated anything that breathed. Even if I managed to survive officialdom, the red tape would strangle me.

He carried a pair of scissors, he said, when visiting a government office, 'just in case there was paperwork to be cut'. He laughed loudly at his own joke. India's bureaucracy had four rules, he explained. First, you're not paid to act but to think; second, if you must act, delegate, so you've someone to blame; third, when you're in doubt, mumble; fourth, if you've nothing to do, write a memo—it proves you're busy. What saved the government, he said, was its inefficiency.

As I got up to leave, he flung his parting shot. 'Son, you were not meant to be a paper-pusher!'

I returned home confused. Although the judge had punctured my mother's illusions about the civil service, she was not deterred. A practical, determined woman, she picked up the phone and told the judge that she was coming over the next day to lunch and to fight with him. She then spoke to his cook and gave him the menu. A widower, the judge didn't take much interest in housekeeping. She told the cook not to make the vegetables too soft—the last time the okra and carrots had wilted on her plate—and to lay an extra setting for her son, who would be accompanying her.

The lunch was a success, but only as far as the food went. The cook had outdone himself—his cauliflower al dente was delicious. My mother opened her attack by claiming that the only decent jobs were in the civil service—it was still called the 'steel frame'. Yes, people talked about coveted, high-paying jobs in the old British firms in Calcutta, but these were few. So why was he determined to ruin her son's future?

The judge conceded that the civil service had once been a 'steel frame'. But it began to rust after Independence, succumbing to the disease of seniority—a person was promoted not on ability but the years of service.

'It still attracts the best talent,' she insisted.

'But even excellent raw material gets spoiled if you don't nurture the good and remove the bad,' replied the judge. 'When you're promoted regardless of performance, you lose the will to excel. You become time servers, captured by a safe system run by small men.'

The jousting went on through lunch. As we were saying goodbyes at the gate, the judge softened. 'This boy is a free spirit with the wind in his hair. I don't want him to waste his life.' Handing me a translation of the *Kathasaritsagara*, a thousand-year-old Sanskrit storybook, he asked me to read the story titled 'Mouse Merchant'. After that day, my mother did not mention civil service again.

I plunged into the storybook as soon as we got home. The hero of 'Mouse Merchant' is a poor boy. His father died before he was born, and his mother cleans houses for a living. When the boy grows up, she advises him to go and meet the richest merchant in town and ask for advice. The following day, while waiting outside the merchant's mansion, the young man sees a dead mouse in his courtyard. When the merchant appears, he asks him if he can have the mouse. The merchant laughs. 'Is that all you want?' The boy nods, picks up the mouse, and goes and sells it as cat food to a widow in his neighbourhood. With a few paise in his pocket, he buys roasted, spiced chana, which he makes into snack packets. With the snacks and a pot of water, he goes and sits under a tree at the city's crossroads.

In the afternoon, loggers arrive from the forest. They put down their heavy load and sit down to rest. The boy offers each a snack packet and water. Since they have no money, they repay his kindness with a log of wood. The next day he sells a log, buys better snacks and repeats the same routine. He does this daily for the next three months till the monsoon arrives, when the logging stops. The price of timber shoots up. By now, our hero has a houseful of logs, and he begins to unload them slowly in the market. By the end of the season, he has made enough money to buy a shop in the timber market. His competitive advantage now lies in his friendship with the loggers, who prefer to deal with him. Before long, our hero is a successful timber merchant.

He is not satisfied, however. He discovers that building ships from timber is more profitable than timber trading and persuades a ship builder to become his partner. Soon, his ship-building business begins to grow and also becomes a success. As the days go by, he learns that shipping companies have a higher margin than ship building. Again, he looks for a knowledgeable partner and finds a shipper in distress. He provides him with capital and common-sense advice, and before long he's running a successful shipping line. Our hero, still in his twenties, has now become the richest man in town. He asks a jeweller to make him a gold mouse, which he presents to the wealthy merchant who had got him started with a dead mouse. The old man is so happy to hear this entrepreneurial tale that he gives his daughter in marriage to our hero.

I was so inspired by the story that I decided to try my hand at business. First, though, I had to learn the ropes. I decided to get a job. It would also relieve my mother's distress over having a 'useless' son at home. I began to look at 'Wanted' ads in the papers. Before long I chanced upon one. It was a company that made Vicks VapoRub. They were looking for trainees. I didn't know what it meant, but I tried my luck. I was called for an interview in Delhi, although the company was based in Bombay. The interviewer was 'America-returned' and spoke with an American accent. He did not beat around the bush.

'What's your goal in life?' he asked.

'To be happy,' I said.

There was embarrassed silence. It was the wrong answer. He had meant my career goal.

'What will make you happy?' he asked.

I got distracted by a stunning young woman who entered the room with a tray carrying tea, coffee and cookies. But quickly, I collected myself. 'There are many ways to happiness,' I replied. 'One is to get married, have kids and a happy family. Another is to make a successful career. A third is to seek adventure. A fourth way is to help the poor. Still another, to find God.' Again, it was the wrong answer.

He suggested patiently that I tell him what side of the business interested me—marketing, production or finance. I did not know, and I told him so. The interview went on in this way. He tried not to show his frustration, but eventually he gave up. Just as I was getting up, he asked if I had any knowledge of business. I told him the story of the mouse merchant. He broke into a laugh, and we shook hands.

The interview had not gone well, and I returned home dejected. I felt I'd had fluffed my chance and began once again to look at the 'Wanted' ads. The bell rang a few days later. It was the postman. To my astonishment, there was a letter for me. I had got the job. I ran to my mother.

'This is for you!' I said, holding the letter up proudly.

I'd become what the Japanese call a 'salaryman'. She was thrilled. I was on my way to becoming a brown sahib with a coveted job in a multinational company. She was delighted with my salary of Rs 750 a month. It was a lot of money in those days. She wrote promptly to the relatives, focusing on the salary in her letters. All week long, she was giving the news to her friends, basking in my success. Although a little squeamish about business, she reassured her friends that I was a professional executive, not a trader. In her status-conscious heart, my job fitted in with her self-image of a high-caste Kshatriya.

My father was surprised. 'Must be your Harvard degree that impressed them!' I confessed that I was a little sad cutting off from the intellectual life. My job, he replied, didn't have to define me. I could still cultivate intellectual interests, especially over the weekend. He was speaking from the heart. He'd been an engineer all his life, but his driving force was his spiritual life. People knew little about themselves, their abilities. I was right to experiment at my age. 'You'll only know the road when you travel on it,' he said. If I didn't like it, there'd be another road. Joining business didn't mean I had to become a cigar-chomping businessman. Society, of course, would try and slot me in a box, but human beings were messy, and they tended to spill out. 'Remember, you've got to make a life, not just a living.'

Three weeks later, I arrived on the island of Bombay seeking gold and glory. The monsoon was leaving, and the city's air was dense with wetness. The yellow-and-black Fiat taxi drove me through soggy quarters, bouncing carelessly over puddles. The streetlights glistened on the asphalt. That night, I dreamt of making whopping deals to the accompaniment of fifteen-foot-tall waves of the Arabian Sea shattering thunderously against the rocks beneath my window. I walked into the company's office the next morning exuding the towering confidence of my twenty-one years.

It was in Queen's Mansion, a run-down yet impressive Victorian structure with a stone facade, along tree-lined Prescot Road near Flora Fountain. The lift was a cage made of criss-crossing steel rods. It took me to the third floor. The offices were not grand—a bunch of rented rooms, nothing like what my mother had pictured. I was led to an area occupied by two other trainees, who looked at me suspiciously. The best thing in the office was my chair—it spun around. I sat in it, and I went round and round, and it cheered me up.

I had been assigned to the sales department. At ten o'clock, tea was served on a tray along with a napkin and biscuits, which confirmed my status as an 'officer'. The clerks and secretaries got sugary tea in a cup and saucer; no biscuit, no napkin, no tray. Soon, my boss, the sales manager, walked in. The other trainees stood to attention. He asked with mild sarcasm if the tea suited me. He was still waiting for me to get up.

The tea was fine, I said. But why did some get it on a tray, not the others? He gave me a peculiar look and asked the three of us to join him in a sales-training session, where he proceeded to tell us to memorize everything— from the price of each size of each product to the names and telephone numbers of our major customers, to the departure times of the trains on our journey cycle.

'Why memorize what you can look up?' I asked.

He gave me another peculiar look.

I had a cousin in Bombay, who he invited me home to dinner a few days later. He worked in a grand old 'Calcutta-style' British company with many factories, thousands of employees, in plush, multistorey marble offices. He asked me what my offices looked like. I felt ashamed.

'How many factories do you have?'

'None,' I said.

'How many salesmen?'

'None.'

I told him defensively that my company was just starting out. We were only a few dozen employees; our office was a little bigger than his house. Someone was making our products under contract; another was selling them under contract. My cousin's talk over dinner revolved around office politics, mainly how to get around the office bureaucracy. After dinner, he confessed that he had met the right girl and was thinking of marrying her, but he said he wasn't sure if his company would approve.

'Does your company have to approve whom you marry?'

'Yes, she has to fit in.'

Looking at my closed-collar jacket, he announced suddenly, 'Get rid of this silly thing!' But it was the only jacket I owned. It was comfortable, light, with a slight yield, as if I wasn't wearing anything. His advice was to look casually stylish. He looked at me again. I also needed a haircut, he said. Hairstyle revealed one's character. He suggested the barber in his club. I agreed to meet him there the next evening.

Colonial ghosts hovered above as I entered the Bombay Gymkhana Club, established in 1875 for 'White only' members. The sun may have set on the empire, but resplendent bearers carrying fresh lime sodas in glasses etched with the club's insignia were not deterred. Brown sahibs, flotsam of the Raj, had comfortably replaced the White sahibs and were moving about with ease. The barber gave me the promised haircut, after which my cousin asked me for my sports credentials. I had none. He was thinking of proposing my name for membership. Since it was a sports club, a form had to be filled stating what sports I played. I hesitated. Why must I join this temple of colonialism? Because, my cousin explained, anyone who is anyone in the multinational corporate world was a member. I was moved by his generous gesture.

The following week, the sales manager's secretary came rushing up to me in a panic. Newly hired salesmen had just walked in, and everyone was away in the field, including her boss. Would I step in and 'warm them up'? I was a trainee, for god's sake, I told her, but she wouldn't listen. So I got up bravely to make the first speech of my life. Walking to the training room, I remembered how I had frozen on the stage in Kaka Nagar. However, seeing the affable faces of young men from different parts of India reassured me. We introduced ourselves—a nice way to kill time, I thought. I asked each one to tell a story. This ate up an hour. When it was my turn, I narrated the story of the mouse merchant. It was an instant hit. They were laughing and applauding. I was feeling confident, and I sought to correct some things I had observed. 'Never memorize what you can look up!' was my subversive advice.

That afternoon, the same secretary brought me a sheet of paper. The boss had left it for me to calculate our salesmen's productivity of the past week and get it typed in the steno pool. I was in a lofty mood after the morning's performance. I sat back and took a round on my swivel chair. I was dreaming of becoming boss, wearing dark glasses to avoid being recognized by my adoring fans. I felt that my job was to look at the big picture and to delegate relentlessly. So, I went to the steno pool, found a willing young typist, and taught her how to calculate percentages while typing the report. After she finished, she handed it over to the boss's secretary, announcing her achievement proudly.

By the following day, word of my heresies had spread. The sales manager was livid, and he marched off fuming to the managing director's office. 'We may have a rotten egg,' he declared. The MD looked puzzled. 'He asks too many questions!' The sales manager recounted my doings, accusing me of not respecting the way things were done. I had to be 'let go' before I infected the others. News of this conversation between my boss and the MD had spread, and I thought everyone was staring at me at lunchtime. I was feeling lost when the company's south Indian accountant took pity and invited me for an idli-dosa lunch at his favourite café. I needed a lesson in corporate morality.

The rasam arrived as soon as we sat down, its pungent aroma opening our nostrils. Every company in Bombay, it seems, had a south Indian accountant, and they had all gathered to listen to me being instructed in corporate ethics. A sensible recruit, he began, stayed on the boss's right side—you never know when you'll need him. Our idlis appeared, served generously with mounds of coconut chutney. It was time to impart deeper secrets of life. 'What is right is what the boss wants!' Senior managers needed to feel comfortable, and a junior's job was to put the senior at ease. Otherwise, the junior wouldn't be trusted and would be condemned to an anxious life. He should keep his boss from making mistakes. 'Never contradict him in public.' To violate this rule was a death wish. 'Don't ever speak out of turn, and make every effort to laugh at the boss's jokes.'

When our dosas were placed before us, the lesson on management principles were put on hold. His eyes shone as he plucked a piece, dipped it in sambar and placed it carefully into his mouth. He burped in satisfaction. By the time our filter coffee arrived I was feeling troubled with the accountant's dharma of hierarchy. My world was going awry. Had I made a mistake in joining this profession? It wasn't the way of the mouse merchant. The judge would have called it 'bureaucracy'. As we were walking back to the office, the accountant farted. Perfect, I thought! He had expressed exactly how I felt about his motto: 'What is right is what the boss wants!'

By the time we got back to the office I was feeling suffocated. Everyone was working with their head down. To put myself in a good mood, I decided to take a spin on my swivel chair. My eyes, however, fell on a message. The sales manager wanted to see me. Like a coward, he began by making small talk about things that had nothing to do with anything. After an interminable lecture, he got to the point. I didn't fit in, he said, and so I was being 'let go'. I had a blank look. He had to repeat 'let go' several times. Soon I got it. I was being fired. He was trying to be politically correct, in the way people say, 'passed away' instead of 'died'. Then he gave me a paper to sign, presented me with a cheque for a month's salary and a train ticket back home to Chandigarh.

Instead of returning to my desk, I went out, wandering aimlessly towards the harbour. It was a clear day, and the mainland of India was visible in the distance. The vast scene coloured my unhappiness. Passing a row of warehouses, I felt defeated by this gritty, impossible city. A dozen merchant ships were moored, waiting to unload. It crossed my mind to ask God to eliminate the sales manager. But since I wasn't much of a believer, it didn't seem like a good idea. I turned around at the docks, took a bus to a wholesale bazaar. The bustle of the marketplace calmed me. I paced around like a monk. I didn't like being fired, but I didn't like the accountant's corporate morality either—all of it a huge letdown after the hopes I'd built after reading about the mouse merchant.

The next day I went to the office to pick up my things, clean up my desk. I was taking the last turn on my swivel chair, trying bravely to look cool when the managing director's secretary burst in. The MD wanted to see me. I walked lightly behind her, almost on tiptoe. He didn't waste any time. The company had made a mistake, he said, in 'letting me go'. I was familiar with the phrase now, but I got the feeling that we were speaking of someone who had passed away. He told me that he had decided to reverse the decision. Would I stay on?

So, I was still alive. I pinched myself to make sure.

He then gave me some advice. Yes, I was an oddball, but he liked my free spirit. I should never lose it. But I had to realize that I was no longer at the university. The office was not a seminar, and I had to observe rules. Before I could get into more trouble, he said, he was sending me 'upcountry' on my six-month field training. He believed that business was learnt in the bazaar. He insisted that I send in a daily report from the field—what I was seeing, what I was learning. I was ready for the new adventure, although I would miss the swivel chair. Before leaving, they reassigned me to the marketing department under a more affable boss.

My first stop was Surat. It conjured bittersweet feelings of my first love, umpteen years ago in Modern School—Alisha's family had come from there. Surat was once a great port of the Mughal Empire, and its bankers had financed Britain's trade with China during its heyday. But it had gone into decline with the rise of Bombay. I began the first morning by calling on our stockist, who was cleaning his teeth mournfully with a neem twig when I arrived. Dozens of open jute bags of chilli stood at the entrance, and they sent me on a bout of sneezing. He gave me a handkerchief, apologizing for his unshaven appearance. He had not slept all night, he said, having lost a fortune with the sudden drop in chilli prices in the futures market. I felt sorry for the poor man.

After checking the stocks of our products, I left at ten thirty to visit retailers, chemists and wholesalers, accompanied by a tricycle filled with our products. While I took orders and collected cash, the poster-cum-tricycle man delivered the stock and put up advertisements of our products. We were an efficient team, although sometimes he would stick the posters upside down. We broke for lunch around two. In the afternoon, the bazaars closed as people slept. I went back to my salesmen's lodge, where I had a leisurely Gujarati luncheon thali and wrote my daily report under the fan.

These reports often turned into long, chatty observations about the market and life in general. I had got into the habit of writing letters ever since my parents left me in America. At Harvard, I had filled a dozen notebooks with reflections on what I was reading. Even when I was exhausted, I still found time to get my head straight and put down my musings. For me, writing was a way to bring coherence and order to my life, working my way out of dark places. This was how I developed beliefs and convictions. This was also how, I think, I began my career as a writer.

In the evening, the stores would be filled with customers; the merchants didn't have time to meet company salesmen. So I decided to visit homes instead to do some informal consumer research. I have a vivid memory of knocking timidly on my first door in Surat. A middle-class housewife opened it. I asked her what her family used to remedy coughs and colds. Her eyes lit up. She asked me in and went to the kitchen, returning with a kettle of boiling water. It was teatime, and I thought we would have tea. But she mixed a spoonful of Vicks VapoRub into a bowl of hot water. This was her answer to my question. Instead of drinking tea that evening, we inhaled medicinal vapours instead. When I told her I worked for the same Vicks company, she was thrilled and presented me with a box of Gujarati sweets. A small present, she said, for all the years of relief and comfort we had given to her family. Thus, I learnt an important lesson. It was she, and millions like her, who paid my salary, not my boss.

The day was not over. After dinner, I walked to a cinema nearby to check if it was showing our advertising commercial. During intermission, I also supervised the distributor's staff as they gave out samples of Vicks throat drops to the audience. During these months in the field, I acquired a deep respect for the Indian merchant, amazed by his acumen, sophistication and purposiveness. He took our products deep into the hinterland, to the smallest village, in vans while conducting local promotions and advertising campaigns, becoming, in effect, our company's ambassador.

In contrast to the vibrant commercial life of the bazaar, office life in Bombay struck me as dull. My cousin's political life at the old British firm seemed stifling. I'd felt defensive at his house that night. But years later I realized that what had humiliated me about our tiny company was, in fact, our strength. All of us were focused on building the Vicks brand without the distraction of factories, sales forces, headquarters staff and industrial relations. A reputable manufacturer made our products under contract; a national distributor with hundreds of salesmen sold them in stores around the country; a finance/legal company did our accounting. We were lean, nimble, focused on creating, retaining and satisfying consumers like the housewife with the tea kettle in Surat. As so often happens in life, by the time I could apply this lesson, our company had built factories, created a national sales force, hired thousands of employees in half a dozen departments, all of whom were having lots of fun fighting over turf.

As I relive my life, I wonder if I really understood myself back then. Twice in four years I had changed my life. I'd gone to Harvard to learn something 'useful', like engineering. Once there, I got seduced by the magical, wondrous world of the humanities. Then, four years later, waiting to become an academic philosopher at Oxford, I had gone off to chase the mouse merchant's dream. Each time, my mother felt her 'dancing star' had thrown his life away. But my father knew better. Books had set me free. I had lost my fear of authority at Harvard. No longer afraid of the future, I had chosen to create myself. My father consoled my mother saying that I was an untamed spirit, born to be free. I could pretend to be cool in a swivel chair even when I had been fired. These were milestones in my moksha journey.

I had hit Bombay running at twenty-one, just as I'd hit Lyallpur running at two and a half. No matter where I ran, I seemed to run into myself. The sales manager didn't think I fitted. The chief accountant tried to stick me in a cage. My cousin was contemptuous of our tiny company. The managing director called me an oddball. But I knew what I wanted. It was the mouse merchant's free life in the bazaar, not bureaucracy. The judge taught me the dharma of work. Yes, both of us were ahead of our times. We were in the Jurassic age of the Licence Raj, whereas we belonged to a future age to come: the age of start-ups. It wasn't going to stop me, however, from being myself.

9

Told to Shut the Door, I Kept Both Open

'To escape boredom, man either works or plays.
If he tires of both, then he invents a third state,
which lets him float like a dancer.'

—Friedrich Nietzsche

'Is this seat 6D?'

The owner of the voice had a familiar face. We exchanged a few awkward words while she tried to locate her seat. After she sat down, we did not make eye contact, although we were sitting near each other in the air-conditioned chair car of the Flying Ranee, the train that merchants of Surat had been taking to Bombay since 1906. Twenty minutes later, I heard the same voice.

'Is it you? Is it really you?'

'Alisha? Modern School?' I exclaimed.

Alisha nodded, her lips curling into a smile. She managed to get her neighbour to exchange seats with me, and we sat together for the rest of the four-hour journey. We were shy, and the conversation was hesitant. I told her that my field training at Vicks was finally over and that I was on my way back to the headquarters in Bombay. She was looking after the family's textile business in Surat while dodging attempts to get her married.

'Time passes quickly in Surat,' she said. 'One is forever busy with customers, suppliers and employees.' But it was a boring life, she felt. You knew exactly what someone was going to say before they said it. After a pause, she said she wished she lived in a big, anonymous city like Bombay, where people valued their time . . . and privacy. Plus, there were museums, galleries, film premieres—the latest in everything! The only excitement in Surat was when you quarrelled. She'd had a row with her family recently because she wanted to live alone.

We were soon chatting in an easy, fluent manner. She pointed excitedly at the strange light outside, the monsoon sky, the long strips of bright orange light falling on the rushing fields in the distance. Gradually, our masks fell off.

'You've changed,' she said. 'So much confidence . . . not the frightened boy I knew in school . . .'

'. . . who brought you roses one day.'

She winced. 'I was beastly then, wasn't I?' she said contritely.

She had grown into a beautiful woman from the thin, wilful teenager I remembered. Her lustrous hair kept falling on her face, and she gently brushed it away with her hand. But there was something sad, melancholic in her eyes. It soon began to drizzle, raindrops falling on the windows of the train. She took out a shawl from her handbag. We talked lightly and easily.

'You have a nice, comforting manner,' she said, peering into my eyes. 'So different from the boys I meet.' She must have been twenty-three.

There had hardly been a difference in our ages. What had been different was her family's status and wealth. And what had seemed terribly important then hardly mattered today.

'You're gentler,' I said.

'. . . and sadder,' she added.

Between pauses we stole burrowing stares at each other. By the time we reached Bombay Central, it was clear to both of us that we were attracted to each other. As we parted at the station, we exchanged numbers. I placed my hand affectionately on her shoulder; she reciprocated by gripping my hands tightly. There were good reasons to believe that we would meet again.

The following day was 27 May 1964. I remember it well because Jawaharlal Nehru died on that day. I was back at work in our Bombay office, assigned now to the marketing department and feeling more relaxed with a mild-mannered boss who smiled easily. At lunchtime, people were congratulating me for completing my field training. We were laughing away when news came of Nehru's death on the MD's secretary's transistor radio. The secretary burst into tears. So did the others. Everyone rushed to her desk. The MD came out, looking deeply sad. We all began to speak at the same time. There was fearful uncertainty in our eyes. 'After Nehru, who?'

Nehru's death was another moment in my political awakening. I was reminded of the day when I'd missed that catch at age eleven: I had muffed a chance to grab Nehru's garland of marigold on Rajpath, not realizing what it had meant. I admired Nehru like everyone else—he'd kept us together, making us into one nation. He had turned our habit of arguing into democracy; he'd taught us to tolerate each other, building an infuriatingly plural, secular India that I so loved. As the years went by, I began to also see Nehru's flaws. His well-meaning state socialism degenerated into 'Licence Raj', taking the economy to a dead end. Under his daughter, his democratic socialism would become authoritarian socialism. Sometimes called the 'last Englishman to rule India', Nehru had the English upper-class bias against business. Add to it a strong dose of Fabian socialism at Cambridge, and this was the key to Nehru's ideology.

In my new role in marketing, I discovered something odd. The company was spending the entire advertising budget of Vicks in the winter, although we were shipping lots of cases during the summer monsoon months. People must be catching colds in the monsoon, I thought. 'Shouldn't we shift some of the spending?' I suggested to my boss. He consulted the 'holy book' of dos and don'ts from our New York headquarters. Sure enough, it commanded us to advertise in the winter. My timid boss felt uneasy. He asked me to write a memo, which he passed on to the managing director without comment.

The MD also hesitated. 'What percent of the budget ought we to allocate to the monsoon months?' he asked. My fainthearted boss suggested 10 per cent. The MD looked at me. I said 50 per cent. We compromised at 30 per cent and he forwarded my proposal to New York. There was a flurry of telexes. At first, HQ was perplexed, but agreed to 25 per cent. I then worked with the advertising agency to make a commercial: it showed six-year-old Raju catching a cold after playing football in the rain; his wise mother applied Vicks on his chest, and all was well. We even coined a new name for summer colds: 'wet monsoon colds.' Sales jumped. New York was delighted, and we were heroes. The company commissioned a study by scientists, which confirmed that people catch colds when seasons change, not just in the winter.

Thanks to my new boss, I felt free to be myself. Seeing me asking questions all the time, the others began to do the same, and office life became roomier. As the days went by, I found there were two kinds of people: those who did the work and those who took the credit. There was lots of competition in the second group, very little in the first. Kamble belonged to the first, and I instantly took a shine to him. He was our night guard. He'd arrive at 6 p.m., looking fresh in his khaki uniform when the rest of us were tired and worn. He was lean, taut, with an athletic build and a neatly trimmed beard. He came from a village in Maharashtra and didn't know much English—everyone laughed at the way he pronounced the company's name with a Marathi accent. Full of childlike curiosity, he wanted to know how everything worked. He discovered the tea- and coffee-making machines in the pantry, and quickly picked up how to operate them. Between his rounds, he would be serving tea or coffee to anyone who wanted it. Despite his broken English, he'd learnt the telex machine and began sending short messages. The same went for the switchboard—he'd be found answering the phone. Before long, he was operating the film projector, and we had the unbelievable luxury of reviewing advertising after office hours.

The MD got a taste of Kamble's magic one evening. He needed to speak urgently to the finance director, who was away, and no one knew how to reach him. He was beginning to panic. Someone said, 'Ask Kamble!' So Kamble made a few calls, discovered that the finance director was staying at Ashoka Hotel in Delhi and connected with him in minutes. Since that day, if you needed anything after hours, 'Ask Kamble' became the mantra. Some managers began to stay late because the office was more efficient after hours. One day Kamble came rushing to me. He'd found a wallet near the men's room containing lots of cash. Worried that the owner might be anxious, he asked if I'd take charge of office security. He rushed in a taxi to deliver the wallet, which belonged to a senior manager. When Kamble reached his home, he found both husband and wife enveloped in gloom. The money was an advance on their 'dream house', and the seller was expected any minute. Never was anyone more relieved to see Kamble. Before the story got out, Kamble swore us to secrecy—he was self-effacing and didn't want to take the credit.

A few months later, our telephone operator went on maternity leave. Through the grapevine, I heard that Kamble wanted her job temporarily while she was away. He was tired of working at night. But the personnel manager turned him down flatly, saying ours was a multinational company where calls came from around the world. How would he cope when he couldn't even pronounce the company's name properly? But his formidable reputation on the night shift must have swung it, because I walked into the office the next morning and found Kamble smiling at the switchboard. At the end of the week, passing me by in the corridor, our lawyer asked if we had a new phone system. His calls were answered now on the second ring—earlier, he'd have to hold for the fifth or sixth ring. Kamble was our new system. I stopped at Kamble's booth and asked why he answered so promptly. His reply took my breath away. It may be a customer, he said, and we might lose an order.

The company realized quickly that Kamble was meant for bigger things. He was promoted, then promoted again and kept rising to bigger jobs. He showed the same curiosity, energy and a helpful attitude of service towards each job, inspiring others around him. He would get so absorbed that he would forget himself; and he never cared who got the credit. He was lucky too—our company was still young and didn't have boundaries, which meant he could play many roles. His secret lay, I think, in an innocent quality to turn every activity into play, no matter how menial or routine. And so, he loved the work he did when others found it boring. You'd think that all companies would want to hire Kambles, but they insisted on recruiting people based on their credentials and knowledge rather than attitude.

My father once told me about the advice in the Bhagavad Gita about the dharma of work: do your job without thinking of the personal reward. I was sceptical. I didn't think that self-interested human beings could act in this way. But unassuming Kamble proved me wrong—he taught me that self-forgetting is the path to high performance and happiness. I haven't been able to achieve it, but the aspiration has been liberating—a marker on my moksha journey. What drew me to Kamble especially was his lightness of spirit. He became my role model.

It was not an easy shift from the academic to the business life. I'd been thrown into business by accident. There were days when I hated it and missed the intellectual life of Harvard. I asked myself: What was I was doing, trudging from shop to shop selling Vicks in hot, dusty bazaars? I wrote to my mother about my discontent. She said the best way to appreciate my job was to imagine I didn't have one. She believed in karma and wanted me to accept that I wasn't a master of my fate. I wrote back saying that it was only a job right now, but if I stayed on, it would become a career, and then I'd have to throw myself under a train. I consoled myself, thinking that I was in a gap year and would soon go back to academic life. That would be a mistake, she said. I ought to shut that door for good.

Nor did I like Bombay at first. Except for a few old Victorian buildings and Marine Drive, I thought it ugly. It was a smug, heartless city—the only thing that mattered was to buy low and sell high. The sun beat down all day on street hawkers, who carried their livelihoods in their baskets on the suburban trains. People worked, loved and died while hanging on to phones giving shipment numbers, bills of lading and discounts. It was soulless and depressing. I missed the India of my childhood—idyllic Company Bagh in Lyallpur, the Himalayan birds of Shimla, the vast grassy spaces of Delhi.

But as karma would have it, I began to gradually enjoy the rough and tumble of the business life. Having Kamble around helped; he taught me the right attitude, grounding me in the moment. I began to see adventure around each corner. I was amused by a salesman travelling with me—he'd fall asleep as soon as the train moved and was wide awake, alert, as soon we arrived an hour later. When it came to money, I realized it wasn't mine; it belonged to the company's shareholders. So, I relaxed—I was an employee, a custodian. I was playing Monopoly, but with real money. Like Kamble, I shed the burdens and began to feel lighter. I found myself fashioning a new self.

So I stayed on. I found spacious rooms with plenty of light on the top floor of a tiny Parsi house near the Colaba post office. It overlooked an orchard and had a view of the sea. The terrace became my open-air living room. On it, I placed a birdcage, a wrought-iron swing and a stone chessboard, all from Chor Bazaar. Inside, I arranged a low but large divan at one end, covered it with a handloom print of frolicking elephants and surrounded it with colourful cushions. I lined the room with books and a small V.S. Gaitonde painting that I got on easy installments from the Chemould gallery at Kala Ghoda. It became a sitting room during the day and a bedroom at night. My terrace flat was ideal for parties on weekends. During the monsoon, however, all partying came to a halt.

One lazy Saturday afternoon, during a break in the monsoon, I caught an unexpected glimpse of Alisha walking idly past Strand Book Stall. She wore a thin, white, almost gossamer sari with white sandals. The pale rays of the afternoon sun fell on the curves of her body. She was looking for a cab. I rushed towards her. She gave me a contrite smile, admitting awkwardly that she had got my messages. Anyway, she was back and wanted to see me. She was staying with her aunt, who had planned a family lunch on Sunday. Could we meet after that? I invited her home. Just as I finished giving her my address, a black-and-yellow Fiat taxi stopped in the middle of a puddle. She jumped into it and disappeared into Bombay's tired streets.

I wasn't sure she'd come, but the doorbell rang late on Sunday afternoon. Alisha stood on the landing, masses of hair framing her face, and a light cotton sari disguising inadequately her slim, round figure. I inhaled her warm smell as she stepped in. Taking off her sandals, she went to the bathroom, washed her feet under the tap in the shower and came out to join me on the terrace. There was a gentle breeze from the sea. She liked my 'open-air living room'. Her eyes had the same melancholy look I remembered from the train. She was in a mood to talk, and I listened, taking an odd pleasure in entering her world of small vanities. She was much concerned with the opinion of her matchmaking aunts and uncles, avoiding anything unpleasant and accepting every superstition. They had recently found another man for her, from a wealthy family of her caste—'a perfect match', they had called it. She'd found him arrogant and insensitive, and was plotting her escape.

It started to drizzle, but she was in no mood to go inside. She seemed a lost soul, prematurely exhausted by life. I took her confessions to be a sign of our deepening relationship. Gradually, the drizzle turned into a monsoon storm, and we rushed inside. I gave her a towel. She insisted on drying my forehead and hair first. At her touch, a feeling of happiness coursed through me. Feeling shy at seeing her wet, partially naked body, I gave her a cotton robe and looked away. But she seemed at ease. The rain eased gradually. Since the air was thick inside, I opened a window. From an overflowing gutter, we saw water pouring in a steady stream on to the street. I made tea.

The rain had washed away our inhibitions, and our conversation over tea was infused with intimacy. I could still hear the raindrops pattering above us, but the force of the storm was over, and only a trickle issued from the gutter. I was conscious of the silence between us. She lowered her head, gazing for a long time into my eyes. Then she gave me a sad smile. I was about to say something when she pressed her hand on my mouth. I felt her mouth on mine as my arms closed on her. It was a long, lingering kiss.

Thus began a warm, happy relationship. Each time she'd come to Bombay for work, she would visit me in my flat in Colaba and fill me with happiness. She didn't want to go out, watch a movie or visit an exhibition. She wanted only to chat and to kiss. Initially, she drew a line, never allowing our intimacy to go beyond kisses, but gradually she relented and nature had its way.

One night, after putting Alisha in a taxi, I was walking home when I found two women arguing on a sidewalk near the Colaba bus station. One of them, Munna Bai, stopped me, complaining that the other woman was trying to usurp her spot. She'd been sleeping at the same place on the pavement since she arrived in the city six months ago. I was face to face with India's poverty. The thought of my spacious flat filled me with guilt and shame. I asked her a dozen questions: What was she doing here? Where was she from? Wasn't it humiliating sleeping on the pavement? Wouldn't she rather be at home with her family and friends in the comfort of her village?

Her replies demolished me. Picking up a handful of soil, she said, 'Sah'b, Bombay is heaven!' I looked at her oval face, straight nose and intense eyes. Bombay had given her a job! She ate well, saved money and sent it home each week to feed her family. She was free here and did what she liked. In her village in Bihar, she had been the prey of upper-caste men ceaselessly. She gave a bold, sidelong glance, and I noticed her earthy physicality. There was dignity in a job, she said, even if she had to sleep on the street. I set about mediating between the two women, and we reached a compromise that satisfied both.

Munna Bai gave me new respect for the city. From the suburban train, I had seen Bombay's urban stain spreading, eating away peaceful old villages, driving back coconut trees, smothering calm lives with chemical fumes, dotting the creeks with slums. The dormitory suburbs were an urban sprawl, mile after mile of sordid apartment blocks. Occasionally, I caught a glimpse of a green field, scattered palm trees, an occasional blue hill. But more often, I saw shanty towns, mud huts covered with tin and plastic sheets. Meeting Munna Bai shattered my negative view of the city. It was another political awakening! I, too, was a migrant like her, I realized. I, too, had come to live, work and seek my fortune here. We were among the millions, who had been migrating for 200 years, seeking opportunity and freedom. For Munna Bai, it was liberation from the oppressions of her feudal village. For me, it was freedom from the expectations created by my academic education. It was another step in my moksha journey! As a result of this awakening, now I no longer minded Bombay's noisy, chaotic bazaars, the exhaust of the tangled traffic. Nor the dismal smoke from the mills in industrial Parel and the empty faces of mill workers. Bombay's capitalism created jobs, opportunity and freedom.

My introduction to Bombay's art world added to my growing admiration for the city. I met the sculptor Pilloo Pochkhanawala, who invited me to the opening of a group show of the Progressive Artists' Group at the Jehangir Art Gallery. I was stunned by what I saw. I had not seen so much beauty in one place! I was drawn to the artists present— Gaitonde, K.H. Ara, H.A. Gade and Tyeb Mehta. I also met the art critic and novelist Mulk Raj Anand, editor of *Marg*, a respected arts journal. I knew him as the author of *Untouchable*, the story of a day in the life of a toilet cleaner. He did not look the Marxist I had imagined.

Pilloo invited me to dinner a few months later at her elegant home behind Worli Sea Face. She was married to the son of Sorabji Pochkhanawala, the founder of the Central Bank of India. There, I was attracted to two persons who would go on to play a role in my political development. One was Sham Lal, who wrote a column, Life & Letters, in the *Times of India*. When I arrived, he was describing in unsentimental words the anxiety that gripped the nation the day Nehru died. It was our first test at leadership succession, he said. The foreign press had raised alarms of upheaval after Nehru, including the possibility of the nation's break-up. Two weeks later, however, India had been greeted with a smooth, painless and mature transition of power to Lal Bahadur Shastri. We'd passed the test.

Ample, high-spirited Piloo Mody laughed at this moment. This Piloo spelt his name with one 'L', and he found the contrast between Shastri and Nehru 'too, too funny'. The latter was handsome and aristocratic, while his successor was a diminutive, village bumpkin in a dhoti. Sham Lal reminded us, however, that it was Shastri's gentle face, his kind, large eyes, that had won the nation's affection, and he had proved Churchill wrong about India's ability to survive succession. But I was captivated by the overweight Piloo, who kept referring to Nehru's 'mixed economy' as a 'mixed-up economy'. Before the evening was over, we'd become friends, and he invited me to join his Friday study group on economic freedom.

We were an eager, motley bunch that met near Regal Cinema to discuss the theory and practice of the free market. Our group included the scion of a princely family from Gujarat—I envied him his striking red Standard Herald sports car. There was a passionate south Indian executive with a sugar company, several lawyers and an earnest accountant. We read selections from the greats of classical liberalism—F.A. Hayek, Adam Smith, John Locke, J.S. Mill—and met on Fridays to discuss and compare what we had read with the current events in India. Minoo Masani, general secretary of the Swatantra Party, dropped in occasionally from his office nearby in the Army Navy building. He was a cold fish, unlike warm and voluble Piloo. Once, Rajaji (C. Rajagopalachari), the head of the party, made a cameo appearance to remind us that classical liberalism had created America, the first modern country. Another time, the glamorous Maharani Gayatri Devi of Jaipur, dropped in, and we couldn't get over her for weeks.

Although I was no longer in the sales department, my job entailed a fair amount of travel. I went to motivate distributors and talk to consumers to get new advertising ideas. But I had plenty of free evenings with nothing to do. I was strolling one evening while chewing paan after dinner, in a bazaar in Hyderabad, when I bumped into an uneasy thought. I'd been reading all these years, taking in knowledge. Wasn't it time to take something out? But how to do it? If reading was 'taking in' others' ideas, maybe, I could 'take it out' by writing. Yes, I would be a writer on the side. It would be a way to pay back. Wasn't this what Rawls and Said had meant when they reminded me that a Harvard education entailed a duty to give back?

The following month I was on a tour in Punjab and stopped to see the family in Ludhiana. Cousin Jeet was curious to know how I was getting on. I began to tell him about my job, but he quickly lost interest. He wanted to know about my 'love life'. I didn't want to talk about Alisha, so I told him about my ambition to become a writer on the side. 'Bad idea! No money in it,' he said dismissively. 'Besides, never put anything in writing.' And he told me about an incident at the railways training school in Jamalpur. He had been so moved by the generous curves of a faculty member's wife that he began to flirt with her. She seemed to like his attention. They began to exchange letters. Being a proud cook, she sent him desserts secretly. In a letter thanking her, he described rapturously her physical attributes. Her husband discovered the dangerous document. Being a jealous sort, and in a superior position, the husband insisted on making Jeet's life miserable.

'Writer? Too dangerous!' Jeet said.

I did not heed Jeet's advice, however. One morning at age twenty-two, sitting in Sri Krishna Lodge in Jalandhar, I began to write my first play, *Larins Sahib*. I told myself, Shakespeare too must have sat down on such a morning to write *Hamlet*. Now, a sensible person doesn't compare himself to Shakespeare, but this is precisely the sort of lunacy you need to get started. Oddly enough, my confidence came from my daily reports from the field, which often turned into musings about life. My bosses liked them. I had also once written a term paper at Harvard as a Socratic dialogue, which my professor enjoyed. He noted, 'You've a good ear.' Thus, my career as a 'weekend writer' was born. I began to write whenever and wherever I found time, in traveller's lodges, on trains, on flights and at airports (Indian Airlines was invariably late). On some days, I wrote only one sentence.

Larins Sahib is a historical play, set in the confused period after Ranjit Singh's death, when the British first arrived in the Punjab in the 1840s. I'd been reading history on my travels and had come across an unusual Englishman, Henry Lawrence, who had the remarkable ability to relate to Indians. I turned it into a drama of hubris. Writing it, I realized how difficult and how amusing the first encounter between the Indians and English must have been. One morning, I opened the *Times of India* to find the announcement of a playwriting competition. Rs 10,000 was the first prize—a lot of money in those days! Greed and the prospect of fame stirred me. I completed the play before the deadline and sent it in.

I was rushing out of my flat when the phone rang six weeks later. I dashed back to get it. It was a reporter, fishing. There was buzz that I'd won. The rumour turned out to be correct. I got a letter a few days later confirming it. They'd received more than eighty entries, some from established writers. For the rest of the week I was flying four fingers above the ground on Yudhishthir's chariot. There was a glamorous prize-giving ceremony at the Taj, where Santha Rama Rau was the chief guest. Alisha also came. I was asked to speak, but I was tongue-tied. My picture was in all the papers, and I was famous. The Bombay Theatre Group performed the play six months later, with actor Zul Vellani as the lead. It was performed in other places as well, including at the Edinburgh Festival, and published by Oxford University Press in the UK. I had a second career as a weekend writer.

My intellectual friends were surprised and envious. They asked why I was writing a play in English. I grew defensive. If I could write memos in English, why not a play? Besides, wasn't English becoming an Indian language? My critics reflected the mood of the '60s, when India's national language was a hot potato. Several states wanted to ban English from schools. Tamil Nadu even threatened to secede if Hindi replaced English as the national language. That put the kibosh on the Hindi wallahs. It would take another generation before English became an Indian language.

My father phoned one morning. He was in town to attend a meeting at the Institution of Engineers. We agreed to meet in the evening. Since it was the opening of Nasreen Mohamedi's show, I suggested we meet at Bal Chhabda's Gallery 59. I liked Nasreen's distinctive line drawings in pencil—precise and meticulous, sometimes in grid-like formations. When my father arrived, I was showing off, trying to impress a critic with my 'Harvard learning'. Even though I'd won a literary prize, I was still an outsider in the world of artists and writers—a crass business type, trying to crash their cultured party.

My father felt I was trying too hard. 'Most of the shadows in our life,' he said, 'are the result of our standing in our own sunshine.'

'What's the point in knowing something if you can't show off?' I protested.

I was a child crying for attention, and he wanted me to relax, do yoga, feel comfortable with myself. Showing off, he said, was a fool's idea of glory.

'You can get people to look at your face but not what's behind it.' Since it was early, we decided to walk to Chowpatty for our Gujarati thali. He approved of my two-hatted existence. It was my way of 'making a life', he said. My mother worried, however. She had wanted me to shut one door, and I had gone and pushed both wide open. There was a long silence as we walked. Just as we arrived at our destination, he said, 'No one can make you feel inferior without your consent.' It was another face of moksha he was pointing to—liberation from vanity.

Piloo Mody never liked to dine alone. He'd grab one of us and take us to the Willingdon Club in his old Cadillac. It was my turn this Friday. He knew everyone at the club and quickly got busy introducing me to old Parsi money. Over dinner, he gave a hilarious account of his first political meeting in a Bombay slum. B.K. Mistry, secretary of the newly formed Swatantra Party, arrived in a white suit, red tie and sola topi, and Piloo in his Cadillac. BK got up to speak in broken Bombay Hindi that upper-class Parsis reserved for servants. He asked the audience to imagine they were chugging uphill on a bus driven by Prime Minister Nehru. All of a sudden, the bus began to slide downhill. The passengers screamed, 'Save us, save us!' Hearing these cries, Raja-ji, leader of the Swatantra Party, swooped down like Superman and singlehandedly saved the passengers and the people of India. Piloo thought BK had made a fool of himself, but the audience loved it. They were in stitches, whistling and clapping.

I was now enjoying my commercial job. My mother was relieved that I had settled down. I also began to work quietly on a second play. I was a man of action Monday through Friday, a man of thought on Saturday and Sunday. While my business friends played golf on the weekend, I wrote. Words gave me pleasure. I'd forget myself, my problems, for hours, forgetting that I was even alive. I thus lived in two worlds. If things got me down in the first, I'd merely open the door and walk into the other. Although the academic world had become remote, I kept alive my ideal of philosophy as a way of existing in the world, giving meaning to my day-to-day life. Having two occupations meant I wasn't a slave to either. It was liberating, another sort of moksha, leading me to a lighter way of being.

I also began to admire Bombay's people. They were nicer than Delhi's. Perhaps it was because Bombay's origins lay in commerce, unlike Delhi's feudal past. Trade taught interdependence: everyone had a customer; both the supplier and customer had to be happy for the transaction to go through. It had to be a 'win-win'. No one could afford to lord it over others—even Mr Tata had to be nice to his customer. This was why Montesquieu called commerce gentle, soft and civilizing, leading to peace. Delhi, on the other hand, had always been ruled by a king with a hierarchical bureaucracy. Now the prime minister had replaced the king, but the ethos had remained. You had to stab a rival to get ahead in Delhi. If you didn't become CEO in Bombay, you merely crossed the street and joined your competitor. Delhi had one CEO; Bombay had 1,00,000.

Amid all the happenings in my life, I received a letter from Alisha. She had succumbed to family pressure and decided to marry. It was to a man she hardly knew, but he seemed acceptable after a single meeting. I was devastated. The pleasurable sensation of her kisses lingered for months, slowly turning into a gloomy ache. Alisha had been beautiful, elusive and unattainable. I had fallen in love with her for the second time. My mother had always found Alisha unsuitable—her family was too wealthy. My father had a different take, however. He said that if I hadn't risked falling in love, I would have lost a chance to awaken to a sense of life and beauty.

Nietzsche says that to escape boredom, man works or plays. If he tires of both, he invents a third state, which lifts him up like a dancer floating. This fitted nicely with my desire to live lightly, with laghima, like my mother's star dancing a billion years away. The third state allowed me to partake in the transient world of the active businessman, who brings bread, butter, clothes, medicines to people to help them live their daily lives; the contemplative life of the writer brings them eternal verities of high culture. Human beings need both.

Although I enjoyed my weekday job now, I did not succeed in bringing to it the playfulness, the laghima, lightness of my weekend job. Kamble, of course, achieved this during weekdays by turning his work into play. He thus escaped boredom by inventing, having fun, not unlike the gods frolicking about above. Kamble had acquired the more difficult skill—to do what had to be done without worrying about who got the credit. It was the charioteer's lesson of karma yoga from the Gita. On the rare occasions when I seemed to achieve this attitude on the weekend, it was liberating.

Joining the Swatantra Party after Nehru's death was also a release. Like my family, I'd always voted for the Congress party—a repayment, I suppose, for winning our freedom from colonial rule. But power changed the Congress as everyone's brother-in-law scrambled for the spoils of office.

I joined the Swatantra Party to seek freedom from the chains of Nehru's socialist raj. Alas, the party turned out to be a short-lived experiment—the only serious attempt in India's political history to institutionalize classical liberalism. It died in the '70s.

It takes foolhardiness to grow up to be yourself, to become who you think you are. My rivals at work began to whisper: How could I be serious if I was writing plays? Self-appointed cultural czars of the literary establishment dismissed my pretensions. I didn't fit their picture of a lean, struggling writer. They tattled: my prize must be a fluke, I must have bribed the jury! On some days, all this would get me down. I had to remind myself that the great Chekov also had a double life—writing stories about futile Russian lives in the mornings and saving those lives as a doctor in the afternoons. 'Medicine is my lawful wife,' he said, 'and literature is my mistress.'

Joining the Swatantra Party made it worse. To leftist literary types, it was a party of landlords, princely families and fat industrialists. They could not understand my genuine desire for freedom from a command economy—they saw only a party trying to preserve the status quo. It is hard to see Adam Smith's 'invisible hand' in a poor country. It's tough to be yourself. I wasn't yet fully grounded and looked to others for approval. Only later would I learn that it is better to be maligned for what you are than to be admired for what you are not.

10

Love, a Temporary Insanity Curable by Marriage

'By all means, marry. If you get a good wife, you'll become happy; if you get a bad one, you'll become a philosopher.'

—Socrates

Democracy is best run by modest persons, and there was none more modest than Lal Bahadur Shastri. What got him the job was his ability to connect with the ordinary person. He did not inspire; he did not offend; he stayed out of everyone's hair. In a party raging with rivalries, he was the least likely to divide. So they gave him the job when charismatic Nehru died in 1964. The gossips quipped, 'Yes, he is modest, but he has much to be modest about.' They had said the same thing about Atlee after Churchill.

Shastri died nineteen months later. I was in a meeting when I got a call from the Swatantra Party office. Minoo Masani was going to address the press, and Piloo Mody thought I should be there. Masani told us that Shastri was healthy at sixty-three but had died mysteriously—his wife thought he had been poisoned. I wish Shastri had lived longer. He was pragmatic, not an ideologue, and he had begun to undo some of the damage of Nehru's faux socialism. Unlike Nehru, who was obsessed with state-owned heavy industry, Shastri returned the nation's attention to agriculture and laid the foundation for a green revolution. Masani's remarks were consistent with his classical-liberal belief in economic freedom.

At 5 feet 2 inches, Shastri was pint-sized compared to Field Marshal Ayub Khan of Pakistan, who must have equated puniness with cowardice and launched an attack in 1965 in Kashmir, not imagining that the little man would counter with an attack on Lahore. India had the clear upper hand when ceasefire was declared three weeks later. Shastri, however, died of a heart attack in Tashkent while signing the peace treaty. He had held his own in a hostile Congress party and died almost penniless—his only possession a second-hand car for which he was still paying installments. It's hazardous to speculate on the what-ifs of history, but I agree with Masani. India's economy would have been stronger had Shastri lived longer. He would have liberalized it, becoming our first reformer. India would have been spared the Nehru–Gandhi dynasty.

Our company's business had been growing nicely, and our worldwide chairman wanted to see it on the ground. His visit with his wife was a first and a big deal for the Indian subsidiary. Our MD spent weeks in planning—arranging meetings with key government officials, dinners with businessmen, plus cultural and social events. I was put in charge of a classical Indian dance performance, which the top man's wife had expressly asked to see. Knowing my peculiarities, the MD warned me, 'No philosophy! Stick to business!' He handed me a stack of magazines— *Businessweek, Forbes, Fortune*—so I'd be able to speak sensibly about the international business scene.

At the performance, I sat obediently next to the chairman's wife, trying to impress her with business jargon. She wanted to talk about Indian dance, but I kept bringing her back to business. It was a farce. Later that evening, she told the MD that she had not come to India to hear the usual talk about business. She wanted to experience a great ancient civilization. He confessed that it was his mistake and told her that I was actually a playwright pretending to be a businessman.

At dinner, she changed her seat from the high table and came to sit beside me. Explaining the mix-up, she plied me with dozens of questions about India. I gave her enthusiastic answers. It was late when we rose— almost everyone had left. Before departing, she told me that God had made me 'an original' and that it took courage to be oneself. Conformity was a prison. We should not be defined by what we do but by what we are. It was good advice—I had to climb alone up the moksha tree.

I was twenty-five years old now and restless. I got a call from a headhunter, asking if I'd be interested in working for the Swiss company Nestlé, in Delhi. It would be a promotion, more money. I was tempted. I flew over the weekend to Delhi to meet its Swiss and Indian bosses. On Monday, I told the MD about the offer. Smiling wryly, he said the Swiss had pre-empted him. He showed me a year-old memo about Vicks's plan to promote me to a job in New York. Nestlé, it seems, had accelerated his timetable. Would I be interested in becoming a global manager at the Vicks headquarters? I was in a dilemma. Nestlé was bigger, more famous and respected, but Vicks was ready to make me a global manager. Also, I was comfortable at Vicks—they'd got used to my eccentricities, my weekend writing. Besides, there was Kamble. By the end of the week, I'd been promoted to a plum job at the Vicks headquarters on 42nd Street in New York.

I gave the news sheepishly to the headhunter. He accused me of using the Nestlé offer to bargain with Vicks. I protested—I'd seen the old memo with my own eyes. He didn't believe me. In the evening, the Swiss boss of Nestlé called. It was a different conversation. He tried to sell his company. Once I'd proven myself at Nestlé India, I too could become a global manager at Nestle's headquarters at Vevey, Switzerland. He conjured visions of the Alps—breathtaking cliffs, glaciers, tranquillity of the green valleys; not to forget, chocolates and Swiss cheese. Compare that, he said, with crime-filled New York! Someone had to defend New York. I told him that NYC's beauty wasn't external; it was inside its people. He could tell I'd made up my mind.

Before leaving for America, I went to see my parents. They were driving to Beas the following day for the season's big satsang, and I tagged along. During the three-hour journey, I tried to hide my godless self. Lurking behind each encounter with my father were big questions, especially the one about God. His world needed a divine arbiter; mine did not. I had been on a steady diet of atheism for four years at Harvard: Marx taught me that religion was the opiate of the masses; Feuerbach maintained that God was a product of the human imagination; Durkheim called it a projection of society and its rituals; Freud thought it was an illusion, although critical to the making of civilization; finally, Nietzsche pronounced famously, 'God is dead.' All this had meant a steady loss in faith. I did not mind losing faith so much as hiding it from my father. I had tried to believe in God but had failed. The more I tried, the less I believed. I began to secretly hope that He did not exist. Frankly, I liked the world without anyone ruling over my destiny. There are always people who want to improve things. Some want to change the weather—Indians want more rain; the English want less rain. Others want to change human beings. I like things as they are, imperfect and uncertain.

My father was quiet and serene throughout the journey. Occasionally, he'd point proudly to a canal with which he had been associated. He was proud of his life's work, bringing water to a parched land that went on to become a granary of the nation. He must have suspected my growing scepticism, but he never let on. We arrived in Beas as a dust storm was retreating. The leaves were falling, circling down with sombre lightness. Seeing me watching the leaves, he smiled. He wanted us to meet the guru and was delighted when we got an audience right away. To see and be seen by an enlightened guru conferred merit, he believed. As we entered the guru's chambers, my mother proudly announced that I had been promoted and would be leaving soon for the company's headquarters in New York. I possessed 'good karma', he said and offered to initiate me. The mantra, he said, would come in handy in distant shores. As we came out, my mother was beaming. She said, 'You lucky boy, good karma!' I must have saved lots of cows in my past lives.

That night over dinner, my father alluded to Pascal's wager. He didn't want me to chicken out of the initiation, I think. Blaise Pascal, the French philosopher, had offered four possibilities regarding the existence of God. If you believe God exists, and it turns out to be true, you've won. If you believe he doesn't exist, and if that turns out to be true, again you've won. A third possibility: if you believe he exists, and He does not, then you merely shrug your shoulders, nothing lost. However, if you don't believe in Him and he does exist, you've lost the bet and the chance of a lifetime. So, the sensible thing is to believe in Him. Pascal had offered this wager in the seventeenth century to a sceptic like me.

'Is it as simple as the toss of a coin?' I asked.

'No,' my father said with a smile. But to a rational Harvard graduate, who needed proof of God's existence, it might help to regain my faith.

By meditating on the mantra, he said, I would experience God and get the proof. Then, I'd no longer need to have faith. I could not dispute my father's logic.

The next day, I obtained the mantra from the guru. Over, the following three days, I woke up early, had a bath, sat cross-legged on the floor and meditated. It was not easy. My body was heavy. I'd been in the West too long, sitting on chairs. Seeing me struggle, my father came and sat beside me; his body was light, in a state of ease, offering no resistance. He asked me to think lightly, to extend myself from my body's centre. I tried to still my mind but could not. The movie kept running in my head; the more I tried to empty my mind, the more thoughts, feelings and memories sprang up. I was frustrated.

'Thoughts! Thoughts! They are the problem,' my father said.

They were not real, just projections of my ego, like an image in a mirror, he explained. Once I realized this, I would stop taking the voices in my head seriously. Meditation would make me see their illusory nature. As I became liberated from my crippling ego, the inner chatter would also subside. My father was teaching me the fine art of self-forgetting. The important thing, he felt, was that I had got initiated; I had crossed a rite of passage.

My mother was anxious about another rite. On the way home, she kept on talking about how I should 'settle down' with a nice Punjabi girl. Did I have a girlfriend in Bombay? She knew the business with Alisha was over. I told her I that hadn't met the 'perfect soulmate' yet. She dismissed 'soulmate' as a silly illusion fostered by romantic novels and Hindi cinema. It did more harm than good, making everyone search for a flawless partner. She'd been reading how girls in the West stayed single for too long, looking for the perfect partner. What worried my mother was that I was going to America, where an American girl might ensnare me, and I'd be lost to her forever.

She asked if I would be willing to meet some girls in Chandigarh. There was so little time, I felt. I was leaving in a few days. Within hours of reaching home, news of an eligible bachelor in the marriage market had spread. Offers began to arrive. My mother got busy filtering them, making a shortlist. Some matchmakers felt that 'going to foreign' was a competitive advantage; others thought the opposite. In the end, my mother's efforts came to naught. I did meet a few girls, but there wasn't time to get to know them properly.

I left home with mixed feelings. I had made my father happy by getting initiated. My mother was, however, disappointed at failing to get me engaged. She would worry. But these thoughts were soon left behind as my flight took off from the Palam airport. I felt a sudden sensation of freedom, like gambolling Hanuman, leaping from continent to continent to another destination of moksha. I flew by Air France because I wanted to see Les Deux Magots, the famous café in Saint-Germain-des-Prés in Paris. It had been the preferred hangout of Jean-Paul Sartre, Albert Camus and Simone de Beauvoir. They drank here, argued here, thought here and wrote their books here. I wanted a taste of the heady early days of Existentialism! On the way to the café, however, I found myself sitting next to an innocent American tourist on the bus. She could not adjust to children on the street speaking French. They were either bragging or being difficult, she felt. Since I'd taken French in college, I too tried to flaunt my French. It didn't go well with her, and I stopped showing off.

A couple of days later I arrived at the JFK airport in New York, where a Sikh taxi driver pulled up in a beat-up yellow cab. He had recently arrived in America and was thrilled to be speaking to me in Punjabi. He didn't know the streets, and I had to guide him in midtown Manhattan. When we reached the hotel, he declared proudly in his best Punjabi–American accent, 'Have a nice day!' The next morning, I marched in a grey flannel suit to our company's headquarters at 122 East 42nd Street, opposite the Grand Central Station. I discovered that everyone was in a meeting—they were always in meetings. When not in meetings, they were writing memos to each other in a bizarre language. My boss wrote that I was not expected to attend a middle-management meeting because I was 'underinvested in experience and had a reputational deficit'. Translated into English, this meant that I was a young nobody who shouldn't be thrown to the lions.

Everyone referred to each other by their initials. My boss, BRC, was famous for turning innocent nouns into active, fighting verbs. In one of his memos, he told our advertising agency 'to language the global footprint of the Vicks brand'. After blinking a few times, I figured it out: he was asking the agency to communicate the international nature of our business. The sales manager spoke about 'swimming in channels other than pharmacies'. He wasn't referring to our aquatic skills but to making our products available in general stores. The division head gave us a pep talk in which he wanted us 'to be 1000 per cent committed to our mission'. One hundred per cent, I felt, would have been adequate. It was wacky, seeing perfectly sober adults duelling in a verbal fantasy land. Since I did not want to be left out, I also plunged in, impressing people with my own neologisms.

Every company has a dogsbody, and HMG was ours. A small, earnest man, he had been passed over many times, but the company kept him on because he was willing to chop the wood and fetch the water. He loved spinning yarns about his past glory. He took me under his wing and promised to make me a 'somebody'. My name had two initials, but this wouldn't do—not enough gravitas, he felt. So, he divided my name into three initials, proclaiming proudly: 'GCD.' He also encouraged me to give thirty-second elevator speeches to the top brass.

'What's that?' I asked.

'It's the time it takes for the elevator to go from the ground to the top floor, where the big guns sit.'

He gave me a new nickname, Gerry—short for my unpronounceable first name. 'If they can't say your name, how will they remember you?'

My first attempt at an elevator speech didn't go well. I stood dutifully on the ground floor at 8.45 a.m., when the bosses usually arrived on the club car of the 7.50 Express from Greenwich, Connecticut. He'd shown me their photos, and I spotted my first target: the worldwide head of sales. I got into the elevator behind him and completed my speech before we reached the top.

'This sounds amazing, Gerry, but it's a bit early in the day,' he said.

HMG deciphered his reply: 'You bored him, Gerry.'

I hated HMG's idea. He looked hurt but was not deterred. He pointed at the marketing head's secretary. 'Go schmooze her—ask her about her baby.' I did. She pulled out a dozen photos and proudly asked, 'Isn't he the best-looking kid in the world?' HMG said that the kid was probably frightful, screaming all the time. 'But guess what? She loves her baby. If she can, you can.' I wasn't persuaded.

The work at the headquarters was 80 per cent time-wasting. The remaining 20 per cent was brilliant. The company had divided the world into three divisions: US, Europe/Africa and Latin America/Far East. I was assigned to the third group to manage Vicks Cough Drops. My job was to ensure that local subsidiaries didn't make stupid mistakes. Since my job didn't stretch me, I had to find something else to do. While reading consumer reports I discovered that there was an unmet need for other therapeutic flavours of throat drops. By now I had made friends with a young colleague in R&D and another in the advertising agency. We decided to work clandestinely on this project—we called it Project X and swore each other to secrecy until we'd confirmed its viability in consumers tests. The R&D guy developed initial prototypes of therapeutic flavours. The ad agency guy came up with potential ways to express consumer benefits. I wrote up a proposal for management approval, suggesting we test the products and concepts with consumers.

The problem was BRC, my boss. He sat on my proposal for months. People at my paygrade didn't go around creating new products. The project languished; I lost heart. I'd almost given up hope until one day it blew up in BRC's face. At the company's annual strategy meeting, the R&D head casually mentioned to the division boss about new, 'promising flavours' they were developing for throat drops—a 'honey lemon' and a high menthol 'ice-cool mint' that helped open the clogged nose while soothing the throat. The big boss was curious to see the management proposal. He turned to BRC, who slipped out quietly and found my proposal collecting dust. Hastily, he typed the front page, replacing my name with his, and handed it to the big boss. Unfortunately for him, the R&D head had already spilled the beans, telling everyone how I had conceived Project X, created a 'ginger group' of three, but there was no formal management proposal. The fraud was discovered. BRC confessed what he had done, but he was not sacked. The big boss liked the project and asked the Mexican subsidiary to test both flavours with consumers before placing them in the market. From a victim I had become a hero, although I got a rap on the knuckles for working clandestinely.

I preferred the people at our ad agency. Whereas our office had the human equivalent of worker ants trying to cling to their jobs, ad folks were mavericks, either failed writers or artists. They didn't care, coming in late, going out for long, boozy lunches and getting big raises when the gods smiled on their creative campaigns. I found I was caught up in New York's energy and electric lightness, believing that the time I spent sleeping was time wasted. It was neurosis, I now realize, which I mistook for energy. Deep inside I was lonely. After work, I'd wander the streets, a Brown man lost in the abstract wilderness of mirrors, mesmerized, and alienated by the riveting windows at Lord & Taylor and Saks Fifth Avenue.

For Americans, reality was the outside world, to be conquered and perfected. For me, an Indian, it wasn't quite real.

Luckily, I found a girlfriend. She, too, worked in advertising. A bright, attractive Jewish girl, she'd studied at Mt Holyoke College. She was crazy about the Beatles and told me that they were in India. She was an anti-war activist, and her political world of the late '60s was wrapped up in a rage. The war in Vietnam had sent her, like so many young people, into a state. Students were trying to seize control of the universities. TV cameras showed people wrecking cars, smashing windows. The police were coming down hard; hard-hat union guys were beating kids with baseball bats. She would drop in at night after a street rally to tell me about a new riot in a new city. The nation was on fire, she claimed. Till then, I had not been able to identify with American politics. I began to realize how profoundly shocking Vietnam was. She had opened the door to a new political awakening.

Both of us lived near Greenwich Village. To relax, we used to walk on weekend evenings down to Bleeker Street Cinema, an art house in the Village that showed mostly foreign movies—French, Italian, German. My girlfriend called it 'her way out of America'. For me, it was a return to an earlier passion from my Harvard days. It felt like visiting old friends—Bergman, Antonioni, Fellini, Truffaut, Satyajit Ray. Together, we watched Godard's savage satire *Weekend*; then, a political thriller by Costa-Gavras called *Z*, about a prosecutor who uncovers the rot behind the murder of a liberal Greek official; we liked Éric Rohmer's *My Night at Maud's*. I was shaken by Buñuel's *Belle de Jour*, featuring the beautiful Catherine Deneuve, who, in the film, has everything—a handsome, loving husband with a promising career, a beautiful home, a coveted place in high society. But her hidden fantasies take over, turning her into a prostitute in a high-class bordello. It all ends sadly.

One warm and easy Sunday, my girlfriend and I discovered we had differing thoughts about our relationship. Traipsing around the kitchen in my chikankari kurta, she asked if I loved her. I hadn't thought seriously about it. 'It depends on what you mean by love,' I replied. She was sad most of the morning. When we were making lunch, she brightened up and started laughing again. We kissed. After lunch, she asked about my thoughts on marriage.

'I suppose it's a good institution to bring up children,' I replied.

'But you don't sound enthusiastic. Then why get married?'

'You're the one keen on it.'

A few days later, she asked, 'What if another girl asked you to marry her? Would you?'

'I would if I really liked her.'

'The same way as you like me?'

'Yes, I suppose so.'

'You'd say "yes" to her as well?' she asked.

'I guess so.'

She felt we needed time away from each other. But it was the end. She walked out, and we never met again. I felt sad. We had been such good friends and lovers. Our last conversation left me wondering about the meaning of friendship, love and marriage. Loving is easier between men and women. Friendship is easier with the same sex. Honest friendship is a gift, a piece of good fortune. Even in marriage, it is a better guide than love. Liking and loving come naturally to human beings, but marriage is a matter of choice. Since I don't make friends easily, I was miserable when I lost her.

I finished writing my second play, *Mira*, in the spring of 1969. It is based on the life of Mirabai, a sixteenth-century Rajput princess–poet who became a saint. Since saints are not particularly interesting on the stage— only human beings are—I had to humanize her. I had to figure out how a human being becomes a saint. I struggled with the problem for months. In the end, I managed to write the play. Then began the labour of getting it on the stage. Trudging from agent to agent, theatre to theatre for months, I felt defeated. No one wanted it. Feeling low, I arrived one evening at the doors of La MaMa, an experimental theatre in the East Village. Ellen Stewart, the exuberant African American founder, took me into her office, where she was stitching a skirt. She told me to leave my script on her desk and go see Sam Shepard's play inside. When I returned after an hour and a half, she was reading my play.

'It beeps to me, honey!' she said.

Two weeks later, I called her. 'We're gonna do it, baby!' she told me. I was thrilled. 'But it'll only work as total theatre,' she said. Total theatre? Ellen wanted to create a rock musical based on Mirabai's songs. I'd have to do rewrites, working with a director. It was all too exciting, but I was also scared. I was not a theatre professional; plus, I had a full-time job.

She reassured me that La MaMa's directors worked at nights and slept during the day. She wanted Tom O'Horgan to direct it (he had done *Hair* the previous year). But he was not available. She then chose Martin Brenzell, who introduced me to the magic of how theatre could be created minimally, mostly out of body movements.

Since naturalistic dialogue was out of the question, I began to rewrite the play at nights with ritualistic, aphoristic dialogue. Brenzell found Equity actors with good voices, trained under Martha Graham. Setting Mira's bhajans to American rock music was a brilliant idea, and Mirabai herself would have approved of it. But Brenzell had other ideas, something ethereal, from another world. He began rehearsals, which lasted from midnight to 5 a.m. We met at three in the afternoon for breakfast (yes, breakfast!) in the East Village, where I handed over my rewrites. I did go at midnight to watch a few rehearsals, and it seemed like a different play each time. The actors complained that they were rehearsing a new play every night, right till opening night.

In the end, it all worked out. Clive Barnes, the *New York Times* critic, came. I stayed up all night waiting for his review, rushing out at 4.30 a.m. to a deli, where the paper's first copies were delivered. He wrote that Mira was 'remarkable in the way it combines Indian legend with the sophistication of Western total theatre . . . [with] all the grace of a lovely voice speaking of eternals in a language just delicately opaque and something of the quality of a dream ritual . . . Mira, you feel, is a modern woman being broken on the wheels of convention . . .' I was in heaven! Over the years, there would be many productions of *Mira*, including Alyque Padamsee's visual enactment in Bombay, using backward- and forward-projected slides. There was even a production in Spanish in Mexico, with Enrique Hett's inspired translation; and one by M.K. Raina, with Jawahar Wattle's music, which brought back some of the energy of the original. None, however, equalled the magic of La MaMa's *Mira*.

Around this time, my education in liking, loving and marriage took a great leap forward. I met Bunu. She had come to see *Mira* with her friends. After the show, my gaze fell on Bunu—not on her friends; only on her. And it stayed there, captivated. She had a thin, oval face and shining brown eyes. What was in those eyes that drew me to her? I kept hoping she'd look my way, but she was busy chatting and laughing. I then spotted a friend, Jasbir, in the group and rushed to meet her. She introduced me to Bunu and the others. A couple of actors from the play came by, showing off, dancing in our midst. 'Actors are always on stage,' said someone. Jasbir invited us all to dinner on Friday. My head was spinning when I got home. I tried to remember Bunu's shining brown eyes, her long dark hair spilling over her face. The more I thought of her, the more unattainable she seemed.

On Friday, I arrived at Jasbir's carrying colourful gerberas. But there was no party. Just as I was turning around to leave, feeling dejected, they burst in, chatting and giggling. All four girls worked at the United Nations and had been playing duplicate bridge. Bunu looked radiant in a deep-green sweater and matching pants. Jasbir apologized—she'd tried to reach me to say that the dinner was cancelled, but no one had answered. While she got busy serving drinks, the others plied me with questions. How did it feel to have a play performed in New York? Another had read the review in the *New York Times* and felt proud that an Indian play was successful in New York. A third was interested in the idea of 'total theatre'. My natural tendency is to show off, but I resisted the temptation. I wanted to make a good impression.

I was asking Bunu about her job at the UN when Jasbir interrupted us. What to do about dinner? While she flitted nervously, fretting about the food, Bunu quietly went to the kitchen, found eggs in the fridge, peeled some potatoes and onions, and whipped up a Spanish omelette. It was delicious, and everyone enjoyed the improvised dinner. It was obvious to all that I was attracted to Bunu. One of the girls even teased Bunu, reciting the old saying about 'the way to a man's heart . . .' Everyone was in a good mood and the conversation flowed easily. Time passed quickly. It was almost midnight when Bunu got up, announcing that she had to rise early the next day. Since she lived only a few blocks away, I offered to escort her.

Downstairs, a mist was forming, and it soon enveloped us. We passed the streetlights, and at the stop sign I took her hand as we crossed the street, and she pressed it gently. I felt I was falling. Falling through time and space in thrilling lightness. She sighed—a faint, soft release of the breath. She did not remove her hand. Drops of rain began to fall. Soon, the rain grew heavy, and we began to run. We were drenched when we got to her building.

I was in love! I desperately hoped she felt the same. I had met many girls, gone out with some, had a longish relationship with a few. But in the spring of my twenty-sixth year I had finally fallen in love. How did I know that she was the one? I did not. My practical mother had warned me that the 'perfect soulmate' was an illusion. It may exist in fairy tales or in poetry books. But in real life, it was about making a commitment and hoping you were right. She didn't realize that falling in love was not about conscious choice; not an act of will with someone 'suitable'. Bunu and I had hardly spoken. I'd fallen in love quietly—not with her words or her omelette-making, but with something in her eyes.

Bunu had awakened me to life. I had become a creature of habit, going to work each morning, returning home in the evenings and writing on the weekends. It was a life of settled routine and deadened sensibilities. She shook me out of my apathy. We began to see each other regularly, and soon we were inseparable. In her presence, I felt weightless, the lightness of my childhood. Love makes you recover the present, bringing you alive to the present moment with your whole being. I had found in love a new state of awareness.

* * *

I finally got to meet Clive Barnes. I'd expected the 'most powerful man on Broadway' to be overbearing. Instead, I found a small, dishevelled, pudgy, self-effacing Englishman. As we were exchanging pleasantries in his office, Russell Baker, the columnist, dropped in. Blowing smoke from his Kent cigarette, he began to test an idea for a column. He asked me if I was serious or solemn. I was confused. Solemn people, he said, took themselves seriously, while serious people took their work seriously. Being solemn was easy; being serious was difficult. Adults were solemn, children were serious. Washington was solemn, New York was serious. TV anchors were solemn, Shakespeare was serious. Using 'one' as a pronoun was solemn. What did we think of his idea for a column on solemn vs serious? Barnes loved it. I thought of Kamble—he was serious, not solemn. BRC was solemn.

Back at the office, it was getting pretty tense. BRC was drumming support to get me out. When he saw Barnes's review of *Mira*, he saw his chance for revenge. He circulated the review widely with a comment: 'Is this guy serious?' Then, he began a whispering campaign. How could a serious person do business in the day and write at night? He called me in, told me I'd have to choose. I couldn't sleep at night. What if I was fired, what would I do? Become a playwright? *Mira* hadn't made any money, although it had got good reviews. Ellen Stewart called it a 'critical success', but she advised me not to quit my job. I trudged to work each morning thinking it might be my last. Eventually, the top man put an end to my misery.

'Why should I care what this guy does on weekends? Hasn't he given us Project X?' he told the personnel head, who had brought him BRC's proposal to fire me. Meanwhile, both therapeutic flavours of throat drops had scored well in consumer testing. The Mexicans were excited and wanted to 'borrow' me for a year to conduct an extensive test market in two cities. Headquarters agreed. I was transferred to Mexico. Instead of firing me, the company fired BRC.

'You got justice, Gerry!' HMG smiled.

More than justice, I was saved the foolishness of becoming a playwright. After La MaMa, I understood my limitations. To write for the theatre, you had to know the theatre—ideally, as an actor or a director. Performance is the thing. One false note on the stage and you are finished. Then there are set designers, electricians and musicians—any of them can mess up the play. Maybe I should try my hand at a novel, I thought. At least, I didn't have to know about printing, publishing or distributing books. Plus, I could write a story about something that happened long ago, and the narrator's reassuring voice would be there to carry the reader. Unlike the stage, where it is all about the here and now.

I was now relaxed, carefree and in love. Should I get married before the illusion disappeared? There was also the Mexico transfer hanging—I didn't want it to separate us. I sounded Bunu out on the marriage thing, and she got a look of distress. I thought I'd made a mistake. 'You'd better check with your parents,' she said. I had to tell them she was a divorcee with a son, a Nepali, not Punjabi. Bunu had taken the courageous step at nineteen to do the unthinkable in 1960s Nepal: she had filed for divorce when it was a matter of great shame. They had taken her son and given him to her husband as per the law.

'Why should anyone want to marry me?' she asked with a sigh.

I was floored by her blinding honesty. I looked at her magical eyes. She was utterly beautiful, and I knew that I wanted to marry her. I sat down to write a letter to my mother. 'This is not what you expected to hear, mother, but I'm thinking of getting married.' And then, my self-assurance left me. I couldn't go any further. After a few days of dawdling, I put down the basic facts and mailed the blue 10-cent aerogram. The reply came promptly.

My mother wrote calmly to tell me that she had harboured a single, unfulfilled wish in her life. It was for a grand alliance for her son. Instead, I had presented her with a dowry-less divorcee with a child. It was either a deliberate act of unkindness or rebellion. She could not understand why her son would give her so much pain. By the third paragraph, she softened a bit. Marriage was serious business, she wrote. It was a matter of judgement. Emotions and upheavals of a love marriage were not a part of our tradition. One married to have children, as simple as that. This was why it mattered which family one married into. At the end of the letter, she presented me with a roll call of appropriate Punjabi families with eligible daughters.

I was hoping for encouragement from HMG, but I got a cynical indictment of marriage instead. He looked at me gravely. 'I'll be honest,' he said. 'If you want to stay in love, do not marry.' Love and marriage were two separate books. There was uncertainty in love; there was deadly routine in marriage.

'Surely it isn't either/or?'

He had learnt two lessons from marrying his wife. One, get married if you want someone to annoy you for the rest of your life. Two, confess when you are wrong; remain quiet if you are right. I asked him if he had considered divorce? He had not. But he'd thought of murder. The biggest risk in marrying was to lose your freedom. Marriage was a cage: the birds inside wanting to get out; the birds outside wanting to get in. For someone dedicated to moksha, it was a devastating verdict.

HMG's cynical observations were bested at the Bleecker Street cinema a few evenings later. I wanted Bunu to see Visconti's rendering of one of my favourite novels, *The Leopard*. The wise, aristocratic hero watches his handsome nephew dance with his fiancée at the grand ball. They make a charming, innocent couple, he thinks. But he knows that they will not find happiness. Why? Because 'marriage is a year of fire and thirty years of ashes'. A devastating Sicilian maxim!

My father's letter, a few days later, explored a different angle. He felt that friendship was a more reliable basis for marriage. 'Yes, it is unnatural for two human beings to be together all the time. So, you must ask yourself: Would I be able to talk to this person right into old age?' Bunu and I took his advice and tried an experiment. We spent a weekend in the confines of my apartment like two prisoners—going out was not allowed. The consequences were unexpected. Bunu proudly cooked three Indo–Nepali meals during the forty-eight hours. While the food was delicious, its powerful aroma drove the neighbours to distraction. Since it was cold outside, they couldn't open their windows. But we had passed the test. We had not come to blows. My concern for my independence was appeased. It was time to get married.

Another message came from my father a week later. The guru, he wrote, was due to arrive in New York in two weeks to begin his US tour. He suggested I get his counsel on the marriage issue. He had, in fact, got an appointment for Wednesday, 6.30 p.m., at the Roosevelt Hotel in midtown Manhattan. Bunu decided to tag along. When we arrived, I didn't know how to introduce her. 'Girlfriend' seemed frivolous; 'beloved' sounded overly intimate; 'lover' was too much in the face. Winging it, I presented her as my 'fiancée'. He was all smiles. How did I like my job? I told him about the play. He was intrigued by Bunu and wanted to know about Nepal. We made small talk, and before I knew it the interview was over.

Bunu gave me a look as we came out. 'Fiancée, hmm . . . An unusual way to propose?' I grew defensive. She smiled and said she'd be happy to be my wife. The decision was thus taken away from everyone. The guru had blessed the 'unsuitable match'; so, it was sacrosanct in my parents' eyes. My mother reconciled to it gradually—she no longer thought it was an act of unkindness, nor rebellion, merely the expression of a free spirit. She blamed my American education. We set the wedding date, and a week later, we picked up our suitcases and our hopes and boarded a flight for Delhi. The Mexican assignment was due to begin in six weeks. Bunu was happy to be going there—a year-long honeymoon, she called it. I crossed my fingers, hoping we would land not in HMG's cage but in the valley of moksha. And so, it came to pass: 'Love, a temporary insanity, curable by marriage,' as Ambrose Bierce put it.

11

Voices

'Your voice is the most potent magic in existence.'

—Michael Bassey Johnson

On the train to Chandigarh, Bunu was nervous, uneasy about the imminent meeting with my mother. I tried to calm her, telling her about my philosophy of laghima. Since we were starting out together, shouldn't we aspire to make our lives lighter, almost weightless, like a tiptoeing cat? If we stopped taking ourselves so seriously, maybe we'd see another side of life. 'So, let's glide through life, my darling, leaving no dents, losing all gravity, shedding all luggage. Let's make our life together into a work of art.'

Bunu did not want to be a tiptoeing cat, nor a work of art. Gazing at the rushing wheat fields, she said lightness was okay for me. I wasn't the one on trial. I wasn't a Nepali divorcee with a child. 'Will your mother approve of me?' was her constant lament. I advised her to be herself. She did not believe me, insisting on making heavy weather. Her wings were heavy.

As the train pulled into Chandigarh, I saw a slim, awkward figure on the platform. It was my father, raising his arm in a clumsy gesture of pleasure as we stepped off the train. We touched his feet. He embraced me with feeling. There was embarrassed shyness as we walked out of the station.

My mother was waiting on the back veranda of the house overlooking a small garden. She poured us buttermilk from a blue ceramic jug as we sat down. She was cordial, not warm; conversation moved slowly. Although we were under a fan, we were sweating. 'You'd better take a shower. It'll cool you down after the journey.'

An hour later, mother and son were seated in a cool nook in the living room. My father had gone to work. Meera had taken Bunu to see Chandigarh's Rose Garden. My mother was hurting, her dream of making a brilliant match gone. Pale and agitated, she was going over the key points that she'd mentioned in her letter. Romantic love was a myth, its emotions and upsets inappropriate to marriage. The main purpose of marriage was to have children—a duty to society and to the species. Like life itself, marriage had its limitations on how exciting it could be. I tried to cheer her up, reminding her that I'd always chosen my own path. I hadn't done too badly, had I? But I also stood my ground. Anything was preferable to marrying without love. She found it disagreeable to confront her son's passion. Behind the conflict between mother and son lay two moral systems: one inherited from the dharma texts of Hinduism, the other from European modernity. The clash wouldn't be resolved in a single conversation.

Staring out of the window, my mother could not see anything beyond her own unhappiness. There were tears in her eyes when she turned to me. 'I don't ask for happiness, just a little less pain.' I began to realize my mistake. Her 'pain' had less to do with me and far more to do with my sister. Meera was incurably sick. She had ceaseless headaches. They'd taken her to doctors, but no one could help her. They said it could be a mental illness, but she didn't believe them.

Meera had been the brightest, most gifted in our family. Ever since I can remember, every teacher in school and college had predicted a brilliant future for her. But suddenly, it all began to evaporate—a tragedy of budding promise, of unfulfilled potential. That's how life is: bewildering twists and turns. Happiness came in one size; unhappiness was in many colours, shapes and sizes. To hit the mark of kismet was difficult; to miss it was easy.

My mother felt life had cheated her. She'd wake up with a start, drenched in tears. Each time she opened her eyes, she'd shut them, wishing she didn't have to open them again. She blamed herself, the guilt too much to bear. After weeks of suffering, she felt weary and drained. My father tried to cheer her up. 'Think of happier things,' he told her. The boys had turned out well. My middle brother, Manni, had done engineering at the prestigious IIT Kharagpur, followed by a PhD in America and had a good job there in a big company. Tutu, my youngest brother, was settled nicely in the government's revenue service.

My father bore his own pain calmly. Every day was not supposed to be cool and pleasant, he'd say. It was nobody's karma to be unhappy—it was a decision, depending on the thoughts you chose to have. Pointing to a mynah flying above, he said, 'The bird doesn't think much about being happy or unhappy.' The secret was not to obsess about happiness. It could set one free. He was teaching us another way to live. To me, he had offered another route to moksha. I tried to imagine if I could be happy by giving up happiness. It seemed more like the ethic of saints, not of human beings.

Meera's own reaction to her debilitating headaches was to act, not complain. She was forever searching for answers, looking for new doctors, seeking new cures. She asked me if there were doctors in America who might help. I promptly wrote to our brother in America, asking him to find out.

In all the mayhem, Bunu's fears of being accepted by my mother waned quickly. She asked it was right to celebrate our wedding in the shadow of such sorrow. My father reassured her—the wedding, on the contrary, would divert everyone from thinking about Meera. It was thus agreed to go ahead. To make it easier for everyone, it was decided to hold the wedding in Delhi, not in Nepal or Chandigarh. With a lighter heart, Bunu flew off to Kathmandu. Two weeks later, her clan arrived exuberant and high-spirited, all set to celebrate the wedding of their daughter.

The wedding itself was a comedy of errors. The exchange of rings at the preliminary *svayamvara* was a high ritual of her Nepali warrior upper caste, unknown to us ignorant Punjabis. The ceremony preserved the illusion that the bride was choosing the bridegroom, not the other way around. Bunu had hinted that I had to ensure the ring was 'special'. I delegated the job to my mother, thinking it would divert her from obsessing over her daughter. Unfortunately, she didn't give it much thought. In the end, it turned out be a cheap, ordinary ring, not an expensive 'special ring' befitting a noble family. Bunu put up a brave appearance at the ceremony, although she lost face with her clan.

The second mishap was the wedding dinner. Deferring to my father's ascetic preferences, Bunu ensured that no alcohol or meat was served. Her own clan, used to eating wild boar at breakfast, were in shock. The solution was a diplomatic coup. A secret non-vegetarian feast, with alcohol, was served to the Nepali guests after the formal vegetarian, non-alcoholic dinner. No one was offended, everyone was satisfied.

The third misadventure was the threesome honeymoon. Bunu and I had planned to honeymoon in Europe, en route to my assignment in Mexico. My brother, Manni, meanwhile, had found a 'headache clinic' in Chicago. So Meera happened to tag along. Bunu was a good sport about it. Thus, it became a threesome honeymoon. We toured Austria in a VW Beetle, stayed at pensions, picnicked in forests and listened to Mozart concerts at the Salzburg Festival. It was all great fun, except both women were headstrong and opinionated. It meant we had lots of anxious moments, which at times needed copious diplomatic skill on my part. After a week, the cold war and the honeymoon came to an end. Manni and his wife, Bina, greeted us warmly in America. They were generous, happy to care for Meera while she took the cure. As soon as she settled in, we flew off to Mexico City.

Our stay in magical Mexico began in linguistic confusion. The Mexicans called us Hindus. 'No,' we corrected them, 'we are Indians.' They were puzzled. No, no, they insisted, their native people were Indians. It was all due to Columbus's fault, of course. When he discovered America he thought he'd found India. So the Mexicans had a point. 'Hindu' and 'Indian' were originally synonymous, words referring to people across the Indus River (Sindhu, in Sanskrit), used by people who lived on the other side. Persians aspirated Sindhu, which sounded like 'Hindu'. The Greeks breathed 'Hindu' softly, making it 'Indu'. Thus, 'India' was born. Centuries later, in the nineteenth century, when European missionaries and scholars needed a word to denote the religious beliefs of the people of India, they picked 'Hindu' off the shelf. What is the lesson here? A name is an arbitrary possession, but human beings fill it with such emotions. Nations are just as arbitrary, but citizens are willing to kill in the name of nationalism.

We soon found ourselves living in captivating Polanco, a leafy neighbourhood where the streets were named after writers. A good omen. Our charming, modest apartment was on the corner of Edgar Allen

Poe and Homer. The grocery store was located on Calle Tennyson; our bakery at Molière; the laundry on Calle Oscar Wilde; our flower shop on Charles Dickens; and our bookstore was on Alexander Dumas. Other neighbourhoods in the city, not to be left behind, had named their streets after artists, musicians, lakes, rivers and mountains from around the world. A person with real imagination must have thought this up! So our first impression of Mexico City was a feeling of awe at its inspiringly literary and cosmopolitan street names. Such a refreshing contrast to most cities in the world, groaning under the names of petty politicians!

As Bunu and I began Spanish lessons, our hearts were lighter. Although Meera's illness had been the provocation, it was my mother's reaction to it that had weighed me down. In distant Mexico, there were no burdens. We felt free, living simply and lightly, like my father's mynah soaring above. Bunu thought I must have got my aspiration for lightness from my father, who seemed to live life effortlessly. In my case, though, it sometimes turned to frivolity, which put her off. 'I don't know,' she complained. 'You always make light of everything. I never know when you're serious.'

I would wake up in the mornings, surprised to find Bunu on the pillow next to me. The sunlight filtered through the curtains, spreading layers of colour around us. The light would fall on her cheeks, and as she awakened her dark eyes would blink at regular intervals.

My office was not far, and I preferred to walk. There would be a spring in my step as I strode to work, without a care, my nostrils filling with the fresh morning air of a city perched 7000 feet above the sea. Mexico City was high in altitude but low in latitude. The sun thus shone brightly even in winter. It was cool in the mornings, but by mid-day it was warm enough to make you want to jump into the swimming pool; it then become cool again in the evenings. We felt we had four seasons each day of the year.

At the office, I plunged into Project X. Working closely with the sales force, I had chosen two Mexican towns to test the two flavours of Vicks throat drops. In Monterrey in the north, we began a test of the high menthol version, claiming, 'Put it in your mouth and your nose knows.' In Oaxaca in the south, we tested 'honey lemon', based on the therapeutic value of its two natural ingredients. I began to visit both cities regularly, where I would get a kick out of practising my broken Spanish with consumers and shopkeepers.

Around one o'clock, I would hurry home for lunch and siesta. Rounding the corner of Goldsmith and Homer, I would spot Bunu waiting at the window. My step quickened as I neared, and I would think, 'I'm a lucky man!' After lunch, Bunu would beckon me with her eyes to the bedroom, and in the time-honoured Latin tradition of the siesta, we would make love in the afternoon. I had someone to love, something to do, something to hope for. What more could a man want?

It was exciting living in a new country, making new friends. I even began work on a novel on weekends. Bunu toyed with the idea of going back to the university, but she felt intimidated by the place, the new language and new ways. She thought of working, but her visa would not permit it. We soon found Alicia to help part time around the house. She quickly became Bunu's friend, and thus her Spanish also took off.

Mexicans were polite but shy. I made friends with Antonio at the office—he was bright and cheerful but formal. A football fanatic, he would invite me sometimes to watch Club America play at the Azteca Stadium. He would never confide in me, however, fearing that by opening up he would be scorned. Irony was his way of dealing with life's battles. As I got to know more Mexicans, I found a strange loneliness in the Mexican soul.

Each morning before leaving for work, I found Alicia sweeping the pavement with a twig broom, her dark hair drooping. Occasionally, she would give me a quick, furtive glance under her brows, her eyes veiled by their own blackness, her dark hair gleaming blue in the Mexican sun. She had rich, dark skin, the richness hiding her lonely life. Later in the morning, she'd accompany Bunu to the wet market on Horace. On the way, Bunu got the latest news about Alicia's macho man—one day, he had stolen her money; he beat her up another day; and he mistreated Lupita, her daughter, on a third. He was her third husband—the others had been no better, leaving her as suddenly as they had arrived.

'Mexican men don't stay long with a woman,' Alicia said.

In the market, they were preparing for the Day of the Dead. Alicia peered at a corner stand, eyeing a pink candy skull in sugar sitting on a white plate. She bought it to take to little Carmelita's grave. With tears in her eyes, she told Bunu how her seven-year-old daughter had been hit by a bus. She wasn't hurt badly and seemed to be fine, but gradually she grew thin and sad, and just died. Each year, Alicia prepared a special meal and took it to the cemetery at 3 p.m., when Carmelita was expected.

Countries have their own smells. India's countryside smells of the dust raised by cattle returning home at dusk, mixed with burning cow dung; it's called *godhulisnanasamayam*. Mexico smells of perspiration mixed with sunburnt earth and urine. Alicia introduced us to more Mexican smells when we visited her in the city's outskirts. Teresa, her sister, was also there, along with Pepe, Teresa's husband. Alicia's own husband was absconding. Pepe was a Huichol from an Indian tribe in Central Mexico. He worshipped peyote, the spineless cactus, with hallucinatory properties, found in the north. Teresa offered us peyote instead of tea, saying that it would expand our consciousness. But before I could reply Bunu declined politely for both of us.

Pepe did not say a single word during the two hours of our visit. I felt uneasy at his silence, but he seemed relaxed. Alicia explained that Huichols do not make small talk, speaking only when necessary. In this way, they conserved their energy. Each year Pepe walked 150 kilometres from his home in Nayarit to celebrate the peyote festival at San Luis Potosi. There he sang, wept, contacted his ancestors and got stoned on peyote. Centuries ago, Catholic missionaries had come and stolen his gods, leaving Pepe and his people bereft and half dead.

I was fascinated and confused by Mexico. Disturbed by Antonio's impenetrable formality, Alicia's wandering husbands and Pepe's unsettling solitude, I was full of questions. A chance meeting with Octavio Paz, the distinguished poet and diplomat, began to clear the fog. He gave a talk at the Indian embassy on the Mexican character. Ninety per cent of Mexicans, he said, were mixed, *mestizo*, and every answer went back to Cortez's bloody conquest followed by centuries of humiliating Spanish colonialism. Human beings are lonely, but Mexicans are the loneliest, wearing a mask of self-denial, rejecting both their silent Indian and honour-obsessed Spanish pasts. They had not forgiven their Indian mother, La Malinche, for sleeping with Cortez; nor had they absolved the Spanish conqueror for abandoning her. Born from this illegitimate union, the Mexican male was still seeking his father. To forget he's a bastard, he lives from fiesta to fiesta, behind a mask that conceals a profound solitude.

All this left me feeling very sad. I wrote a long letter to Paz comparing our two countries, both victims of colonialism. We were luckier, I felt, because the British were mostly interested in our money. They did not steal our gods—only 2 per cent of Indians became Christian.

Finding someone from India lost in Mexico, Octavio Paz took pity on me. He invited us to tea in his elegant apartment in the stylish Zona Rosa. He'd been Mexico's ambassador to India in the 1960s. He told me to read Juan Rulfo's *Pedro Paramo*. I picked it up the next day from our bookstore on Calle Dumas and plunged promptly into the world of magic realism. It is about a son searching for his hateful, dead father in an enchanted village among dead madmen.

In Paz's apartment, we met other Mexican intellectuals, including Héctor Azar, the powerful head of the Institute of Fine Arts. Paz told him about my play *Mira*. He had read it and liked it. Fascinated by the idea of Indian sainthood, Azar wanted to publish it in Spanish. My excellent Spanish teacher, Enrique Het, translated it for him, and he brought it out in a nice, slick paperback with photographs.

Before we realized, our stay in Mexico was coming to an end. Project X had delivered mixed results, failing in Monterrey but performing strongly in Oaxaca. The test markets gave the company, however, many learnings, and it decided to launch the products nationwide in the winter. My work was done. They threw a going-away party for us at the office, where they announced my transfer and promotion to marketing manager in Bombay. We also decided to host a dinner for some Mexican intellectuals, who had been kind to us during the past year. Bunu slaved all day over an Indo–Nepali feast, assisted ably by Alicia. I picked up drinks from Bodegas Alianza at the corner of Victor Hugo and Shakespeare. We were ready by eight o'clock. But no one came. We waited till nine thirty, and then I started phoning. Each one had a meek excuse—someone had a cold; a stomach ache in another case; still another had a last-minute pick-up at the airport.

We were devastated, confused and maddened by what had happened. When Bunu recounted the disaster to an American colleague's wife, she said it had happened to her as well. I was angry and continued to feel depressed. But something very strange happened a few days later, which took our minds off the disaster. Bunu and I were returning home after our favourite walk in Gandhi Park nearby, behind the Chapultepec Zoo. For some reason, we had got separated—she wanted to pick up bread, I think, from a new bakery that had just opened; I decided to wait on a bench nearby on Calle Lord Byron.

I was alone, gazing at the cloudless sky. A car swept past, and then a man appeared clutching a bag of groceries. Mexico was getting me down— its impenetrable men, its sorrowful women and its cruel Aztec gods. Then, nobody showing up for dinner—who'd do such a thing! I began to grow depressed again. It was unexpectedly quiet among the surrounding jacaranda trees. After a pause, another uncomfortable question sprang in my head. What was I doing with my life anyway, so far away from home? Well, I was selling cough drops to the Mexicans. The absurdity of my answer left me reeling, and I grew infinitely sad.

A few minutes later, without warning, I was talking to myself. Not just an odd obscenity or remark, but a long, loud conversation with myself. Luckily, no one heard. It was quiet outside, a holiday afternoon, people on siesta. But who was I talking to? I looked around; there was no one. The voices must be inside me. I turned my attention inwards but didn't find anything. There were only thoughts in my head. But I began to pay close attention to them. A fresh thought arose: it was Bunu at the bakery, explaining in broken Spanish that she wanted sourdough bread. This thought vanished soon, replaced by a sound: it was a bird chirping. This sound was definitely *not* inside me. I looked around, relieved when I spotted an Inca dove cooing on the purple jacaranda on my left. This sound, too, disappeared, replaced in my mind by the sudden memory of the peas pulao that we'd had last night—I wouldn't mind having leftovers today, I thought. I kept observing this flow, rising quietly, then falling, a continuous movie in my head.

My mind returned to the insistent question: What am I doing in Mexico? Big things were happening back home, and I should be there. Indira Gandhi was breaking Pakistan into two, creating Bangladesh. Loathsome Nixon, upset because Pakistan was his ally, had sent the Sixth Fleet to intimidate India, while hinting to China to invade India from the north. When a reporter asked Nixon how he could support murderous Pakistani generals who had killed 3,00,000 of their own citizens and forced 10 million refugees to flee to India, Nixon replied impatiently, 'They're just a bunch of Brown goddamn Muslims!'

I looked at myself, sitting on a bench in Mexico. And here I was, peddling cases of Vicks cough drops in faraway Mexico. Time to go home. Just then, an elegantly dressed elderly lady went past with an annoying black Chihuahua. She must have heard the voices too, because she turned around. They were loud. She came up to me, gently asking if I was feeling okay. I was puzzled at her concern for me. Just as she was preparing to offer some advice, Bunu arrived. I introduced them. The Good Samaritan was apologetic. 'I'm sorry. Your husband was talking to himself, and I thought maybe a hot cup of tea might help . . .' There was also a 'nice clinic' up the street; she'd be happy to take us there. They had good doctors, even a psychiatrist. Bunu was bewildered. Jolted back to reality, I recovered my composure and put on my best laghima mask to conceal my nervousness.

I suggested other possibilities to the old lady. Yes, I did sometimes talk to myself; I found it better than listening to myself. But I generally reserved these moments of self-speak to when I was writing, especially dialogue. The woman was puzzled, not knowing what to say. Bunu was still in shock. Her instinct would have been to apologize on my behalf, but she didn't know what was going on. The Chihuahua came to our rescue. It began to pull and yelp, becoming a total nuisance. Everyone got distracted, the magical voices were forgotten. I rose and thanked the kind lady. She left us quietly, leaving us her card and a blank smile.

Bunu joined me on the bench after the lady left. We were silent. She was waiting for an explanation. It isn't easy to talk about the futility of life. She suggested we head back home. As we were walking, I too began to worry about the voices. Was I really losing it? Would I have to go to a doctor? I was scared. But my overactive imagination rescued me, diverting me from my fears. I began to imagine that I was primitive man, blurting incoherent sounds because I had not yet discovered language. As those sounds evolved into words, I began talking in sentences. But since no one was around, I began to hear myself talking to myself.

By now we had reached home. Bunu went to make tea. She could tell I was still in no mood to talk. By the evening, she could not hold any longer. 'What's wrong?' she asked insistently. Nothing, I lied. The history of consciousness begins with a lie. But I'm no good at keeping secrets, and it came out gradually. She was worried, but she made light of it, asking jokingly if I'd taken Pepe's peyote. Talking to yourself is okay; it's the answering back that's the problem. She tried to console me—everyone talked to themselves from time to time. Why, she was often rehearsing past conversations, thinking about she'd said, what she hadn't and what she should've said. In the same manner, I was speaking to myself when I was writing on weekends—she could hear me clearly across the house. No big deal! Yes, I agreed, a writer was many persons disguised as one person.

The matter rested there. But she was obviously worried inside, seeking insistently for an explanation. She wondered over the next few days if it had something to do with Mexico's blood-curdling Aztec gods, its hallucinatory plants, and the dead returning to feast each year. Gradually, she seemed to settle on a more mundane explanation: I must still be upset about the no-show dinner. I listened to her quietly, touched by her genuine concern. But she had missed the point, I felt. Yes, the no-show might have been the immediate trigger for the voices, but the real cause was a nagging sense of the futility of my job, of my life. I didn't want to dwell on it. That would upset her even more.

Our plane took off a few days later from Benito Juárez International Airport. As the seatbelts came off, I began to calm down, my distress over the voices left behind. My anger had also subsided by now, dissolving into another uncomfortable emotion. It might have been my fault, I realized suddenly. No one on the guest list at our dinner could be called a 'friend'. They had been acquaintances, interesting intellectuals whom I had met during our Mexican sojourn. Finding them stimulating, I had filed their names in my address book. In some cases, we had also enjoyed their hospitality, and I had felt a desire to reciprocate.

When we had been making the guest list, Bunu had remarked, 'But where are your *friends*?' I had grown defensive. 'What about people at the office?' she had asked. None of them were friends, I had told her. 'What about Antonio?' she had asked.

'He won't fit in with this group,' I had replied. Besides, he had never invited me home.

She had wondered why all the people on the list had to be 'interesting'. Couldn't they be just nice, ordinary people? I had told her that I didn't find ordinary people interesting.

'Well, I'm ordinary, and I like ordinary people. So, where do I fit in?'

I did not have an answer. She told me I would never have real friends if I insisted on collecting only 'interesting people'. She was right, of course. I faced the depressing truth: I had almost no friends. Was I incapable of friendship, then?

I looked warily around the airplane cabin. Bunu was asleep, as were most of the passengers. The captain's voice came on, saying that we would be landing in Chicago in forty-five minutes.

After landing, we visited my brother's family and see how my sister was faring. Manni, smiling cheerfully, was waiting at Arrivals. On the way to his place, he told us that the news about Meera was mixed. Her headaches had reduced, but she now suffered from chronic fatigue. She was optimistic as ever, determined to make something of her life. She was thinking of applying to Princeton to continue her studies. There was melancholic tension, however, throughout our visit. The burden of looking after my sister had fallen on Bina, my sister-in-law, who was not emotionally strong. Our hearts went out to her.

There is no education like a tragedy: Meera's illness introduced our family to itself. You don't judge a family by how it celebrates good times but by how it copes in bad times. My mother would have exchanged her own health to give her daughter a chance. Manni was generous in providing my sister with all the conditions to turn her life around. Meera herself evinced huge courage; she did not give up even for a day. The more she focused on her illness, the unhappier she became, making those around her also miserable. My father had tried to teach us to live our lives without needing to be happy all the time. Not caring about how you feel sets you free, he used to say. As for me, I had found happiness in love.

12

The Two Birds

'Two birds nestle on a tree.
One eats the fruit of the tree,
the other looks on.'

—Mundaka Upanishad, 3.1

The goals we pursue are mostly veiled. What gives our daily moves meaning is not understood until many years go by, if ever. I was thirty now, responsible for all the marketing activities of the Indian company. Although I had the trimmings of success—more money, power and respect—I did not feel a sense of achievement. I wonder sometimes if my search for another sort of moksha was an attempt to be free of the things I did not like in order to be enslaved by the things that I did. Was I like the young man who craves fame not knowing what he is after? The voices that had shaken me in Mexico must have been related to this dilemma, but mercifully, they had subsided now, pushed perhaps into a dusty, unused drawer of my memory.

I was happy to be home, where momentous events were unfolding. The world's largest democracy had reposed its faith in a woman to steer the nation. The old guard of the Congress party had propped up Nehru's daughter, Indira Gandhi, after Shastri died. Thinking she would be pliable, they had called her *gungi gudiya*, a dumb doll. What they got instead was an 'iron lady', who understood power far better than they did. She had gained huge popularity after she split Pakistan into two.

Pakistan, of course, had it coming. Its problem began when Jinnah imposed Urdu, an alien language, on the proud Bengali people far away in the East. It led to a movement of secession. When Pakistani generals unleashed genocide in 1971 to stop East Pakistan from seceding, millions of refugees flooded into India. Indira Gandhi was forced to intervene, and in two weeks, India defeated Pakistan, and a new state of Bangladesh was born. A cautionary tale for arrogant leaders who impose linguistic whims on their people. Sri Lanka would make the same mistake, imposing Sinhala on the Tamils, and it would lose a generation in a civil war. India may have made mistakes, but imposing language was not one of them. Although Hindi nationalists had tried to impose Hindi on the rest of India in the '60s, they backed off quickly when the Tamils threatened to secede.

The city of Bombay was nervous when we arrived. It was troubled by Indira Gandhi's sharp turn to the left. Guided by a Marxist coterie, she had aligned with Soviet Russia and begun nationalizing banking, insurance, coal, steel and more. My boss was worried: What would be her next move? Talk about the nationalization of the trade in food grains was in the air. As were fears of more socialist controls on the private sector. I met Piloo Mody a week after I arrived. The 'Indira wave' had wiped out the Swatantra Party and the rest of the Opposition in the 1971 polls. Minoo Masani called her a 'commie dictator'. She claimed to be doing it all for the poor—*garibi hatao* (eradicate poverty) was her slogan. Ironically, she would end up doing very little for the poor.

Jawaharlal Nehru, her idealistic father, had wanted a caring, egalitarian society, but the bureaucracy had given him a command economy, a 'Licence Raj', which took away our economic freedom. It is difficult to blame Nehru—he had been a product of a socialist age. One must squarely blame Indira Gandhi, however, for not changing course when Japan, Korea and Taiwan had already shown the way. They had opened up, adopted export-oriented policies, while India persisted with a closed economy, wallowing in export pessimism. These nations would become 'Asian Tigers', while Indira's closed, command economy would suppress growth, keeping India poor. When individuals blunder, their families go down. When rulers fail, it is a national tragedy.

I was now a middle manager. One of life's truths is that almost everything seems to be a failure when you're in the middle. As companies grow big, they insert layers of middle managers between those at the top who run the business, and those at the bottom who do all the work. Middle managers get so caught up between managing up and down that they become bureaucrats, entangling everyone in paperwork, losing touch both with customers as well as their own products. As a result, bright and hungry youngsters are forced to deal with layers of bureaucracy before they can implement fresh, innovative ideas of their own.

Our company's model middle manager was the head of personnel, who was always dressed in a sharp suit, a white shirt and an elegant tie. He noticed one day that one of my product managers had shown up in tennis shoes. It was bad enough that I (and my team) had shed the necktie a few weeks ago. When the personnel head had complained, I had told him to lighten up—after all, ours was a hot, tropical country, and one had to be comfortable. He had conceded reluctantly on the tie issue, but tennis shoes . . . this was taking things too far.

The offending young man, I discovered, had blisters on his feet; leather shoes aggravated them. I was satisfied with the explanation, but the personnel manager was not. He began to keep a close watch on my department's attire. When the same offender showed up a few days later without socks, he hit the roof. His blood pressure rose, and he stormed into my office, declaring, 'There ought to be a law!' To calm him down, I gave him some background. The man without socks had executed a brilliant promotion the previous year, which had had a significant impact on the company's profits. As a result, everyone had received a bonus. The offending young man didn't have to come to work with sores on his feet, I argued, but he had put the company's work ahead of his comfort. The personnel middle manager went away fuming, shaking his head. The blisters went away soon, and so did the tennis shoes.

Despite my apparent success, I felt imprisoned by my impressive title, my company flat and the company car. I was spending hours coordinating activities, shuffling papers and writing long reports that no one read. One morning, I was giving an important presentation to some big shots from the headquarters. I'd done my homework, got all the facts and figures; my shoes were shiny, my delivery perfect. Only one thing was wrong: no one was listening. They were all preoccupied with a recent change of guard at the headquarters. They were worrying about their careers, about where they would fit in.

The futile labours of the middle manager came to a head the following year. There was a flu epidemic in India. As a result, sales of the entire line of Vicks cough and cold products shot through the roof. The factory worked overtime to meet the demand. At the end of the season, the company declared record profits. Everyone was happy, except the legal department. The company secretary, with fear in his eyes, came to my room, accompanied by two lawyers with long faces. Our sales had exceeded the production capacity authorized in our official licence. We had broken the law, and it might mean a jail sentence. They wanted my help to draft a defence. From heroes we had become criminals, and a pall of gloom descended on the office.

Sure enough, we received a summons from Delhi. It was a preliminary hearing, but I had to be present. Two lawyers accompanied me to the joint secretary's office, where we were made to wait for hours. The officer was reading a newspaper as we entered. He gave a cold look that said he didn't want to be disturbed. I was afraid but tried not to show it. Eventually, he looked up.

'What?' he asked impatiently.

One of the lawyers handed him a copy of the summons. He glanced at it irritably. 'What?' he repeated. I explained nervously that the flu epidemic had resulted in extra demand for our products. We had merely done our duty in keeping the shelves stocked at pharmacies. Our products had come to the rescue of millions of mothers whose children had suffered from the flu.

He stopped me, irritation showing in his voice. 'But you have broken the law!' he thundered. I replied politely that something was wrong with the law that punished one for producing things that had benefitted millions of sick people. Anywhere else, one would be applauded for treating the sick, especially children. The joint secretary pushed his chair back noisily, signalling the end of the interview. We had broken the law, and the law would now take its course.

As I reached the door, I don't know what came over me. I turned around defiantly and asked him how our country would appear to the world if news got out that our government had punished the executive of a foreign company for helping to produce products that alleviated peoples' misery during an epidemic. Imagine such a story on page three of the *New York Times*.

'Are you threatening me?' he thundered.

'No, sir. I was merely appealing to your common sense as a fellow citizen. By punishing us, you'd be making our prime minister a laughing stock of the world outside.' He gave me a venomous look and gestured me to get out of his office.

The lawyers were trembling as we stepped out, convinced that our goose was cooked. I was calm, although I wanted to get as far away as possible from the stink of the Licence Raj. The joint secretary was ready to kill anything that breathed of spontaneity or human achievement, the opposite of my ideal of moksha. I'd rather battle a demon in hell than have a face-off with such a bureaucrat. It was my first experience of Indira Gandhi's bizarre regime, which gave you a licence to produce a specific quantity of a product, in a specific location, with specific technology and on a specific machine. Instead of looking after your customers' needs, you could spend a lifetime idling outside Delhi's government offices.

In the end, the lawyers' verdict on our meeting turned out to be wrong. The government never wrote back, dropping our case quietly. But not before giving me many sleepless nights.

The absurdities of India's command economy added to my growing unease with a middle manager's fussy life. Just as I concluded that I hated being a wage slave, I got a phone call. It was Matilal, a nostalgic voice from my Harvard days. He was giving a lecture at the Asiatic Society. 'Of course, I'll come,' I told him, adding that I would also take him out to dinner. He wanted to taste Gujarati food. I suggested Chetana, near Kala Ghoda, which offered the bonus of a bookshop filled with the books that were right up his alley—on the Vedas, Upanishads, Hindu and Buddhist philosophy. We agreed to meet at the Strand Book Stall, my favourite bookshop. I called Bunu, asking her if she'd like to join. Curious to meet someone from my Harvard days, she agreed readily.

As our car turned on to Marine Drive that evening, I thought of Kamble, who had been rising continuously in the company to positions of increasing responsibility. Some people love their jobs, and he was one of them. Why couldn't I be like him? We reached the busy roundabout at Horniman Circle. Lots of people, black-and-yellow Fiat taxis going past, people minding their own business, no one interested in my problem.

I was soon at the door of the bookshop, where I spotted Matilal at the counter. He looked the same as ever—tall, thin and dignified, not too different from when I'd known him in Ingalls's class at Harvard. I smiled at Shanbagh, the store owner whom I knew well. I looked around appreciatively at two levels of books piled to the ceiling. Matilal smiled on seeing me, and we walked briskly to the Asiatic. There, he spoke on *nyaya* and Buddhist logic, a dry and esoteric subject, but he made it interesting for the audience. He spoke rapidly in a soft voice with a charming Bengali accent, his curly hair flying under the fan. He had a quiet manner as he moved with ease between Eastern and Western philosophy.

Bunu was already at Chetana when we arrived. She'd chosen a table near the window. Matilal gave her a big Bengali smile. As we settled down, he turned to me and asked casually if I had found my calling. I confessed about my growing feelings of discontent. The phase had begun in Mexico. Bunu blurted out about the voices. Matilal exclaimed in Bengali, 'Ah! It's the two birds!' We were puzzled. He jumped up and ran to the bookstore section of the café and grabbed a copy of the Mundaka Upanishad. Opening it to the third chapter, he began to read aloud a verse in Sanskrit. I looked around nervously. We were noisy, but the diners didn't seem to be bothered—they were busy devouring Chetana's 'all-you-can-eat' thalis.

The verse was about two birds perched on a tree, one eating the fruit, the other looking on, watching. The voices in Mexico, he claimed, were of the two birds, both inside me. One was the 'I' who was acting, doing things. The other 'I' was looking on, judging what was happening. I could relate to that. A human being is not only conscious, Matilal said, but he's also conscious that he is conscious. The second bird was my reflexive consciousness—watching me, questioning what I was doing, judging me. So I had been talking to myself, that's all.

'All of us do it,' Matilal reassured me. 'Mostly we talk to ourselves quietly, but sometimes the voices burst out, especially when we're troubled.'

'Why, I do it all the time,' Bunu said and smiled.

Feeling much relieved and suddenly lighter, I kept repeating, 'The two birds, hmm!' Matilal had solved the mystery of the voices. I remembered now that my father had also told me about the same birds on the train to Beas. What I had experienced in Mexico, then, was an Upanishadic moment.

Matilal would go on to become the Spalding Professor of Eastern Religions and Ethics at the University of Oxford; the chair was previously occupied by Sarvepalli Radhakrishnan, the first President of India. Although the mystery of the voices was solved, the voices themselves did not go away. But I no longer viewed them as a threat. They were mere curiosities, like the ritual of an ancient religion. What brought them on was some mundane, often disagreeable, feature of my daily life, such as our 'Mancom' meetings.

The boss was away on an extended assignment at the headquarters, and his decision-making powers had devolved to the Management Committee of department heads (Mancom). These meetings were always at two thirty in the afternoon. They were usually tedious, with everyone wanting to blabber on for hours. It was bad timing because our business was in trouble, there was competition at our heels, and we were wasting time on inter-office issues. One of these meetings related to the appointment of regional manager for the northern region. I liked a candidate who was bright and hard-working, but he spoke English poorly. The committee rejected him.

The national sales manager and I put up a strong defence on his behalf, arguing that the job was in the field and mostly required interaction with traders in Hindi. Eventually, we brought the others around, but I didn't feel triumphant. I was sad. Trudging back to my room, I wondered what sort of country we lived in. The British had left twenty-five years ago, but the major decisions here were still deliberated over in English, when only 10 per cent of the people spoke the language. Had an ordinary person, a non-English speaker, walked into our Mancom meeting, he would have felt like an outsider—an outsider in his own country! I was unable to face the absurdity of this situation.

Bunu announced one morning that she was having a baby. It took a few seconds to register. I was happy but also wary about raising a child in a world that was growing ridiculous. My mother was, however, thrilled to get my letter. She promptly wrote back to say that it was her duty to help around the house, given Bunu's 'delicate condition'. So she was coming along with my father. Bunu groaned—she would now have to look after the baby and her mother-in-law. She went around muttering, 'The best mothers-in-law live far, far away.' But when my parents arrived, her attitude changed. She went out of her way to be nice and was always on her best behaviour. When I remarked about the astonishing harmony in the house, Bunu replied that only a mother-in-law and daughter-in-law could have an all-out war without anyone knowing it. When I insisted that all seemed nice and pleasant, she sighed and said, 'Men are so simple, bless them!'

As the day of our baby's birth neared, Bunu grew more nervous. She asked my father how he happened to be so calm and relaxed about his children. He smiled and began speaking in a light, easy manner. 'We are the children,' he said, 'not of our parents but of what we were in our past lives. Parents are only a medium through which life expresses itself.'

'What an odd idea!' my mother exclaimed.

Ignoring the interruption, he said that children came into the world carrying past karmas and future destinies. They are temporary guests in our home. They grow up one day and leave. We should love them, not think of them as our property and especially not try to impose our ambitions on them. A parent's attachment to his or her child was a handicap. It was bad manners to harp on your child's achievements. My mother gave him a look, as though he was a bit cracked.

A few weeks later, our child was born at Breach Candy Hospital. We were there in full force, waiting since early morning. By dinner time, my mother decided the baby was delayed and that we might as well go home for a quick meal. Well, of course, the baby decided to emerge right when we were on our second roti with saag-paneer. The baby had timed its entry perfectly, my mother said. Her daughter-in-law would tell the world that her mother-in-law had chosen dinner over her baby.

The baby was a boy, and we called him Kim Kanishka. 'Kim' is an interrogative in Sanskrit, a question mark, and we hoped the boy would grow up with a searching outlook on life—in the spirit of the Rig Veda's 'Nasadiya' verse on creation, which inquires into the origin of the universe and concludes sceptically that no one really knows the answer. When Kim grew up, he asked, 'Do you mean I'm a question mark?' His name was an unplanned tribute to Rudyard Kipling—Kim was also the eponymous hero of his famous novel. Kipling, with his colonial outlook, was out of favour at the time, and our anti-colonial friends thought us disloyal. But we weren't fazed, believing that art trumped politics. The second part of his name, Kanishka, commemorated the Buddhist emperor of the

Kushan dynasty that had ruled in the second century over north India and Central Asia.

Thus, Kim Kanishka entered the chaotic, colourful world of Bombay, a city teeming and stinking, wealthy and stylish, poised between the East, the West and Bollywood. He arrived just when builders of crass high-rise buildings were flattening genteel Parsi bungalows, the last vestiges of art deco were fading and Bombelli's was giving way to bhel puri parlours. Kim would go on to attend Cathedral School, much like the snotnose Saleem Sinai in *Midnight's Children*. But unlike Rushdie's hero, Kim hadn't been exchanged at birth at Breach Candy Hospital, nor did he possess the gift of telepathy. We hoped our boy would live a sensible, uneventful life, again unlike Saleem, who went on to become a metaphor for India's confused contemporary history.

Puru Pulakesin, our second son, would enter a year and a half later. His double-barrelled name also carried history. His ancient namesake, also known as the Indian king Porus, had fought and lost Punjab against Alexander the Great in 326 BCE but had won the Greek conqueror's grudging admiration for his courage. We hoped our Puru would inherit not so much the king's martial but his human qualities. Further back in time, there was another inspiring Puru in the Puranas, who had sacrificed his youth for his father Yayati's sake and had been rewarded with the throne. Our Puru had a lot to live up to.

My father's quiet words about not 'owning our children' must have made an impression. Bunu and I were surprisingly relaxed, easy-going parents. We neither fussed over our kids nor pushed them to perform. Our friends were surprised at, and mildly critical of, our laidback attitude. But we were following laghima's spirit in light parenting. We sent our kids to good schools, made sure they grew up healthy, but we did not stay up till midnight helping them prepare for their exams. Had we done so, they might have won more prizes; become millionaires. But they managed to turn out all right, growing up free in the spirit of moksha. Our style of parenting meant less worry, more peace in the house.

My mother wanted to meet our glamourous friends. Bunu suggested a party. Mother jumped at the idea, a chance to show off her grandson. It was also a celebration of a new production of *Mira*, which had just been successfully restaged by the director Alyque Padamsee a few weeks before my parents came. I sat down to make a list, filling it with 'famous people'—Mulk Raj Anand, Sham Lal, Gerson da Cunha and other eminences from the fields of theatre and politics.

'Where are the ordinary people?' lamented Bunu.

I had still not learnt my lesson from the no-show party in Mexico. She quickly added to the list her friends, our neighbours and people from the office. We had a typical boisterous Bombay party with lots of fun, laughter and noise. Its notable feature was Pali, our young Labrador, who chewed up a new pair of Gucci shoes that belonged to Dolly Thakore, the star of the play. They had been a present from the director, who was courting her at the time. Pali had shown good taste, but Padamsee was not amused and didn't speak to me for months.

My boss had still not returned, and the business was in trouble. Mancom meetings remained a nuisance, eating up valuable time. Apart from competitive pressures, the market for cold-related products was changing—adults were moving away from rubs to more convenient tablets for cold. I arrived early one morning at the office to put the finishing touches on a strong competitive response. Our R&D had developed a superior cold tablet, Vicks Action 500, which had just been approved by the government. We were launching it that day, backed by a massive advertising campaign. Sales managers had arrived from across the country for a briefing. I was feeling nervous; a lot was at stake.

I looked at my desk, and my gaze fell on a memo. They had called a Mancom meeting to discuss a 'serious issue'. I groaned, praying that it would be a short one. At 2.30 p.m., the personnel manager, impeccably dressed, rose to his feet and turned on the slide projector. The serious issue was a proposal for a private lunchroom for senior executives, where we would be served by uniformed waiters wearing white gloves. He had come from an old British, colonial-style company in Calcutta, where this had been the norm. There were smiles—everyone liked the idea. The sceptical finance manager wondered if the timing was right, given that company profits were under pressure. But the men around the table were happy. They had worked hard for this well-deserved perk.

I was irritated. 'For heaven's sake, liveried waiters in white gloves!' We had an important new product launch in a few hours. And what were we doing? Blabbing on about a relic of the Raj? Yes, the current lunch situation was chaotic, I admitted. Everyone getting *dabbas* from home; some eating at their desks, others in a dingy, nondescript hall. That wasn't nice. I suggested that we—officers and staff—eat together. 'Let's have a nice cafeteria, serving delicious, piping-hot food to everyone.'

My idea was not popular, but the Mancom had to agree with my logic. The faces around the table turned glum as the vision of white-gloved waiters began to fade. The personnel manager knew he had lost and withdrew the proposal in a huff. They gave me dirty looks as I rushed back to the product-launch meeting. My team had just completed the briefing. The sales group was filled with excitement, convinced that Vicks Action 500 would succeed.

Instead of going home that evening. I went to Haji Ali nearby. The waves were splashing against a rock. They always calmed me as I gazed at the Arabian Sea. I was troubled. Almost the entire Mancom had turned against me. It isn't a pleasant feeling, taking the moral high ground. But the executive lunchroom had been a preposterous idea in a new, democratic country. Privilege in any age is the enemy of the good. Yes, of course, I was privileged in a country of vast poverty. But honestly, it never sat comfortably with me. I always felt guilty at winning the birth lottery. Perhaps it was my American upbringing. But frankly, that afternoon, I had surprised even myself. The irony of suddenly becoming a champion of the proletariat did not escape me. It was an odd feeling, finding myself in the same camp as Marx.

The lunchroom saga did not end there. The personnel manager returned with a new strategy. At the next meeting, he sneaked in the executive lunchroom as a part of the general office renovation, including upgrading officers' toilets. Again, it didn't go well for the poor man. I was his bête noire yet again. I had always felt uncomfortable with 'executive toilets', and I recounted an adolescent experience to the Mancom. I'd been sent by my high school to Alabama in the south to compete in a table tennis tournament. Needing to pee before my match, I found two toilets, one marked 'Coloreds', the other 'Whites'. Since I was brown, I thought I must be coloured, and so I went in. But coming out, I felt strangely humiliated.

'Shouldn't we also think of integrating staff and officers' toilets?' I suggested. They agreed again, reluctantly. The privileged were clearly wounded. The haves could not admit they were the haves. Sensing defeat, the personnel manager sighed and withdrew the proposal.

Look for the ridiculous and you shall find it. Our business was suffering, but our management committee was engrossed in things like white-gloved waiters and perfumes in officers' toilets. I didn't feel triumphant so much as sad, growing more and more alienated at the job. The feeling of life's absurdity returned. I needed to breathe, and I went off to my usual spot at Haji Ali. The faithful rock was still there, ready to comfort me. It had been around for a long time, I thought, never judging, nor trying to make sense of life. I was seeking a cohesive self, but it kept slipping away. Each time I tried to seize it, it seemed to disappear through my fingers like the water of the Arabian Sea.

The next morning, I woke up with the alarm at 6.05 a.m. I tried to cover my face with a pillow but felt weak and couldn't move. The ringing of the alarm grew louder. Eventually, I managed to reach over and shut it off. I told myself I'd laze a bit, give myself a few more minutes before getting up. Suddenly, I had an odd sensation. I tried to move my arm, then my hand, but there was no feeling. I touched my legs, my arms. I was inert. My body did not seem to be mine. I was a stranger to myself. I remembered that I had fallen asleep last night, exhausted by the Mancom meeting and my visit to Haji Ali. So it must be me. I was aware of involuntary thoughts passing through my mind. I tried to pay close attention. A new thought arose spontaneously in which I was both subject and object. It must be the voices—so, they had returned.

Sure enough, I now knew them as the two birds. One was feeling self-satisfied, congratulatory, for having taken a principled stance at the Mancom. The second was cautioning me about taking the moral high ground, feeling superior. It's not nice to be smug and self-important. Just as the voices were getting interesting, an unrelated thought danced into my head. It was the first bird in a panic, telling me not to dawdle in bed. Get up, take a shower. I was late for work. The other bird piped in, telling me to relax. No need to rush and get worked up. Wasn't my job a bit of a joke, anyway? Besides, in the big picture, I was insignificant—one of 4 billion people on earth, only a speck in a universe of billions of galaxies. No one would miss me if I died. A few relatives and friends maybe, but they too would forget after some time. I felt depressed.

I must have dozed off. Soon, I heard a baby crying. Was it another thought? No, the noise was coming from the next room—Kim exercising his lungs. Bunu was trying to calm him. A few minutes later, I heard my mother's voice, offering to take the baby and give her daughter-in-law some rest. I now became aware of the sounds on the street. Children were racing their way to school. Then, the musical voice of the vegetable seller, announcing the day's bargains. The morning sun was peering into the room through the curtains. I got up reluctantly. The world outside, at least, was real. When you change the way you look at things, things seem to change.

I did not go to work that day. My father sensed something was wrong. In the middle of small talk at dinner, he asked me nonchalantly, 'So, have you found your calling?' It was the same question as Matilal's. I answered by turning the question around. Had he found his calling? He replied matter-of-factly that his real calling was 'searcher for God'. But yes, his mundane occupation was that of an engineer, and he seemed satisfied with the two-hatted arrangement.

'My father, the mystical engineer!' I exclaimed.

He smiled, embarrassed. I confessed that I had had no such luck. I was bogged down. My job was becoming more and more tedious. On some days, I felt like quitting. My mother was shocked. 'Be thankful, you have a job!' she said. Millions would give anything to be in my shoes.

Disaffection at work was common, according to my father. Earning a livelihood was dreary, monotonous work much of the time. But if one accepted that, life became easier. He'd observed many of his colleagues and friends. The majority were decent and conscientious, but their work didn't interest them. Some were lucky to have a sunny temperament, and they had made the most of it. Others had coped because they enjoyed the people they worked with. But he and I were lucky, he felt. Both of us had found a third way. He'd developed a passion for the spiritual life; I had found writing. Having two selves meant two ways of being, and this was almost better than having one. When you got tired of your working self, you could turn to your other self.

Preoccupied with her own thoughts, Bunu had not been listening. Discontent at work was her trigger, and she burst out with a full account of the voices. My mother grew alarmed, but my father had the same reassuring reaction as Matilal's. I'd stumbled on my consciousness, he said calmly. The voices were the two birds inside me. The first bird, eating the fruit, was the acting human self. It was doing what I did all day. The second bird was the witness; it was my awareness that stayed awake even while I slept at night. This was how I knew that I was the same person today as I had been yesterday.

At this point, my father's spiritual interpretation of the voices began to diverge from Matilal's philosophical one. The witness bird, he claimed, was my atman, 'pure spirit', the divine in me. By meditating on my consciousness, I'd be able to discover how to transcend my day-to-day existence. The analogy of the birds captured the wonderful capacity of human beings to be both participants and witnesses of their lives. By meditating on the divine inside me, I would be able to go beyond my slavish life. I'd be able to liberate myself from the demons of my 'I-ness' and the effects of karma. I would then shed my individuality and merge my consciousness with the Universal Consciousness and Absolute Being. This was his spiritual ideal of moksha, the ultimate freedom. It left me cold.

My father laughed nervously, and there was an awkward silence. He swung his arm lightly, suggesting we need not take him too seriously. I had listened to him intently, but I could not make his leap of faith. I was turned off by talk of the 'spirit' and the 'divine'. 'Universal Consciousness' and 'Absolute Being' were only words. They did not mean anything to me, because I could not accept anything that I could not perceive. I could not accept my father's idea that by discovering my consciousness, I was on my way to God. I was not a spiritually ambitious *mumukshu*, searcher for moksha, like my father. I felt more comfortable with Matilal's philosophical explanation about the reflexive nature of human consciousness. I was happy to believe that I'd merely been talking to myself—that was all that the voices were.

'Everyone has three lives: a public life, a private life and a secret life,' says Gabriel García Márquez, the Colombian writer. So far, I'd thought I had only two—a public life in business and a private life as a writer. But now I realized that I might have a third one. It was the secret life of an involuntary explorer of my consciousness. I, too, was a mumukshu, but of a different kind from my father. It was a secular, non-transcendental moksha that I was after. But it was not clear to me where this third life was heading, or if it was heading anywhere at all.

13

A Quixotic Age

'The only way to give finality to the world
is to give it consciousness. For where there is
no consciousness, there is no finality, no purpose,
no meaning to the universe.'

—Miguel de Unamuno

I came home early one summer afternoon in 1975, bursting with news. India was about to become a dictatorship. The Allahabad High Court had found Indira Gandhi guilty of corruption: she had misused the services of government officials during her personal election campaign. It seemed like an impropriety, somewhat like a traffic violation for speeding. After all, she had gone on to win the election by 1,00,000 votes. But the judge had taken a tough stand. Instead of resigning, she declared a 'state of emergency', suspending constitutional freedoms. Before dawn, the police woke up her political opponents and locked them up. In the next thirty-six hours, India did, indeed, change from a democracy to an autocracy. The number of Mrs Gandhi's political opponents in jail soon climbed to 1,00,000.

Since she distrusted everyone, power shifted to her son, Sanjay Gandhi, who let loose a reign of terror. One of his pet projects was population control. He hit upon the idea of sterilizing men—anyone with more than two children would be vasectomized mandatorily. With monthly quotas to fulfil, petty officials scrambled to catch any male in sight, young or old. A reporter in Bihar found only women in the bazaar. The men had all run away, hiding from officials, afraid they would end up on a dingy operating table, their genitals cut off. Around 6.2 million men were sterilized in the drive.

During this ghastly period, I was promoted to a bigger job in Mexico. Ironically, the more alienated I grew from business, the better I seemed to perform. I had mixed feelings about leaving India, however. I certainly wanted to run away from Mrs Gandhi's nightmare, but I didn't want to miss history in the making. The first thing dictators do is to establish censorship, finish off the press. So we didn't know what was happening in the country. The newspapers were full of blank spaces because the censor would have stopped political stories at the last minute. Or there would be a recipe for cucumber raita on the front page that a more creative censor had substituted for an inconvenient story. Mrs Gandhi claimed that she had saved India from anarchy, from Opposition leaders like Jayaprakash Narayan, who were all funded by a 'foreign hand'. Unafraid, my friend Piloo Mody walked into Parliament with a placard saying 'I'm a CIA Agent'. Mrs Gandhi was unamused and threw him into jail. The Congress president D.K. Barooah proclaimed, 'Indira is India, India is Indira.' But we knew better: the state of emergency was a lie nurtured by lies.

Some of my friends, however, found reasons to celebrate. 'How wonderful!' they exclaimed. 'Trains running on time, everyone working, streets neat and clean.' In the end, the bad dream would last only twenty-one months. Mrs Gandhi would call a hurried election and lose it. Why did the dictator make this rash mistake? A deeply insecure woman, she wanted desperately to be loved. Her sycophants told her she was massively popular, predicting a landslide victory in the election. Common sense would have told her the opposite—the mass-sterilization drive had been an evil act of idiocy. The people's verdict proved that they preferred a democracy. Dictators are never as strong as they imagine and people never as weak as they think. The nation's spine did not bend in the end. Luckily, nothing is permanent, and the state of emergency is a distant memory now.

Our second sojourn in Mexico began on a high note and ended on a low one. I was now a general manager, heading the nutritional foods business of the company. We were also a bigger family, and we found a bigger house in Las Lomas de Chapultepec, not far from our old haunts. While literary Polanco's streets had been named after writers, Lomas's streets got their names from mountains. Our house was aptly situated on Calle Himalaya, surrounded by other colossal piles—Mont Blanc, Sierra Nevada, Andes and others. We had the luxury of a garden where our two boys frolicked with Pali, our Labrador. Before long, they were speaking in three languages: in English to us, in Spanish to each other and in Nepali to Bajai, our maid from the real Himalayas. Their personalities also began to emerge in the new environment. Kim was turning out to be a sports-loving, 'Hail fellow, well met' extrovert; Puru was more introspective, reserved.

We were delighted to be back among old friends, acquaintances, having long forgiven the 'no-shows'. The Mexicans seemed pleased to see us too, welcoming us with a brilliant party, where Octavio Paz spoke about his experiences of India. He spoke like a poet rather than a diplomat. India, he claimed, was an excess of reality filled with riddles. The Indian had a split personality between Tantric plenitude and Buddhist emptiness. More worrisome was the uneasy coexistence of rich, polytheistic Hinduism and strict, monotheistic Islam. From his days as ambassador, he evoked memories of passionate, worldly encounters with Mumbai and Delhi, filled with images of sensuality. He closed with a generous memory of Mrs Gandhi, eschewing the temptation to condemn her horrid state of emergency.

Our business was centred on a popular chocolate powder, Choco Milk, fortified with vitamins and minerals, that our company had acquired in the '60s. Since the 1920s, the brand had been spoiling Mexican children, who refused now to drink plain milk. My boss was a charming silver-haired American, the best sort of liberal that sprouted on the East Coast of the US. He had three general managers under him, heading three distinct businesses: over-the-counter drugs, chocolates and candies, and nutritional foods. Mine was the third.

Soon after arriving, I found that Choco Milk, the market leader, was under competitive pressure from Nestlé's Nesquik. We had to defend our leadership, but I felt we also had to expand our offering. Listening to a focus group of middle-class Mexican mothers, I got my first clue. A mother was describing the mad rush at home on school-day mornings. Pepe always woke up late; the school bus was due any minute; no time for breakfast. Her answer was to pour a glass of milk into the blender, add Choco Milk powder, crack an egg into it and throw in a banana. Pepe drank it rushing to the bus stop. He jumped on the bus, and she returned home, happy about having given him a nutritious start to the day. She called the drink 'liquado', after the Spanish word for blender, *liquadora*.

Here was a nifty idea for a line extension of Choco Milk: a ready-to-mix powder with eggs and fruit, and fortified with vitamins and minerals. Our team was excited. 'Liquado Instante', we called it. The R&D head got busy developing the product. Our market research manager began to test the concept. The guy at the advertising agency suggested a clever packaging idea—resembling a blender, ubiquitous in Mexican homes for grinding chillies. All was going well, but we had not taken into account an insecure, bureaucratic headquarters.

Trouble had been brewing at the headquarters for some time. The top boss was under budgetary pressure. Thinking his flagging fortunes were the result of giving too much autonomy to the subsidiaries, he wanted a more formal, centralized system of control. He called in a team of consultants. They asked for a mission statement. He didn't have one. So, a conference was called to thrash one out in Hawaii—an attractive get-away, but hugely extravagant under the circumstances. After three days of deliberations, we came up with some weighty sentences. Lots of time went into wordsmithing, getting the right adjective. Did we want to be 'superior' or 'cutting edge' or 'foremost'? An Australian manager was obsessed with the adverb 'passionately', wanting it everywhere. I was confused. Passion had to do with love. Business ought to limit itself to making good products, having satisfied customers and happy employees. When my turn came, I said quite simply that our mission ought to be to survive, to be fair to our employees and make lots of money. The rest was corporate white noise.

After finalizing the mission statement, the consultants delivered a masterpiece of red tape: Continuous Planning and Review System (CPR), with a six-step process for developing new products. It was enshrined in six intricate manuals called Product Marketing Guides (PMG), requiring HQ approval at each stage. Unfortunately, Licuado Instante became the scapegoat and I the fall guy in the first test case.

One innocent spring morning, I got the bad news—HQ had stopped the Liquado project. They liked the idea, but I was found guilty of flouting the CPR/PMG paperwork. My punishment was to write up the six PMG manuals, one at a time, and seek retrospective approval for each by HQ apparatchiks. As I hunkered down to perform the futile labour, I felt like Sisyphus, condemned by the gods to push a boulder uphill. Just as the rock reaches the top, it rolls back down. Sisyphus must begin again to push it up. Again, it rolls down, and again and again for eternity. After three weeks, I had rewritten history, and I flew to New York, where I waited patiently outside each apparatchik's office and obtained the required approvals. I had been disciplined, but the Sisyphean ordeal did not kill my spirits.

Since I was in New York, I decided to visit my sister, who now lived nearby at Princeton University. We were all proud of Meera. After months of suffering and treatments, she had won a full scholarship to Princeton. I got on the train at Penn Station, and in a little over an hour, I found myself on a glorious ivy-covered campus. Meera was delighted to see me and showed me proudly around her stunning Gothic lecture halls set amid breathtaking gardens. We spoke about her courses in mathematics and economics. I was beaming throughout until I realized something was wrong. She was out of breath, and we sat down on a bench. It wasn't the headaches but extreme exhaustion. The strong drugs she had taken at the headache clinic in Chicago had left her without energy. I took her to her room, where she lay down uncomplainingly for the rest of the day. There were other problems: an eating disorder. For the first time, I detected mental issues. Not being a psychiatrist, I couldn't be sure. Beneath her physical disorders there might have been a deep psychological problem.

Liberation comes not from repressing sorrow but from experiencing it. Meera was forced to leave Princeton a few months later. The university was decent about it, offering to keep her place for three years till she got better. But she never returned. Desperate, she would see all kinds of doctors, physical and mental. The headaches did not reappear, but she remained exhausted for life. She was not able to study or work again. She lived bravely for many years in the counterculture of California. On the face of it, she would always be charming, alert, articulate and far saner than the bureaucrats at my company's headquarters. Instead of cheering me up, the visit had left me depressed.

A Harvard Business School professor, meanwhile, got wind of 'L'Affaire Liquado'. He decided to write a case study, for which he interviewed the various players, including me. It was an old conflict, he said. The tension between headquarters control and local autonomy went back to the East India Company, once the most powerful corporation in the world. It had struggled with this issue in the seventeenth century, when it took six months to get a reply to a letter, provided the recipient answered promptly. As a result, its headquarters had no choice but to cede autonomy to employees in faraway lands. The professor's case study (HBS #179-068, 1974) became a popular offering, and the top boss was invited to Harvard. He strode proudly into the lecture hall to defend his side of the story. But to his dismay, he was crucified. The students were mainly on my side, chewing him out for killing innovation. Coming out of the lecture hall, he was heard to say, 'Bunch of commies!'

The old feeling of life's senselessness had begun to hover once again. My warm, liberal, silver-haired boss was soon transferred from Mexico. They replaced him with someone who had risen to his level of incompetence. He was well-meaning but found it difficult to cope. He loved long meetings—people who enjoy meetings shouldn't be put in charge. When power and incompetence meet, disaster is not far behind. Day by day, the office became politicized and ineffective. I oscillated between Apollonian lightness and Dionysian darkness. On some days, my mind would be clear, razor-sharp, when I would feel bursts of energy convulsing inside. On other days, I would be devoid of ambition, mostly in a grey fog. As the days went by, the fun drained out of life. For someone born to live lightly—whose mother had called him a dancing star—I was now shuffling iron in my blood.

It was time to quit. Unceremoniously, one Friday evening in October 1978, I wrote a few lines on a yellow pad, put the paper in an envelope and walked over to my boss's office. It was locked. He was gone; as was his secretary. I slipped the envelope under the door, picked up my things quietly and left. Instead of going home, I drove around. I was suddenly light-hearted. It felt like another kind of moksha. Not a born executive, I had sort of slid into the role like an actor in a movie. Over fifteen years, I had sleepwalked through my part. People had been happy to slot me thus, saving them the trouble of getting to know me. I had gone along, doing what I was expected to do. The movie kept running, and I kept forfeiting more and more freedom. The weekend writer's role was a bit part, a palliative, making me forget that I had to engage in the hard work of creating an authentic self.

Eventually, I reached home, parking the car in my usual spot on the corner of Himalaya and Reforma. As I got out, I asked myself: Is there such a thing as an 'authentic' me? Or do we just wing it, creating ourselves on the fly, improvising roles while the film projector whirrs on? I had always wanted to play the main character, a streaming meteor, like Karna in the Mahabharata. Opening the gate, I realized that I had finally stepped out of the movie. Having discarded a tired role, I had to find a new one. I wasn't in a hurry—I just hoped it wouldn't be another lie.

I needed a suitable time and place to break the news to the family. I walked quietly into my study and put on my weekend writer's hat. I was longing to escape into another movie, one that I would have more control over. I had begun a novel about three generations of a Punjabi family. The characters were coming along nicely, hurling me into a world of my own making. But I had got bogged down by Partition. Instead of providing a healing touch, the memories had reopened old wounds. Still, the book-in-progress helped to distract me.

The next day was Saturday. I announced that we were having lunch at a grand colonial restaurant, La Hacienda de los Morales. Bunu gave me a searching look, wondering why we were going to such an expensive place. I was nervous, not knowing how to break the news. Finally, over Sopa de Fideo, I mustered up the courage and told Bunu and the children I had quit my job. There was a long silence. They did not take it well.

Bunu was horror-struck. No more monthly checks. I told her that change is painful but not as painful as staying stuck where you don't belong. If you have the guts to say goodbye, life will reward you with a 'hello, there's something ahead'.

'What shall I tell my friends?' Kim moaned. 'And what does your father do? Oh . . . nothing.'

'How about lion tamer?' I suggested in jest.

'But you're not!' he said bitterly.

Bunu was sulking when I paid the bill. 'I could have fed you all for a week from just the tip,' she said.

The next day, to stop herself from thinking, Bunu prepared a big Sunday lunch. She decided to try out new Mexican recipes from her cooking class. We had tortilla soup, guacamole, chiles en nogada, enchiladas, quesadillas and flan. It was all delicious, but no one was in the mood. By the afternoon, she was tired and grateful when I offered to take the kids to the park. We took the soccer ball, found a nice green spot in magnificent Chapultepec Park, once a refuge of Aztec kings. Soon we were kicking the ball. Other kids joined in. I was panting, trying to keep up, when Kim spotted a pony. The action stopped as both boys clamoured for a ride. Out of breath, I agreed readily. Soon, they were off, wearing sombreros in a procession. The hats, loaned by the pony man, were his way to attract gringo tourists. Other kids kept playing with the ball. I found a bench in the shade from where I kept an eye on them. Children are serious when they play, and if adults want to reclaim the same seriousness, they must be willing to turn life into play.

It was while I was sitting on the bench that the voices returned. They had been silent a long time. I had almost forgotten them. 'The Upanishadic birds', meanwhile, had become a code between Bunu and me for my occasional outbursts at life's general silliness. Oddly enough, Chapultepec Park was close to Calle Lord Byron, where I first heard the voices during our earlier Mexican sojourn. I looked around suspiciously. There were people about. Not surprisingly, the voices were about my job; faces from the office popping randomly in my head; the dominant voice asking insistently what I was going to do. Didn't I have to support the kids and Bunu? The dialogue between the birds went on, one thought replacing another until the movie in my head came to an abrupt halt.

I was back in the park. The kids were returning—talking to the ponies, laughing at each other and having a good time. I envied them. Unlike me, they were living lightly, secure in their reality. Both Matilal and my father had reassured me that the voices were merely self-talk in my consciousness, nothing to worry about. But I continued to fret. I peered inside my head, searching in my consciousness. All I could see was one thought rising, giving way to the next much too quickly. I wondered if my consciousness existed *between* my thoughts. But there was no gap. One thought led to another. I looked again, seeking for the thinker behind my thoughts. I failed again. I only experienced a stream of thoughts. Soon, I grew tired of the mental gymnastics and let it go. The kids were back from their ride; their pony talk had shut the voices for now.

It is astonishing how much panic a single man can cause. On Monday, I got frantic phone calls from the local office, then from the New York headquarters and finally from the Bombay office. The script was identical. They were shocked: Why was I leaving, and so suddenly? Why don't we meet and talk? Maybe I'd like to work in another country or at the headquarters? Or return home to work in India? I was flattered but adamant. They were polite, I was polite; politeness is acceptable hypocrisy.

Within a week, news of my leaving had spread. I started getting calls from headhunters. It surprised me because I was considered an 'oddball'. The call that intrigued Bunu came from Europe. General Foods, the American consumer giant, was seeking a general manager in Spain. Would I be interested? I was not, but Bunu and the kids insisted that it would be fun to live in Europe. So two weeks later, Bunu and I were on a recce in Madrid. The head of General Foods Europe was flying in from Brussels to check me out. While he interviewed me, their personnel team showed Bunu the schools, houses and stores in Madrid. It was a typical expat pitch, to which we succumbed easily. The next day was a holiday, and we walked in charming Retiro Park, looked into the Prado to see the Goyas and Velázquezes, and lunched lazily on the patio of Sacha, the Basque bistro.

In the evening, we drank glasses of Rioja and ate tapas in Plaza Mayor, listening to Lorca's songs of the *revolución* (this was possible, now that the fascist Franco was gone). Bunu was relieved that we would have a monthly salary again. We were both relaxed, looking forward to living in a freer, democratic, post-fascist Spain. We loved Madrid's elegant boulevards, its expansive, manicured parks and the portico-lined plaza in which we sat. I was amused to learn that this great European city had been founded by Muslim Arabs during the Emirate of Córdoba in the ninth century. While Bunu listened to the street singer, my mind wandered into the darker corners of my head. The poet's cry for freedom was in dramatic contrast to my unheroic bourgeois life. This historic, cultured city seemed suddenly a veneer hiding yet another meaningless job. Instead of selling Vicks and Choco Milk, I would be selling Maxwell House instant coffee under a local brand name, Tang vitamin C drinks and Jello desserts. I ordered another glass of Rioja, hoping to bury these uncomfortable thoughts under the flamenco rhythms and the poet's cries.

The feeling of emptiness refused to go away even after we returned to Mexico. We were packing for Madrid the following afternoon when Bunu reminded us not to be late for Raul's birthday. Seven-year-old Raul was Kim's best friend at school. We arrived at his apartment on Lord Byron 721 just as they were breaking the piñata. Blind-folded Raul was beating the suspended papier-mâché figure to cries of 'Da-le, Da-le'. He broke it on his last hit. Candy, fruit and toys fell to the ground. Everyone burst into Las Mañanitas and rushed to fill their pockets. An avant-garde poet standing next to me observed casually that the rite symbolized a Mexican son beating his pregnant mother for sleeping with the Spanish conqueror. Sickened by the thought, I needed air, and I slipped out quietly.

I spotted a bench on the street and found myself being drawn to it like a magnet. Noticing the purple jacaranda tree, I remembered. This was where I had first heard the voices. I was scared as I sat down. Luckily, the voices did not return; nor did the kind lady with the Chihuahua. Instead, my life seemed to surface before me. I was watching a movie in which I was the hero. Scenes began popping up randomly: Cousin Jeet was returning the stolen bicycle in Ludhiana; Alisha, the snob, sniggering at the roses I'd left on the lunch table; even Miss Allen, my history teacher, made a cameo appearance; then, five-year-old Ayan emerged, protesting his innocence over the pencil box. I was in a sweat. Fortunately, the motion picture stopped. I found I was sitting on a bench in Mexico. Had the movie of my life been a simple play of light on a white fabric hanging in a cinema? Had I been performing to an empty theatre?

And who was the moviemaker? Presumably *me*. The movie was in *my* head. Closing my eyes, I looked inside, but I didn't find myself. I found only my thoughts and memories. If I could think my thoughts, there must be someone thinking those thoughts. It was frustrating not finding myself. The 'I' must have vanished in the hidden space between my thoughts. It felt weird. I took a deep breath. The only certain reality seemed to be the bench on which I was sitting beside the jacaranda tree. Suddenly, I remembered the birthday party. I got up in a panic and ran back. Luckily, no one had noticed my absence. I couldn't have been away too long. There was lots of noise and laughter. I turned to look at my arms, my legs. They must be mine. And the memories in my head, racing in *my* consciousness, had to be mine. So no need to worry. What a relief! I wasn't a fantasy, after all!

The freedom between my jobs lasted only six weeks. During the first few weeks, there had been anxiety and gloom in the house. I may have got my freedom, but I did not have a salary. It isn't easy to cope with the uncertainty—hence, people choose unhappiness over insecurity. Society cannot accept a man doing nothing. Bunu was ashamed when her friends from her bridge group saw me at the supermarket one Monday morning.

They gave me a strange look. To keep myself busy I started doing yoga. Bunu tried to avoid her friends. But she was pleased to see one of them during our last week in Mexico.

'How's your husband—still unemployed?'

'No, he's got a job,' said Bunu, beaming. 'We're moving, you know.'

'Some good news, at last.'

Bunu's friends wouldn't have understood that I was only wearing the mask of a business executive—only playing a role. The truth is that when I quit my job, society stripped me of my identity. Bunu and the kids could not cope with this. So I had taken the easy way out. I had slid back into the same role, resigning myself to sleepwalking for the rest of my life. It's not easy to handle the uncertain freedom of this sort of moksha.

Before long, we were settled comfortably in La Moraleja in Madrid. It was an easy transition for the boys, moving from one Spanish-speaking country to another, from the colonized child to the colonial mother. They quickly adopted the Castilian accent and idioms, smartly uttering 'vale'. Knowing they would have to be fluent in English, we got them enrolled in the American School of Madrid. My job, however, was a let-down. I was pushing water uphill, because Nestlé practically owned the coffee market in Spain. There was little hope for General Foods' other offerings like Tang and Jell-O—Europeans were not into American-style processed foods. Nevertheless, I continued bravely wearing a mask. My job was a joke, but then, life is also a joke.

The compensation of working in Spain was that I got plenty of glorious weekends. We travelled to Moorish Andalusia, faith-inspired Galicia and ironic Catalunya. The landscape of Spain is stark, especially the heartland of Castile. There's hardly a tree for miles where a bird can alight. It's a land of long silences, and this has made the people stern and insular. They see the world in black and white. We were especially attracted to the Romani gypsies in the south, heavy with the lament of blood and death. One of them told us that they were originally from Rajasthan. Alas, they were persecuted souls in Spain, like Dalit outcasts in India, relegated to the margins. We were moved by their outbursts during the Holy Week: 'I don't want this Christ in wood; I want the one who walks on water.' It could have been Kabir singing.

Spanish politics had oscillated between the left and the right, climaxing in a civil war that had killed a million people in the late 1930s. Revolted by the history of absolutism, inquisition and militarism, young Spaniards were more pragmatic, detesting the old live-or-die philosophy. My Spanish teacher was one of them. He was a devotee of Cervantes, and we used to speak for hours about *Don Quixote de la Mancha*, about a supreme idealist who was unwilling to accept the reality of a fraudulent society. In this alternately tragic and comic narrative, he dreamt the impossible dreams of another sort of moksha. From Don Quixote, I learnt to speak to others in a language that one speaks to oneself when one is alone. He spoke to my fears about my fragile identity, teaching me that it is not intelligence but the will which moves the world. The barber's basin was a knight's helmet to him. The more you believe in a thing, the more it exists. It is not learning but the will which imposes the truth.

My old company, meanwhile, had never quite accepted that I had left. To woo me back, it sent several emissaries. One of them was an irrepressible Gujarati colleague. Seeing him, I was filled with nostalgia for the old days. Things got emotional over sangria and tapas. He confessed that the Indian company was in trouble. Some of my colleagues missed me. Would I come back, take over the reins and rescue the firm? I was tempted. General Foods in Europe wasn't going anywhere, barking up the wrong tree. Europeans had a superior attitude, bordering on contempt for fast, processed American foods. Set in their sensible ways, they insisted on a fresh, wholesome diet, eaten unhurriedly in a relaxed ambience.

Added to this was my own unease—seeing our children growing up deracinated in golden expat ghettos. There was a time when I believed that I was a citizen of the world. I strutted about proclaiming like Diogenes the Cynic: 'A blade of grass is a blade of grass in one country or another.' But Don Quixote taught us that glory lies in one's backyard. Home from conquests, he proclaimed that the more a man belongs to his own time and place, the more he belongs to all times and places. I felt dejected seeing Kim and Puru glued to Mickey Mouse and Donald Duck speaking in Spanish on Cartoonito channel. Our boys had no attachment to the grand heroes of the Mahabharata and Ramayana. So it was time to return to our backyard. And we packed up and left one evening, watching from our Iberia jet the immortal figure of Don Quixote growing smaller, merging with the Spanish evening sky.

Thus, the '70s came to an end. It was a quixotic age that taught me that nothing is quite what it seems. I laughed and wept with Don Quixote as he fought windmills that turned into giants, saw a herd of sheep that grew into an army and witnessed inns becoming castles. Thanks to him, I learnt to view the Emergency in India as a quixotic, tragicomic farce authored by the adored heroine of the Indian masses. In my personal space, my enviable job as a global manager turned out to be pointless. But I had to yield to the reality of having to make a living. As a sibling, I experienced the pain of my sister's chronic illness, leaving me feeling infinitely sad at life's unfairness. As an explorer of the human consciousness, I got caught in the drama of the two birds that left me shaken about my fragile identity. And yet, I had a vague sense that the stream of thoughts in my head may one day open the door to another sort of freedom. The possibility was at once enchanting and frightening to a secular mumukshu.

14

Improbable CEO

'A leader is best when people barely know he exists; not so good when people obey and acclaim him; worse, when they despise him. But of a good leader, who talks little, his work done, his aim fulfilled, they say: we did it.'

—Lao Tzu

I was now thirty-seven and sitting at the top of the heap. I had become CEO of Richardson Hindustan Ltd, the company where I had started at the bottom. I was happy to be among old colleagues, but everyone didn't seem pleased. Envy, I suppose, is the side effect of success. I've known envy since kindergarten, when I grabbed the rich kid's pencil box and got poor Ayan into trouble. The Greeks exiled their heroes, allowing them to return only after the public's envy had cooled; Chinese heroes coped with envy by self-deprecation; Indian heroes, by renouncing the world.

I may have got to the top, but I wasn't sitting pretty. The company was in serious trouble, a real mess. I didn't know to which port we were sailing; no wind was favourable. The socialist government had instituted severe price controls on medicines, threatening to bankrupt us. Our labour force was hostile, coming out of a seventy-seven-day strike. The chemists' association had just announced a boycott of our products to force higher trade margins. With sales plunging to zero, we might go bust. I called a meeting of the management committee. Although I hated meetings, this was a dire moment. Some in the Mancom had long memories— they had still not forgiven me over executive toilets and white-gloved waiters. Nevertheless, sharing our difficulties might help to lift us out of a bottomless pit.

Gloom filled the room when I finished outlining our ominous situation. I suggested a free-flowing 'brainstorming', a novel idea that left my colleagues cold. They were suspicious. I might have a hidden agenda before I plunged in the knife. There were long silences, lengthy intervals. One person felt that since I was the boss, I should be giving orders, not asking for help. Another feared that I was trying to steal their ideas and call them my own. Normally talkative, they were tight-lipped at the meeting. Soon, they began to fidget, grow restless, visit the toilet. No one spoke. Someone had a sensible idea: As we weren't getting anywhere, why not end the meeting and the pain? I was confused and didn't know what to do. The uneasy quiet rolled on until, one by one, making excuses, they all left.

The brainstorming was a disaster. I chalked it to our differing mindsets. Theirs was more traditional, hierarchical style; mine was consultative, participative, maybe because I had grown up in democratic America. Nevertheless, I wasn't deterred and called for a second brainstorming session. This time, I did a better job. They had also begun to trust me a bit more. I guided the discussion more confidently, focusing sharply on the key issues. Ideas began to flow. At one point in the flowing stream, the Gujarati head of marketing said almost absent-mindedly, 'What if Vicks Vaporub had been an Ayurvedic medicine, not a Western drug?' Someone snickered, thinking it a joke. But behind the 'what-if' was a hope—Ayurvedic products did not fall under price control.

Then, the Tamil head of R&D spoke, as though he was speaking to himself: 'Vaporub's ingredients *are* natural. I wonder if they're in the Ayurvedic formulary.' The Marwari company secretary thought it worth confirming if Ayurvedic products were indeed free from price control. The Punjabi sales manager wanted to check if Ayurvedic products were limited to pharmacies or sold by general merchants. The Bengali finance manager, ever cautious, felt that even if Vaporub's ingredients were in the formulary, it would be illegal to make the switch. Would the government ever allow it? The wishful Gujarati, who had started all this, confessed that the idea had been put into his head by an official of the Gujarat government. Someone announced a headline from the *Times of India*: '100-Year-Old American Product Becomes a 2000-Year-Old Indian Medicine!' Everyone laughed. The ice had been broken.

Everyone seemed to know what to do. The R&D man rushed to the Bombay University library to check if Vaporub's ingredients were in the ancient formulary. The finance manager went off to the lawyers' office to confirm if Ayurvedic products were indeed free of price control. The company secretary called our government-relations man in Delhi to check if Vaporub's registration could be changed. The sales manager was off to the bazaar to ascertain which sort of stores sold Ayurvedic products. We met in the evening. There were smiling faces. It was a 'yes' on all counts. All of Vaporub's ingredients were in the formulary; Ayurvedic products were not price-controlled. We looked at each other in disbelief. The advice from Delhi was not to ask for a change in registration but to make an application for a new product and make the switch only after the approval. Over the next few days, we worked day and night, preparing a dossier, backed by endorsements from Ayurvedic experts.

When the application landed on his desk, the regulator practically fell off his chair. He had guessed what we were up to, but he couldn't stop us—it was all perfectly legal. After weeks of prodding daily, the authorities handed us the prized licence to manufacture an Ayurvedic rub. From that day onwards, the factory stopped manufacturing the old Vaporub. Our Maharashtrian purchase manager ordered labels for the new Vaporub. The sales manager recalled the entire inventory from the market for relabelling. Two weeks later, shiny bottles of 'All Natural Ayurvedic Vicks Vaporub' were sitting proudly on store shelves. Nothing had changed, except our profits. They soared. The sales force began to expand distribution to the non-drug trade. Within six months, outlets carrying Vicks jumped from 60,000 pharmacies to 7,50,000 general stores. The trade boycott collapsed. Consumers were happy, finding Vicks now at every street corner.

We received the new registration and set up a plant for Ayurvedic Vicks in a tax-advantaged area of Hyderabad, with lower costs and higher productivity. Thus, we escaped the clutches of a hostile union in Mumbai. Since it was impossible to close the old factory in those days of the Licence Raj, we merely stopped production. Workers came to the factory; they were paid full wages but did not work. Soon, we offered them a generous voluntary retirement plan. Most of them found it attractive and accepted it. The few who were left lodged a complaint via the union. The authorities tried to stop us. But they were helpless—we had not broken any law.

With higher prices and better costs, we invested aggressively in marketing. Our after-tax profits rose from 1 per cent to 14 per cent of sales. Soon, we were a blue chip on the Bombay Stock Exchange as the share price zoomed from Rs 30 to Rs 400 over the next eighteen months. (We were owned only 40 per cent by the American company; the balance 60 per cent was widely spread among the Indian public.) Having anticipated this outcome, we had offered shares of the company to all 1248 employees, including factory workers, secretaries and cleaning staff. All shared in the company's prosperity and many ended up buying a home from their capital gains. This had not been easy, since no one had heard of stock options in those socialist days. The controller of capital issues thought it a scam—employees trying to steal the company's money. However, we prevailed in the end and were allowed to offer 5 per cent of the share capital to employees.

The story doesn't end there. We proposed to create an R&D centre in Mumbai to prove the efficacy of all-natural Ayurvedic therapies for common ailments. There were many sceptics at the headquarters. But it helped that we were now flush with funds, having become one of the most profitable subsidiaries in the world. After much debate about Ayurveda's efficacy, the headquarters agreed, and a cheque for $2 million arrived one morning.

Around this time, I got a call from Delhi, inviting me to an industry–government roundtable. With all the goings-on in the company, I was reluctant to accept the invite. But when I learnt that a breakfast with Mrs Gandhi was on the cards, I was easily persuaded. The lapsed dictator was back on the throne. She had returned to power riding a wave of sympathy in 1980, after the post-Emergency coalition had made a mess, getting bogged down in petty squabbling. She reverted to her brand of populist socialism and pro-Soviet foreign policy. *The Times* (of London) called her 'slightly left of self-interest'.

At the roundtable, I found myself surrounded by the 'greats' from both industry and government. But it wasn't a dialogue. Arrogant ministers spoke; meek captains of industry listened. The only exception was L.K. Jha, adviser to the prime minister, who was remarkably open, confessing that the government had made 'some mistakes' and that it was time to change. The next morning, we were ushered into the prime minister's garden. Mrs Gandhi was smiling in an elegant grey-and-pink cotton sari. She was surrounded by spring flowers, and it was hard to believe that this amiable woman was the lapsed dictator who had broken Pakistan into two. She spoke smoothly, always coming up with the right phrase. During question hour, a few sycophants from the industry rose to eulogize her achievements. There was embarrassed silence. I decided to take my chance. I asked her about three of her prized policies: Why did we need licensing when competition would do a better job of allocating resources? Two: Why were our tax rates so high, rising to 98.75 per cent at the top? Three: Why didn't we follow the Asian tigers by opening our economy and exporting labour-intensive goods, rather than insisting on making everything uncompetitively at home?

Thinking I was a bit unhinged, Mrs Gandhi threw me a look of mock sympathy and said, 'We'll need a day-long seminar for this young market wallah's questions.' There were sniggers. She decided to indulge me, nevertheless. Since India was a poor country, she said, it didn't need frivolous cosmetics and luxuries; licensing ensured we produced only necessities. Two, high taxes for the rich, low taxes for the poor—this was simply a matter of being equitable. Three, Indian industry was in its infancy and could not compete in the world. Since we did not export, India did not have the foreign exchange to pay for imports; hence, the only alternative was to make as much as possible at home.

It was the typical defence of Fabian socialism. She had been well trained by her Marxist economists. I was about to jump up and rebut her arguments when my host signalled me to sit down. India's private industry did not want to lose the great leader's goodwill. He launched instead on a never-ending, apple-polishing tribute to Mrs G's leadership. Thus, amid shining marigolds, she had preserved that morning three myths of the Licence Raj. India would have to wait almost a decade before it would be liberated by the reforms of 1991.

Meanwhile, a busybody in the personnel department at the headquarters had been rummaging through the company files. He discovered that the head of their Indian company had a background in philosophy, not in business. HQ decided to send me back to school—a summer course at the Harvard Business School. A needless expense, I felt.

I had managed reasonably well with a liberal education, but they were insistent. The problem of going to business school was that Mrs Gandhi's intrusive government needed to approve the payment of my fees. The deputy governor of the Reserve Bank of India called me for an 'interview'. Suspecting me of being a scamster, he threw a volley of questions. Since I was already head of the company, why did I need to study further? I should relax, enjoy the power.

I asked him politely where *he* fitted into this scheme. I was the one going to school, and my company was paying my fees. But why was the mighty deputy governor wasting his precious time 'interviewing' me? He gave a malevolent smile and said, 'But it is *my* money.' The bank's foreign reserves would be paying for my 'academic holiday'. I finally got it. He thought I was gaming the system, setting off on a foreign junket paid for by the government's precious reserves. 'If it is a holiday, sir, I'd have chosen a nicer place,' I told him, adding that I'd always wanted see Tuscany and Umbria. Perhaps he would like to join the holiday party? A few days later, the bank sanctioned the foreign exchange.

Just before leaving for my 'academic holiday', I learnt that Piloo Mody was sick and decided to visit him. Walking into the grand mansion built by Sir Homi Mody on Cumballa Hill, I found a broken man. I'd known him and the Swatantra Party when both had been at their peak. From being the second-largest Opposition party in Parliament, it had been wiped out in the 1971 election by the 'Indira wave'. Although the party had disappeared, Piloo continued bravely in politics, almost the sole voice of classical liberalism. Now in his eighties, he was still a member of the Rajya Sabha but sickened by the internal feuds in the Janata Party. He was thinking of starting another party. Since he was old and sick, he wondered if I would like to run it. More than a genuine offer, it felt like an admission of futility of this task. He died soon after, leaving me infinitely sad. The Swatantra Party had been a beacon of light in a socialist age, far ahead of its time. All other parties had stood for a particular interest—a caste, a region or religion. But Swatantra had stood steadfastly for its ideology of economic freedom.

* * *

Harvard Business School is situated on the wrong side of the Charles River, which divides Cambridge and Boston. Harvard College, the original Harvard, is on the Cambridge side and has been teaching young men for 400 years (and women since 1975) how to 'make a life'. The business school came much later, almost an afterthought, when someone realized that graduates also needed 'to make a living'. Not wanting to be too close to the smell of business, they plonked it on the Boston side of the river. Professors and students of the arts and sciences still don't cross the river, except to play sports, the facilities for which are located on the Boston side. The business school went on to become wealthier, paying higher salaries to its professors—an injustice that still gives heartburn to the tweedy academics on the other side of the river.

I was happy to be back at Harvard. One summer evening, I decided to visit my old haunts across the river. While browsing in the Harvard Bookstore on Massachusetts Avenue, who should I see but my old friend Donald J.! He had shaved his head and was wearing the saffron robes of a Buddhist monk. He was still the same jovial flatmate, however, with whom I had shared the flophouse during the summer between my junior and senior years. Why had he shaved his head? He had got tired of standing before the mirror in the mornings, he said, trying to decide how to style his hair. We walked across Harvard Square and caught up with our lives over inedible vegetarian dim sums. I confessed to him about the voices and my anxiety at not finding my 'self'.

'No self, no problem!' he quipped.

It was the same Buddhist maxim that he had thrown at me sixteen years earlier. 'So how much "self" do you need anyway?' he asked. Then he answered his own question, 'Just enough, so you don't step in front of the bus, right?' I looked at the bus going past the window. He was laughing, enjoying his own Buddhist humour. But he could tell that I was impatient for answers. As we walked along the river, he explained that I couldn't find my 'self' because the 'I' was a psycho-physical process created by the mind, not a fixed being. A practical convenience, helping me to navigate the world. Like a third-person narrator in a novel, it held the story together but didn't exist. It all sounded crazy. Did he really mean that neither he nor I existed?

'You can't be serious,' I protested.

'No, not on a regular basis.' He smiled.

Both of us turned to look at a passing airplane. 'If I'm nothing, how do I refer to my body, my mind, my emotions? Who's the agent for my actions?' It was all too bizarre. With a twinkle in his eye, he mentioned a helpful English word, 'person'. It came from the Latin *persona*, a mask or a character in a play. He wanted me to think of my I-ness as this character, who is playing many parts, wearing different masks on different days, depending on whom I am with.

'You're only an actor,' he said. 'You don't *own* the characters you're playing. So why do you need your illusionary "self"?'

A couple of bicyclists, dressed in athletic gear, had been waiting patiently behind us. We moved aside, and they waved as they went past.

'But what does all this mean for my day-to-day life?' I asked.

'Quite simple: you don't need to be so self-obsessed.'

The penny had dropped. I had finally understood. If I was merely playing a role, I didn't need the baggage of a permanent I-ness. Since my role was changing all the time, my 'self' was also changing. If I didn't have a permanent self, I didn't have to shine all the time. Didn't need to feel envious, angry. I was no longer competing with others and didn't have to insist on premium treatment for myself. I didn't need to be afraid or even unhappy. The boundaries with others had also dissolved. Empathy is an overused word, but I think it conveys the sensation of connectedness. I could experience myself more democratically. As one among others, it was easier to feel compassion, behave more benevolently.

Donald J. stopped suddenly. He looked at his watch. 'Gotta go, wake up early to meet three Buddhists in the morning—all of them cats. Let's hope there will be enough milk.'

I asked him if he took anything seriously.

'Not if I can help it.'

I don't know if Donald J. realized the profound effect he was having on me. We met a number of times again. We even went to the movies together at the Brattle, just like the old days. After a walk along the river, I began to feel not quite real. I felt like—a bit player on the stage of life, playing many parts, each with his exits and entrances, as Shakespeare says. It was just as well that I was at school, not at work.

At Harvard Business School, I found I was learning more from my classmates than from professors. From the CEO of a small midwestern company I learnt to say 'no'. It is much easier to say 'yes', he explained, but it takes character to say 'no'. Each time, you disappoint someone when you say 'no' (for speaking at a luncheon, for example). But the 'no' was often an invite to a younger person to step into your shoes. And if enough people said 'no' to these ego-massaging activities, the activities themselves would disappear. The trick, of course, was knowing when to say 'yes'. The CEO's simple rule was to say 'no' to all invitations except those that helped his company or enriched his family life.

One of my classmates was a member of the European aristocracy and ran a successful German company. He was formal, always impeccably dressed. He was also reserved, spoke only when spoken to. I was feeling uneasy sitting next to him at dinner one night. To break the ice, I asked him about the secret of his company's success. He perked up suddenly. It was all about attitude, he said. 'When hiring a person, look for attitude. You can teach skills, but you can't change a person's attitude.' He felt determination was even more useful than intelligence. But how does one uncover 'determination' in an interview? His answer was, by hiring people temporarily, for a 'summer job', for example. It gave you three months to see how they solved problems, grasped opportunities, faced adversity. Most companies were careless when it came to recruiting. I found myself nodding vigorously. I told him about Kamble. He said he would like to fill his company with Kambles.

When I returned to Bombay, some of my colleagues felt I had changed. Although I'd never been the command-and-control type, they saw even more conviction behind my participative approach to managing. It must be the impact of business school, they said, but I knew better. It was the 'Donald J. effect'. Since I was only *playing* a role, why go through the charade of strutting around office like a peacock? It was not easy to adopt Donald J.'s philosophy. My mind may have accepted that my 'self' was an illusion, but I could not act on that basis. I couldn't accept that I was just one among others. I still felt I deserved premium treatment. Kamble is the only one I know who never cared about who got the credit for his work. But he was an exception.

I could not leave my ego at the door. All my work was driven by it. To be human, I felt, is to have ambition. As one climbs the ladder of success, however, the ego tends to get bigger. And there's nothing more tiresome than egos throwing their weight around. Although I couldn't erase my ego, I could see the value of diminishing it. When that happened, I found I was freer, lighter. It also reinforced my conviction that the consultative style of working was the right one. The more I practised it, the more the atmosphere changed in the office. Less command, less control meant less hierarchy. It brought laghima to the office. Yes, one should try and not take oneself too seriously.

A young trainee remarked one day that he couldn't work in an office with dirty walls. I looked around and saw for the first time that the walls in our Worli offices were, indeed, shabby. We had been so busy coping with crises that we had forgotten to get them painted. Finally, we got around to it. The walls were now stark white, looking suddenly bare. The contractor suggested covering them with paintings. He showed us some rubbish. Since I knew something about contemporary art, I checked around. I found that for the same price as the rubbish we could surround ourselves with real art, real beauty. This was decades before prices of Indian art climbed to stratospheric levels. Building an art collection gave me the chance to reconnect with old friends from the Bombay Progressive Artists' Group. I began to visit galleries over weekends. Kekoo Gandhi at the Chemould Gallery helped. So did some of the artists, especially Nalini Malani. Before long, we had a decent collection of almost fifty works, some of which we exhibited at the Jehangir Art Gallery in 1985.

I was disheartened, however, by the reaction in the office. People were puzzled by the splotches and stains; some were upset, even angry. They accused me of snobbery; I let it pass. It is true, modern art can be unnerving. People feel that they have to respond instantly. If they would look at a painting as they look at a flower, and not fret about what it meant, they would be more relaxed. I told my colleagues to dismiss the blotches as the feelings and imagination of the artist, a sort of free, undirected mental activity. Since art originates in our intuition, not our rational faculties, it doesn't have to mean anything—nothing more than the accidental play of light and shadow on a wall. Once one gets used to it, one enjoys what one is seeing.

The three paintings closest to my heart were Gieve Patel's *Off Lamington Road*, which celebrated the street life of Bombay with a medieval passion; the second was *Nullah*, a brilliant cityscape by Sudhir Patwardhan, set in suburban Thane; and the third was Gaitonde's greenish, Zen-like abstract work of mysterious hieroglyphics, before which I would go stand once a week and meditate quietly.

The art collection, alas, had a sad ending. It fell into neglect after I was transferred to Procter & Gamble's world headquarters. No one in the company seemed to care after I left. I suggested gently donating it to the National Gallery of Modern Art, but there were bureaucratic hurdles, both in Delhi and at P&G's headquarters. The company eventually sold it wholesale to the Glenbarra Museum in Japan in the late '90s. Alas, just a few years later, prices of contemporary Indian art went through the ceiling. Had they waited, they would have made a killing.

There was relative calm now in my professional life, and during the stillness, Indira Gandhi was assassinated, on 31 October 1984. It was an act of revenge by her Sikh bodyguard for desecrating the holy Golden Temple—she had allowed the army to flush out Sikh militants who had set up a 'parallel government' at the shrine. She was succeeded by the 'wrong' son. She would have preferred her younger, more ambitious son, Sanjay, who had achieved notoriety during the Emergency, terrorizing people in the forced sterilization programme. But he had died as dramatically as he had lived, performing a reckless aerobatic manoeuvre in an airplane.

The democrat in me was offended when another member of the Nehru–Gandhi dynasty ascended to power. The gentler, apolitical Rajiv Gandhi, however, won me and the country over with his winsome smile. He came in as Mr Clean in a nation tired of corruption, and he led the Congress party to a landslide victory. I was euphoric at his first moves to liberalize the economy and reform the bureaucracy. On a visit to Delhi, I happened to meet Lovraj Kumar, a charming man who had made a successful career in both the private (Shell) and public (secretary, petroleum) sectors. He invited me home one evening, where I also met his charming wife, Dharma Kumar. They could sense my youthful excitement over liberalization. Rajiv Gandhi wanted to bring in younger people from the outside. Would I be interested? asked Lovraj.

'Yes,' I blurted out.

My answer took me by surprise. As I think about my motive, it might have had something to do with the discontent I had been feeling for a long time in regard to my own job. The nagging sense of my job's futility had brought on the voices. Luckily, they had been quiet in recent years—and especially in the '80s, amid all the excitement of rescuing and then turning around my company.

Lovraj Kumar quickly brought me down to the ground. They were looking for the head of marketing in one of the oil companies, he said. I was disappointed, and it showed. After being CEO, it sounded like a comedown. He understood and added that he would explore if there were openings to head a smaller public-sector company. I was young by government standards. He warned me that it wouldn't be easy—the civil-service lobby was powerful and didn't like outsiders intruding on its turf. Our conversation came to a halt as guests began to amble into the drawing room. I rose, but Lovraj asked me to stay. Sensing my unease, Dharma explained that theirs was an open house in the evenings.

The room was soon filled with intense intellectual conversations among scholars, journalists and writers; they passionately discussed issues of the day. At the centre was my hostess. I was in a daze. I felt as if I'd been transported to a salon in early-modern revolutionary France. Dharma was an economic historian, and I found her chiding a Marxist for not valuing democracy and freedom. The next moment, she was gently coaxing a civil servant to read novels, not just files—he would find more fiction in the files, more reality in novels. The following day, I went to Faqir Chand's bookshop in Khan Market and bought a copy of Dharma's book, *Land and Caste in South India*. I became her lifelong admirer.

A few weeks later, I heard from Lovraj Kumar. There was an opening to head a public-sector company in infrastructure. It was my chance to escape from the farcical world of consumer products. It would be a more purposive life, I felt. But Lovraj advised me not to get my hopes high. The civil-service establishment would try to keep me out. But anything was possible, since Rajiv Gandhi had just brought in an old school friend from another consumer-products company. Bunu thought I was mad. What was I thinking, going from being the CEO of a high-performing company on the Bombay Stock Exchange to becoming a cog in the wheel of India's byzantine bureaucracy? I sounded out the top brass in America, and they were happy to give me a leave of absence. In the end, wily bureaucrats in Delhi found a stratagem and pushed my appointment into a subcommittee, which never met. And with it vanished my hopes of leading a more purposive life. Just as well, Bunu said. The vile air of Delhi's officialdom would have snuffed me out.

My disappointment did not last long, however. I was soon caught up in another sort of euphoria. Penguin published my novel, *A Fine Family*. It was a thirty-year saga of three generations of a Punjabi family, from Partition to the Emergency. There was lots of publicity—almost too much, thought Bunu. It was unusual for a businessman to write a novel. Expectations ran high, but the reviews were mixed. The favourable ones said that I had come to grips with the pain and anguish of Partition.

India Today thought the book's success lay 'in making people ordinary without making them dull'. I was chuffed to read that my prose was 'lucid, restrained, and even elegant'. However, some critics panned the book. One called it 'old-fashioned', contrasting it to the innovative writing of Salman Rushdie. Another thought the characters were two-dimensional, 'made of cardboard'. I lapped up the good reviews and tried to ignore the bad ones. In the end, I had to face the fact that it was not a great book. I had at best delivered a 'readable, reflective book with some warm and sympathetic characters', as one reviewer put it. Not bad for a weekend writer, Bunu consoled me, but I was disappointed.

I then made a social gaffe. A charming historian at Bombay University decided to have a party in honour of the book. She and her husband invited a few academics, some journalists and common friends to a lovely evening at their home in Bandra. At the end, as we were leaving, she turned to me and asked, 'And where is my signed copy?' It was a reasonable request. But I spoiled the evening, replying insensitively, 'Buy a copy, and I shall sign it.' She thought I was mean and ungrateful. I was shocked at her reaction. I had innocently followed the advice of an older, more famous writer, Santha Rama Rau, who had once advised me, 'Never give away free copies—it cheapens your book.' My historian friend did not speak to me for a year.

In the midst of all this, my professional world was about to go topsy-turvy! My parent company, Richardson Vicks, had been faltering in the mid-'80s, becoming a plum target for a takeover. One Friday morning, Unilever, the Anglo–Dutch consumer products giant, made a hostile bid. I was nervous all weekend, fearing I would lose my job. Lever had been in India for a century and had built a formidable enterprise with an army of outstanding managers. If its bid succeeded, most of us at Vicks would become redundant in India. But on Monday morning, I woke up to the news that a white knight had entered the arena. Procter & Gamble, Lever's main competitor, had put in a higher bid and successfully bought our company worldwide. In the acquisition, many Vicks employees in America would lose their jobs. But in India, P&G was absent. Instead of being gobbled by Lever, we became the eyes and ears of P&G—we became P&G India.

P&G had long eyed India's huge consumer market but had been deterred by Lever's dominance. But now, all of sudden, a high-performing consumer company had fallen into its lap. India was the third-largest market for laundry products (after the US and China), and soon it became the theatre of a major soap war. A detergent war is not dissimilar to a military war. We at Vicks, trained in the art of peace, began to learn the art of war.

It is foolish to mount a head-on attack on a fortress—you need a flanking strategy. We spent months trying to understand the laundry market, fishing for Lever's vulnerabilities. We watched housewives wash clothes, talked to retailers and wholesalers, and conducted product and concept tests. Washing machines were rare; the typical Indian housewife, we discovered, washed clothes by hand, in two steps. First, she soaked the dirty clothes in a bucket of water, adding a cup of detergent powder to loosen the dirt. Then, she scrubbed each garment with a detergent bar. It was backbreaking drudgery. Husbands didn't help.

What if we gave her a product so powerful that it would do the job in a single step? She would save toil, time and improve her life immeasurably. We tasked P&G's research labs in America with the project of coming up with this product. A bright, young scientist there had, in fact, created such a winning compact formula. A *spoonful* of his detergent cleaned better than a *cupful* of Lever's Surf; plus, the clothes didn't need scrubbing with a bar. The problem was its price. Its ingredients had to be imported under punishing customs duties, and the consumer would end up paying Rs 60 per kilo, as opposed to Rs 27 for Lever's Surf. It was lunacy, my colleagues argued, to sell one of the world's most expensive and technologically advanced detergents in one of the poorest countries.

If you're going to attack a fortress, you need surprise and disruption. We had found the disruption in our compact formula and confirmed its superiority in a thousand house-to-house tests. But to make economic sense for the consumer? We redid the sums, this time factoring in the savings in not having to use the bar. To our happy surprise, the cost per wash came out lower with our 'great white hope'. The challenge was how to stop the consumer from thinking in 'price per kilo' and encourage them to think in terms of 'price per wash'. We tested many ideas. The winning TV commercial showed a modern daughter-in-law trying to convince her tough, sceptical mother-in-law. When the latter sees the proof she is so thoroughly converted that she throws the detergent bar out of the window.

We now had a viable proposition and decided to test a limited quantity under the name Ariel. We chose faraway Vishakhapatnam, on the east coast, hoping thus not to draw attention. Lever ignored us initially, thinking we were crazy. Who would buy such a ridiculously expensive detergent? But consumers were delighted—they had understood the arithmetic and had never seen clothes so clean. Month after month, Ariel compact's share began to climb. Eventually, Lever got wise and responded by buying up Ariel's entire stock in the market. Housewives clamoured for more; the test market got spoiled. By then, we knew Ariel was a winner and decided to make a major investment in a detergent factory near Bhopal in Madhya Pradesh. Lever, too, began to develop a compact detergent, similar to ours. It was a race: Who would get to the national market first? They tried to slow us down, taking us to court. Because our TV commercial showed the mother-in-law chucking a blue bar out of the window—Lever's Rin was also blue in colour—they sought an injunction on the grounds of disparagement. But their case didn't hold in court, because other bars were also blue.

Our factory was ready at last. We had hired and trained more than a hundred workers. Raw and packaging materials had been delivered. Trials of the machines were completed. P&G's global CEO and the state's chief minister were both coming for the inauguration. But then, the bomb dropped. An engineer at the government's electricity company refused to supply power unless we paid a bribe of Rs 50,000. I balked. Was it another Lever trick to slow us down? No, our factory manager had checked—it was standard practice; other factories had paid similar bribes. What my colleagues regarded as a simple cost-benefit issue I saw as a moral dilemma. Although the bribe was tiny, compared to the millions we stood to lose, it was illegal, against India's laws and America's Foreign Corrupt Practices Act.

I refused to pay the bribe and informed the headquarters that the inauguration and launch were postponed. The global CEO phoned. He was unpacking his bags. After congratulating me, he said that while millions may be lost, I had done the right thing. My respect for P&G soared. Days went by, then weeks. We didn't budge, nor did the bribetaker. Six weeks later, I realized, the cost of keeping the huge, expensive plant idle was mounting. Opinion in the company was also turning against me. My colleagues thought I was selfish—acting for personal glory, jeopardizing their futures. I could not make peace with the unacceptable. In the end, I went public. The corrupt engineer was transferred, and the power was restored immediately. But we lived in fear of retaliation, worried that someone might cut off electricity at any time.

We launched Ariel nationally, backed by heavy advertising and house-to-house demonstrations in a million homes. Lever counterattacked, playing dirty again. They hired teams of demonstrators, who followed us from house to house, proving to housewives that Ariel discoloured clothes. Their scientists had discovered that a white cloth turned pink briefly, for a minute or so, in a concentrated Ariel solution before returning to the original colour. It was long enough to make the point. We cried foul and took them to court. But the damage was done. Meanwhile, their compact detergent was also ready. Surf Excel was almost as good as our Ariel. It dampened our launch, taking away some of our punch.

There would be many dogfights in the years to come between Lever and P&G in India. Both companies would invest lots of money in these battles, competing either with lower prices or superior quality. Reputations of young managers would be built fighting to gain 1 per cent market share. We also fought another war around this time when we introduced Whisper sanitary napkins. It was against Johnson & Johnson's Stayfree and Carefree, the market leaders. Again, we did well because of our technological superiority. Ultimately, the Indian consumer was the winner.

The socialist commissars of the Licence Raj could never understand why we were wasting the nation's resources in a futile competition. But we learnt many lessons from the soap wars. A deep understanding of consumers is the starting point. Technology gives one competitive advantage. But it doesn't last, and the other fellow catches up. Hence one needs to keep innovating, even in an old-fashioned, businesslike detergent. It's not enough to have a superior product—the job of advertising is to persuade the consumer that one company's product works, while the competitor's fails.

What gave us the confidence to take on a giant like Hindustan Lever, a company twenty times larger, was the quality of our people. Our college recruiting programme was just as good as theirs, and our managers trusted us that promotions would come their way if they delivered results. Yet my friends at Lever thought we were soft. They pooh-poohed my style of managing. What I called 'participative–consultative', they dismissed as 'fuzzy-wuzzy'. They prided themselves on being tougher, superior and disciplined. But in the end, I think, we were a happier place to work at, which gave us another competitive advantage.

As I look back on these competitive wars, what I remember is the spirit. It felt as though we were in the middle of a military war, with lives and national territories at stake. I ask myself: Why do sensible, peace-loving human beings engage in what seems like a boyish sport? Is it a desire for wealth or fame or power? Is this the only way to be a hero in our commercial age, when the glory of kings and empires from an earlier, feudal time has become a faint, nostalgic memory? Pale, boring economists explain it as 'maximizing utilities'. But Adam Smith termed it as 'bettering our human condition', something, he felt, that came to us from the womb and never left us till we went to the grave.

15

The Mask Falls

'If at first you don't succeed,
try, try again. Then quit.
There's no point in being a damn fool.'

—W.C. Fields

In the golden summer of 1991, India finally won its economic freedom. It dawned on me that we had only been partially free so far. When the British left in 1947, we had only got our political independence. We had to wait another forty-four years to become properly free. A human bomb had killed innocent, idealistic Rajiv Gandhi earlier that summer. Since no one in the dynasty was ready to take over, the Congress party chose Narasimha Rao as prime minister. He was quiet, dull and seventy, threatening no one. They saw him as a 'stopgap' to head a minority government that no one thought would last very long. But he surprised everyone, unleashing the biggest revolution in India's economic history. His finance minister, Manmohan Singh, embarked on a bold programme of economic liberalization, which opened the economy to foreign investment and trade, dismantled import controls, virtually abolished licensing in industry, broke public-sector monopolies, lowered tax rates and customs duties, and devalued the currency.

The collapse of communism in 1989 had pulled the rug out from under the domineering Soviet Union. India's anti-statist reforms did the same. They exploded the myths of the Licence Raj that Mrs Gandhi had so lovingly peddled with such charm on that spring morning in 1984. With the opening of the economy, India did not lose its sovereignty, even though foreign investment rose thirty-fold. The Indian entrepreneur, freed from controls, responded with investment, creating new jobs. Demand rose; markets and competition grew. By 1993, inflation would fall from 13 per cent to 6 per cent a year and foreign exchange reserves would shoot up from $1 billion to $20 billion. The economy's growth rate was rising. Government revenues also grew, despite lower tax rates. It was quite an achievement—as important a turning point as Deng Xiaoping's revolution in China in December 1978.

But I'm getting ahead of myself. When Narasimha Rao came to power India was bankrupt, and his first decision was to get a good finance minister. His choice was I.G. Patel, who had returned recently, having headed the London School of Economics. But it did not work out, so he settled for a younger man: the reticent and soft-spoken economist Manmohan Singh. Rao also brought in a tough, action-oriented principal secretary, Amarnath Varma, who had championed delicensing in the previous government. Under Varma, Rao set up a steering committee of secretaries that met on Thursday mornings to push the reforms forward. I recall my excitement on Friday mornings, opening the *Economic Times* to find the announcement of a new reform. It felt like Diwali every Friday! But once the crisis passed, the pressure diminished, and the reforms stopped. There was no national soul-searching about the failure of the state socialism of Nehru and Indira Gandhi. The commissars of the Licence Raj quietly become liberalizers. The reformers didn't bother to sell the reforms. It was all 'hush-hush', for fear of the Left, particularly the powerful left wing of the Congress party. 'Reform by stealth' became India's new mantra.

While history was being made, my company decided to transfer me to its global headquarters to head worldwide strategic planning for the health and beauty business. I was reluctant to leave at this crucial moment in our country's history. But I had already spent the previous ten years running the Indian company (during which span I had added South-East

Asia to my sphere of responsibility). It was unusual to spend a decade in
a single position in a multinational company. The company suggested a
headquarters assignment to prepare me for a role of higher responsibility.
Bunu was not keen on moving either, feeling nicely settled in Bombay.
But she quickly changed her mind, realizing that she would be closer to the
boys, who were both in college now—Kim at the University of Chicago
and Puru at Vassar College.

The company agreed to let me take a short sabbatical before the
shift to 'recharge my batteries' So, Bunu and I found ourselves spending
the autumn semester of 1991 at Harvard. The master of Quincy House
had read my novel, and he thought it would be nice to have a 'writer-in-
residence' (especially when he didn't have to cover my costs; the company
was paying my salary). He offered us a comfortable faculty suite that
had been occupied in the past by the legendary poet Robert Lowell and
the famous theologian Reinhold Niebuhr. The neighbouring suite was
assigned to Mario Vargas Llosa, who would go on to win the Nobel Prize
in Literature and run for the presidency of Peru. Surrounding us were,
thus, stirring vibrations from the past and the future. I sat in on a number
of courses in history, economics and philosophy. The highlight was a
seminar on inequality by Amartya Sen, John Rawls and T.M. Scanlon.
Bunu attended lectures on Renaissance painting and Chinese ceramics.
Time passed quickly, and before long I had to get back to work. The only
thing I had to show for my sabbatical was an article, titled 'Local Memoirs
of a Global Manager', in *Harvard Business Review.*

'If youth is a defect,' says Lowell, 'it is one that we outgrow too soon.'
In my case, I never outgrew my youthful enthusiasm for ideas, remaining
a perpetual undergraduate. Lowell also wrote, 'In the end, there is no end.'
And I would soon discover this truth.

On my first day at the headquarters in Cincinnati, I arrived dutifully
in a white shirt and dark suit. Colours were frowned upon at HQ, I'd
been warned. There was an elaborate ritual before I got to my desk. I
announced myself to the suspicious guard at the reception. After asking
me a battery of questions, he phoned Human Resources. He got clearance
to issue me an electronic card allowing temporary access to certain parts of
the building. I then made a fool of myself trying to operate the electronic
door. I inserted the pass into the slot one way. Nothing happened. Then I
tried it the other way. Still nothing. Meanwhile, a harried assistant arrived

from Human Resources, apologizing profusely. She explained that I was using the card back to front and swiped it correctly. She was remorseful that someone had forgotten to inform reception about my arrival.

It was weird to find that fortress, secured with electronic cards and unfriendly doors, in the open-hearted, neighbourly Midwest. After this creepy welcome, I felt nostalgic for our Bombay office, where a smiling young woman at the reception directed you to where you had to go—no electronic cards, no signatures, no nothing. Admittedly, we were a smaller operation in Bombay. But first impressions do matter, and a consumer products company like ours ought to be more relaxed, offering old-fashioned courtesy, not an excess of suspicion. Yes, if we made fighter airplanes for the military, one could have understood. But even so, the threats of espionage, corporate theft, hacking came from disgruntled employees or from the Internet, not from day-to-day walk-ins.

I soon got absorbed in my work and settled into a routine. I had carried all my three lives with me—my public, private and secret lives—and this made the transition easier. Each morning, I would arrive in a white shirt, wearing the mask of a successful headquarters staffer. It was a convincing disguise that managed to conceal my discontent. After running a tempestuous business for ten years, it was not easy to get used to the humdrum life of a headquarters staffer. My boss was a sensitive man who quickly sensed my disaffection. He thought it might have had something to do with the provincial world of Cincinnati, where people were decent but dull. He suggested a compromise. For some time, he had been looking for a person to lead a team near London for the development of an important new health product. He felt I could do both the jobs, dividing my time between London and Cincinnati. My boss had a name for it: 'Dual-role, dual-located, bridged by Delta Airlines.' Bunu and I soon found a smart pied-à-terre in Kensington, London, right next to the gardens, conveniently situated near the A4, the route to my office. It was a glamorous global manager's life, but Bunu thought it would be disconcerting to live in two places.

It was not a bad life for a couple of years, until my mask decided to fall off one hot, muggy July morning in Cincinnati. The sky was a blaze of light, and the wind was picking up rapidly. The NPR reporter on my car radio was going on about how the reforms had ground to a halt in India.

The powerful left wing of the Congress party had reasserted itself. The PM was on the back foot, and there was the danger that liberalization would soon be unravelled. I was sickened by the news. On entering my office I found a stack of documents on my desk that my secretary had placed there that morning. They were Nielsen market shares from around the world of some P&G brands. I sat and stared at the pile for what seemed an eternity. Eventually, I began to scan through the figures, and a feeling of nausea came over me. I wiped the sweat running down my face and went to open the window. I could not because of the central air-conditioning. I looked helplessly at the cloudless sky.

Back at the desk, I struggled to focus on the paperwork. Wanting to make some notes, I tried to open the drawer of my desk to get out my yellow pad. But I found my arm was frozen. A cold object in my hand held my attention for a time. Eventually, I opened my hand. I was holding the knob of the drawer. It scared me. Trying to calm myself, I kept repeating, 'It's nothing, nothing is the matter with me. Perhaps, I ought to divert my mind.' So I pulled out of my briefcase a new translation of the Gita, which I had picked up at the Ohio Book Store on Main Street. At random, I began to read Chapter 5 of the two-thousand-year-old philosophical poem. It didn't help. I continued to feel anxious. I didn't think I would be able to last through the morning, I decided. So I told my secretary to cancel all my meetings, and I fled.

I should have gone home, but I drove around randomly. The sun was strong, the glare off the road unnerving. I could smell the reek of the gasoline. At Skyline Chili on East Fourth Street, I turned on to Main Street. Passing Walgreens, I found myself on Vine Street, facing Kroger's. It was strangely quiet that morning. On Saturday, it had been buzzing with shoppers pillaging the aisles. I spotted a Dunkin' Donuts and was tempted to stop for coffee, but a raffish-looking man in the window put me off. I turned on to Route 22, where I passed the Greyhound bus station on my left. Soon, I was going past Eden Park in Walnut Hills. Still feeling uneasy, I decided to stop to cool off. It was a working day; the park was empty. I spotted a bench under a shady old willow oak that someone must have planted fifty years back; they never got to sit under its shade, I thought. The air was throbbing with the hum of insects on the warm grass. I felt a wave of heat on my back.

I must have been a sight: a Brown Hindu sitting alone in a suit on a working day. A scruffy man was coming towards me, limping slightly, wiping the sweat from the crown of his head.

'Sun's pretty bad, ain't it? Not a good day to bury someone.'

His cousin had died. He hadn't been so old, the man said. 'They said, he'd live to be a hundred.' He looked again at the sky and began to fan himself with a handkerchief. I watched as he moved on with his limp. I stretched my legs, thinking it would ease the crowded feeling in my chest. Suddenly, I remembered the pile of papers sitting on my desk. The company had a 'clean-desk' policy—one had to put away all papers before leaving. I had broken the policy. The lunacy of my situation hit me again. A grown man in a starched white shirt, with a pointless piece of cloth tied to his neck like a dog collar, going to work day after day to sell a few more cases of Vicks, Oil of Olay, Pantene shampoo—all good products, but there is a limit!

'Is this what life is all about?' I asked myself.

Meanwhile, historic reforms at home were in danger of crumbling, threatening to dash the hopes of a billion Indians. I was in the wrong place at the wrong time, once again. I was almost fifty and weary. I had gone to work each day, fed and looked after my family. My wife and I had raised two children. Gradually, I had moved up the corporate ladder with higher pay, more responsibility. My children would probably follow me on this path, and their children after them. But to what end?

The absurd is born when the human need to know confronts the unreasonable silence of the universe. The human always loses. The universe, nature, animals and plants—they were normal, not needing to know why they existed. Then, as if on cue, the voices arrived. I wanted to laugh because I could not cry. But how can a man laugh alone? One of the voices was accusing me of worrying about Vicks's market share in Belgium when a fire was raging back home. To escape the screeching voices, I rushed to the toilet near the parking lot. I splashed water over and over again on my face. I looked in the mirror. What I saw was a look of shocked incomprehension. Next, my life flashed by before my eyes.

It is kindergarten, I've stolen the rich kid's pencil box, the blame is falling on Ayan. All of a sudden, it is Alisha sniggering at the roses on the lunch table. Next, it is the school vice principal's turn at Roosevelt High; he is advising me that coloured boys are not s'posed to get too big for their boots. Out of the blue,

*it is Mexico: Bunu has slaved all day over dinner, but no one is showing up.
It's a nightmare, and it isn't ending. I am being threatened now with jail for
overproducing VapoRub!*

I was scared. All I could think of was how to shut the nightmare off. I
had to quit my job, get off the rat race. The trouble with a rat race is that
even if you come first, you're still a rat. I had to go home, speak to Bunu.

The hot air was still blowing when I came out of the men's room.
I looked at the green of the park, the sunlight bouncing off the waxy
leaves. The light winked off the cars going past the strip just beyond the
curb. The parking lot was empty. Instead of going home by the direct
route, I meandered. Then I discovered I was lost. Eventually, I found my
way home through Cincinnati's most depressing strip. It was wide and
flanked by K-Mart, CVS, Taco Bell and Pizza Hut. The assault continued
with gas stations, banks, home suppliers, law offices, chiropractors and
knee replacement centres. I was in a daze—stopping now, starting again at
each overhead light. Finally, I reached leafy Indian Hill, where the grand
houses seemed to mock me. It felt like I was at a movie set, a place that
was unnatural and synthetic. The previous week I had read about a man
who had bought an opulent apartment on the ninety-first floor of a new
skyscraper in Manhattan. A week later, he had quietly opened the window
and jumped to his death.

Bunu was surprised to see me. How come I was home early? I wasn't
in the mood to talk, but she was insistent. So I let it out slowly. She grew
concerned when I mentioned the voices. When my tale came to an end, she
announced baldly, 'Oh, it's only a mid-life crisis. Happens to everyone.'

Well, that's a relief, I thought sarcastically. Bunu knew all about
midlife crises from post-war American novels. The hero gets to the top of
the ladder, then realizes the ladder is perched against the wrong wall. This
was supposed to happen to White, middle-aged American males in grey
flannel suits. Not to Brown Hindus? She looked at me: yes, I was the right
age. Her eyes made a broad sweep of our surroundings. Yes, I was at the
right place. She looked at our sprawling house, across five acres in a posh
suburb, with a green Jaguar XJ in the driveway. Yes, the symbols of success
were everywhere. We had money, position, even a nest egg for retirement.
Plus, two grown-up boys, both doing well in college. I played tennis at
the country club, she played bridge with her friends. Yes, I was the perfect
candidate for a midlife calamity!

'You don't think this candidate is me, actually *me*, do you?' I protested. I was merely a second-rate actor playing a role in a play—admittedly, a long-running play. The midlife crisis was happening to the character I was playing, not to me. It had been draining, frankly—always playing a part, forever wearing a mask to hide the short, Brown Hindu kid, who had fled with his life and his family at Partition. I had been running ever since: getting good marks in school, paying attention at the university, climbing ladders at work. Again, to what end? 'Is this what life is all about?' I repeated.

Trying to humour me, Bunu said that I had done a pretty good job of my one-man show, all things considered. Yes, I had. I had made everyone believe, including myself, that the parts I had been playing were, collectively, my true self. No one had bothered to see beyond the performing self. Even I had forgotten if there was anything beyond the performance. 'And why?' she asked impatiently, adding, 'Because you are good at your work.' Not only good, but she felt that I actually enjoyed it, despite my protests. She reminded me of my last job, the time when adrenaline rushed through my veins as I helped to rescue my company in Bombay.

'So, stop moping around!'

I fell silent. I could only feel my pain. She went to the kitchen and returned with a glass of warm milk and cookies. It had happened before, she reminded me softly. The voices would go away, and I would bounce back as I always did. 'It must be the two birds, raising hell again!' she tried to reassure me. As we were turning in that night, she repeated, 'Don't worry, this too will go away.'

But it did not. I did not go to work the next day. She called my office and told my secretary that I wasn't feeling well and wouldn't be coming to work for a few days. The few days became a few weeks, and I did not get better. I felt exhausted, growing more and more unhappy with each passing day. I felt I had wasted my life.

'Wasted? That's a bit strong, isn't it?' she said.

She adopted an indulgent tone, as one does with a difficult child. She asked if I wanted to see a doctor. On hearing 'doctor', I felt a sense of doom. She could tell I wasn't all there. 'You're sounding different—so distant!' I refused to see a doctor, spending my enforced holiday mostly lounging about the house. I tried to don my writer's hat, play a different

part, in a different play. I had begun work on a new book, but it hadn't
been going well. It failed totally to engage me now. Bunu realized that I
wanted to be alone and gave me a lot of space.

I felt thirsty one morning when she was out at the supermarket. I went
to the kitchen, opened the fridge and poured a glass of lemonade. I went
outside and sat in the shade. There I got a sinking feeling as I looked at
the house, which wasn't mine. Going to the bedroom, I felt the bed wasn't
mine. I rushed to the children's rooms, and the boys were not mine. It
was someone else living my life. Someone had got my job, become my
wife's husband and my children's father. The moorings of my life had
disappeared.

A few days later, I found myself in the afternoon beneath the deck
of our house. I was mesmerized watching an ant struggling to climb up a
heap of sand. Did it realize how comical, how absurd it was? I turned to
look at myself. Who was I judging when my own life was similar? Except
one thing: I was aware of my ridiculous situation. Bunu had reminded
me of the Upanishadic birds. Unlike the ant, I was able to step back and
observe myself. What made my life absurd was the gap between inflated
pretensions and the stark reality. The acting bird couldn't help taking
his day-to-day life seriously, playing the role with energy, diligence and
full attention. The witness bird, however, was telling me that I was
only a speck; my projects did not matter to the universe. Why, then,
take myself so seriously? The more I watched the ant struggle, the more
ludicrous I felt.

As the days went by, I felt more and more hopeless. Hopelessness,
however, can give birth to a new hope. One night, I lay on the grass
behind the house and watched the stars. Soon, I was lost, rapt in awe
of their beauty. It was astounding that I was seeing the light from the
stars and galaxies that had perished billions of years ago. It was the first
time in weeks that I had felt anything. Over the years, my professional
life, living out the rhythms of the day's transactions, had pretty much
killed all sense of mystery. Even the word 'awe' had lost its meaning
in America—people used 'awesome' for anything they liked. But that
night, looking at the stars, I paused in wonder. The universe was larger
than I could ever imagine, full of brightly lit and countless galaxies and
solar systems beyond, and, who knows, even civilizations, with people
like us thinking the same thoughts, fighting their own wars.

In a very real sense, I was insignificant. What better reason than that to not take myself too seriously? I had grown weary of seriousness. All the talk of a midlife crisis was making me believe that I was awfully important. Slowly, questions began to pop up in my head. What did I really believe in? I circled around God. People had been circling there for thousands of years. And where had that got them? In any case, I was too far from the sacred, unable to make the leap of faith. There was also a nagging feeling that my sort of moksha entailed freedom from imprisonment by religion. And so, beneath the silent beauty of the stars, I continued to question. This went on for a week, night after night of wonder. There were only questions, no answers.

These nights of awe and wonder began to fill me gradually with new energy. The universe was not cold, silent and mute—it was a noisy place. Yes, my problems were negligible in the big picture, but there was something comforting to know that there were innumerable beings here and elsewhere, who might be asking the same questions. Absurdity and awe might be two sides of the same existential coin. The first led to lonely nihilism; the other led to wonder. One needed to experience absurdity to see the senselessness of life; one needed to experience wonder to make sense of it.

I informed Bunu that the time had come. I'd had enough of hovering between the fool and the sage, and I was ready for action. She was relieved until she realized that 'action' meant quitting my job.

'But how will we live?' she wailed in horror.

Now was the time to do what I really wanted, I told her, not what others expected. I would need a new mask, of course. Putting on the same one would mean repeating the same old mistakes. I was guilt-ridden for being so far away from my real home, where history was unfolding, where the economic future of a billion people was on the line.

'What can *you* do about it?' she moaned. 'You're not in politics or government. You're no policy expert. Who'll listen to you?'

All good questions. I had thought about them. I told her that I would write and speak and try to convince people about the reforms. After all, I had been honing my skills for twenty-five years as a weekend writer. I would write columns in newspapers, persuade people by the strength of my ideas and arguments. Now was the time to find out how good I was at convincing people.

I wrote a letter that afternoon to Manmohan Singh, the finance minister. It was a shot in the dark, although I had met him casually when he was a small fry. He knew about me from my encounter with Indira Gandhi. He remembered that I was the only businessman who had dared to question the Empress about the holy grail of Nehruvian socialism. I wrote to ask him if I he had any use for me. Could I help him 'sell' the reforms to people? I also wrote to Dilip Padgaonkar at the *Times of India* and T.N. Ninan at *Business Standard*. I had written a few pieces for both in the past. I told them that I was thinking of returning to India. Would they be interested in a regular column?

The rest of the evening I spent adding up our savings; then, calculating how much income they would generate if we invested them sensibly. Next, I sat with Bunu to figure out what our expenses would be each month. Like an accountant, I worked for hours, making what is called today an 'Excel sheet'. After copying the numbers on a single sheet of ruled yellow paper, I took it to Bunu.

'We can do it!' I announced proudly. Our standard of living wouldn't go up from here onwards, but it wouldn't go down too much, hopefully.

She was sceptical. We already owned a house, thanks to her prodding years ago. 'Everyone needs an address,' she used to say, trying to convince me. So we had bought a house in Delhi. 'Why Delhi?' she had asked at the time. We had lived most of our married life in Bombay—all our friends were there. It must have been a premonition! I must have known deep down that I would quit the corporate rat race one day to become a commentor on national issues. I agreed with her that Bombay's people were nicer, but Delhi had a richer intellectual life. It was also closer to Chandigarh, where my parents lived, and to Kathmandu, Bunu's home.

The idea of being a full-time writer was exciting, I felt. But to her, it was a scary thought—too much work, too little money. And those sarky columns in the *Times of India*? At first it would be thrilling to see my name on the edit page, but that too would soon lose its shine, she said cynically. She couldn't understand why I was chasing a crazy ephemera. Here I was at the top of my career. Shouldn't I be harvesting all the years of hard work? I had reached a high enough level at my job, where money, stock options would now come rushing my way. I had fifteen years left for this bonanza before retirement. It was senseless, giving it all up. And for what?

An uncertain career in journalism, so late in life. It was not a brave act—it was madness.

'But don't we have enough?' I protested. I had just proven it to her on the ruled yellow sheet.

In her heart, Bunu knew I was burnt out. For years, I had been asking the same question: What am I doing peddling Oil of Olay, Pantene, Tide and Pampers and Vicks? The voices had been insistent. Others might value what I was doing, but to my mind it had become rubbish work. As to my new-found career as a full-time writer, I felt that life was not so much about finding oneself but about creating oneself. Even if I failed, I would have given it a shot. If life is supposed to be a low-stakes game, this was a low-stakes decision. It was an opportunity, in fact, to live with a different attitude. I wanted to try and live my new life with cheerful amusement; relearn the old mantra of laghima—lighten up, live lightly, like a bird.

In the end, Bunu was a good sport, and she agreed. She would miss the big house, the status, the first-class lounges and being the wife of a somebody rather than a nobody. What eventually convinced her, she told me, was my genuine desire to do good, something beyond myself. She could tell that what was driving me to become a cheerleader for the reforms was love for my country and my people. Economic liberalization was a ticket for the poor to cross the poverty line to a decent life of dignity. We phoned the children in the evening. They were not surprised and were generally supportive.

The next day, I went back to work to resign. I wasn't sure whether to knock or walk right into my boss's office. Should I tap deferentially or rap loudly enough to be heard at once and command admission? I had rehearsed my resignation speech and was building up the courage to deliver it. I had formulated earnest, self-righteous answers to accusing questions about my reasons for leaving. As I waited, my mind jumped ahead.

They would soon forget me once I was gone. They would give my office to someone else. They would file me away, all traces gone, in some green cabinet in a dusty warehouse across the river. Just as I was getting lost in those thoughts, the door opened, and my boss came out. He was solicitous and wanted to know how I was feeling. Putting his arm around my shoulder, he led me into his office. His secretary brought us coffee.

After she left, I gave my short speech. He leaned back in his chair and laughed. 'Let me get this straight. You want to quit a job that is high-paying, that you're good at, that gives you the flexibility to live on two continents. And for what? For something badly paid with no status, doing something that you've never done before?' He was genuinely concerned. He felt I was throwing away a lifetime's work and a chance to rise to the top.

'I don't want the top?'

'Everyone wants the top!'

If I was bored with what I was doing, there were other jobs in the company. I could head one of the larger countries. I wanted a different life, I explained. He was genuinely trying to help me, trying to understand what I was going through. I explained that I was tired of this sort of life.

'Really?' He was surprised. 'I find this life quite good enough.' Humans had conquered so many diseases. Everyone's standard of living was going up. Yes, there were problems in America, but nothing that couldn't be fixed by America's institutions. I asked him if he really was comfortable in the corporate world. 'Right at home,' he said. Maybe I just needed a break. I should go back home, think things over and come back when I felt better. A change of scene would do me good.

I got up to leave. He was staring out of the window, happy in his gilded cage. But the door to my moksha had sprung open, and I was ready to fly out. As I reached the door, he gave me a final piece of advice. Why only be a cheerleader for the reforms? I should become a reformer. Go into politics, spread the message of free markets.

'If you leave politics to fools, you'll be ruled by fools,' were his last words.

By that evening I had quit. The company had been generous. Convinced that I was intent on a different sort of life—I wasn't going to join a competitor—it decided to designate my separation as 'early retirement'. This meant that I would receive all my retirement benefits. Driving home that evening, I looked out the window at the leafy suburb of Indian Hill and felt a stab of guilt. Had I made a mistake? If I had stayed on, I would probably have continued in this tranquil world of suburban respectability among people who valued me and my abilities. It would have been a private, anonymous life of understated luxury. If I retired at sixty-five, I would transition into a life of ease amid corporate boards, golf and opulent travel.

It was a passing thought, and it died quickly. It might have been an attractive life for many, but it wasn't for me. It could not have satisfied my new-found hunger and imagination. There is an Ancient Greek word, *thymos*, which means 'spiritedness', and it captures the ambition I was feeling to become the new kind of man I wanted to be. There are few people like Kamble, blessed with sunny temperaments, who love any sort of work, and they make a life of it. There are others who are craftsmen, and they make a life getting better at their craft. Well, writing is a craft, and my experience as a weekend writer had shown me that I, too, could make a life of it. But how could I be sure? Because I had experienced it over countless weekends when I could quickly get into the zone, forgetting myself and the world, remaining absorbed for hours together.

This chapter of my life was a critical milestone in my journey to another sort of freedom. When my mask fell, I was reminded that I am two people. One is the person who appears to others, a successful man of the world. The other is hidden, not only from the world but also from myself. The inner me sometimes subdues the outer one, but it doesn't happen often, because the outer person wears a mighty social mask. Ever since I can remember, society has conspired to create this convincing disguise, and I have grown so attached to it that I feel naked without it. This is why my inner self is a secret.

There are many who earn a livelihood and who must have experienced similar misgivings with their work. They will find echoes of their own life here. Lifetime jobs are increasingly rare now, and there are HR counsellors to deal with such issues. My boss had, in fact, suggested meeting one, but it was too late—I had made up my mind to quit. If my experience holds, here is a lesson on coping with disaffection at your job: cultivate a vocation, wear a second hat over the weekend. It must be an authentic and serious pursuit, however, which so deeply absorbs you to be capable of becoming a lifelong commitment. One must keep at it diligently, giving one's best. It will not only serve as an insurance policy against boredom or disaster at the workplace, but it can also become a second career, as it did in my case.

My midlife crisis was at its heart a moksha crisis—a desperate cry to be free from the many burdens of human bondage. To begin with, a duty to make a living. I couldn't have quit my job earlier because the kids were young, and we didn't have a nest egg. Another was a sense of obligation towards my company, which had been good to me, nurturing me, giving me opportunities in good and bad times. There was also a conflict between the two sides of my own nature—a hunger for the life of action, which I inherited from my mother, versus a wish for a life of thought, which I got from my father. I struck some sort of balance by wearing two hats—one on weekdays, another on weekends. In the end, the contradiction between the two impulses became too great—the balance got lost. I kept running into the absurd, feeling trapped by the utter meaninglessness of my day-to-day existence. The mask eventually fell off in sultry, suburban Cincinnati, of all places.

16

Possibilities

'... we know what we are,
but know not what we may be.'

—William Shakespeare, *Hamlet*

We landed in the early morning of 1 January 1995 at Delhi's Palam airport. To our surprise, we were out of the customs hall in seconds, smiling and wheeling our trolleys towards the taxi stand. It was our first encounter with the reforms. The next day's newspaper offered a clue. Customs had loosened up because India's foreign exchange reserves had blossomed, touching $25 billion (compared to $1 billion during the 1991 crisis.) It explained why we were not subjected to a humiliating search for dutiable goods in our luggage. How quickly attitudes can change!

We gave our address to the taxi driver. I was still drowsy, but I got a warm feeling to be among brownskins again. They were my people, and I liked being among them. As the taxi got on its way, I was seduced by memories: I am ten, bicycling to Modern School, and before I know it monsoon rain is breaking over my head. The taxi came to an abrupt stop at Safdarjung's tomb. It was a red light, jolting me into the present. I looked out of the window as we passed Lodi Gardens. A boy was walking to school. One of a billion Indians, he was the sum total of all who had come before him and all who would follow him. His story was his own—there were as many Indias as there were Indians. My love for India has mostly to do with memories of growing up; of fabulous gods and kingdoms; of the holy Ganges flowing down from Shiva's tresses. It has little to do with the nationalism of power that would soon take hold in India with the rise of the right-nationalist BJP.

Liberated from my job, I could now shed my mask, along with my dark suit and tie, and tightly laced black shoes. I replaced them with a loose kurta and sandals. Breathing freely, with nowhere to go in the mornings, I felt another sort of freedom. I was in life's third stage, Vanaprastha, and was expected to live a quiet, meditative life of ease after a noisy quarter century of business. Working to the clock had made me a creature of habit, diminishing my faculties to a dull apathy. Release from deadly routine meant new possibilities. I could wake up late, read the newspaper unhurriedly over tea, go for a walk in the park, delight in Delhi's spring flowers. I could follow this up with a slow, luxurious bath; then, answer a few letters to friends on the veranda, shaded lightly from the morning sun. All this before a leisurely lunch and a nap in the afternoon. It was an alluring prospect.

I actually tried to live this fantasy for a few days. But I got bored. Pleasure was not enough. The good life needed purpose. Rather than pursuing pleasure deliberately, it was better to let it descend on one, surprise one. To make myself whole again, I began to ditch my old self. But my new self was unknown terrain. To be a full-time writer seemed scary. The uncertain fate of the 1991 reforms had summoned me home. But where to begin in this ludicrous quest? Cervantes's words gave me courage: 'To attain the impossible, you must attempt the absurd.'

Going by the headlines, India was in a free fall. The minority government was beleaguered, facing regular no-confidence motions in Parliament. The Congress party was hopelessly divided, with a new rebellion breaking out each week. There was no clear leadership. Prime Minister Narasimha Rao, father of the reforms, was under attack by his own party. It was incredible: this was India's great moment, and neither Rao nor the Congress party wanted to take credit for saving the country from an economic disaster and setting it on a path of high growth. Why didn't economic success translate into political gains?

I decided to find out. Donning a new hat of a frisky freelance journalist, I began interviewing people—politicians, technocrats, business leaders. Barring a few exceptions, no one in the political class was enthusiastic about the reforms. Government officials complained that the reforms were not 'Indian', implemented under pressure from the World Bank and the International Monetary Fund. The Left's reaction was predictable: the rich were getting richer, the poor poorer. A Bengali member of Parliament couldn't understand why India needed more than one airline—competition was a waste, a plot of the imperial West. Businesspeople had mixed views. Some were delighted that licensing was gone, business was freer. Others grumbled about the lack of a level playing field against foreign competitors. An influential group, the Bombay Club, was afraid that foreign companies would wipe out Indian companies.

All this was very discouraging, especially when the numbers were telling a different story. Inflation had fallen, exports were up, foreign exchange reserves were comfortable, state revenues had risen despite lower tax rates, and the economy's growth rate was rising. It was a real turnaround, and Narasimha Rao and Manmohan Singh were heroes. But this was not how Delhi saw it. Politics was going one way, the economy another. I couldn't understand why everyone was down on the prime minister, and I decided to meet him. It wasn't easy. I had to pester Amarnath Varma, his principal secretary, for days before I got an appointment. Rao met me at his home one day at 7 a.m. He had just come out of his bath, looking fresh in a starched white lungi.

As we sat down, Rao was at pains to convince me that he was a loyal Congressman, merely continuing the party's socialist legacy. He was cautious, defensive about the reforms, insisting that he was merely trying to bring efficiency to the system. He kept talking about 'reforms with a human face'. It was a bizarre conversation. While I was applauding him for being a hero like Deng Xiaoping, he was trying to hide his achievements. Ironically, communist China had embraced capitalism more enthusiastically than socialist India. Deng in China was leading from the front, making historic changes, shedding Mao's legacy openly. Rao, in democratic India, was defensive, secretive about changing India's path from Nehru's Fabian socialism to a free-market economy.

Narasimha Rao was a reluctant liberalizer, I concluded. If he couldn't convince me, what chance did the poor voter have? Manmohan Singh did try to sell the reforms, but he was not a charismatic speaker. He couldn't articulate in simple language the significance of economic freedom. He had sent an enthusiastic reply to my offer from Cincinnati, but it only reached after I had left. He was warm and welcoming—he asked if I wanted a job. I did not. Instead, I planned to write vigorously about his reforms, and he encouraged me to do so.

It is not easy to appreciate the market. Adam Smith called it an 'invisible hand'. This is why Britain's passionate reformer, Margaret Thatcher, claimed that she spent 20 per cent of her time doing the reforms and 80 per cent selling them. Rao failed even to convince his own party. So, in the 1996 elections, the people booted out Rao and his party, and this happened in the midst of the best years in India's economic life. Many in the Congress party blamed the reforms for the loss. Even today, India's political class believes that reforms come at an electoral cost. The invisible hand is, in fact, invisible. Thirty years after the 1991 reforms, Indians cannot distinguish between being pro-market and pro-business, and India continues to reform by stealth. All political parties are populist, and I feel nostalgia for good old Swatantra, the only classical liberal party that India ever had, which had the courage to sell economic freedom.

Although no one in Delhi celebrated, Rao and Manmohan Singh's liberalization had set in motion profound changes across India. After the interviews, I wrote a series of op-eds in the *Times of India*. They must have left a mark because I was asked by the editor, T.N. Ninan, to travel around the country and write a long essay on how the reforms were changing the nation. I jumped at the idea. Promptly packing my bags, I left in less than a week. Before I knew it, I was breathing a different air. Unlike Delhi's politicians, ordinary Indians seemed freer, more optimistic, confident that their lives would be better. One of them was fourteen-year-old Raju. Hustling between tables at a roadside café in a small Tamil town, he mentioned casually that he was taking computer lessons. Why? Because he was going to run a computer company one day. I heard such stories again and again. It was the age of possibilities. The last time I had seen this optimism was when I was ten. I had seen it in my father's eyes and in the eyes of his team—they were building the Bhakra Dam.

Once again, I felt I had landed in another India—an India of the twenty-first century. What was happening in the bazaar could have been a chapter in world history. The turn from state socialism was a liberal revolution sweeping the globe after the fall of communism as country after country turned democratic and capitalist. Eric Hobsbawm, the Marxist historian, claimed that the 'short twentieth century' had ended in 1991, when communism collapsed with the fall of the Soviet Union. It had begun in 1914, at the start of the First World War. And during those seventy-seven years, democratic capitalism had defeated decisively its two main competitors, fascism and communism, heralding a new world order for the twenty-first century. Although a market-based liberal democracy wasn't perfect, it was better than any other, as it was all about securing personal liberty while delivering prosperity. Could one turn free trade and investment between nations—that is, globalization—into a force for good?

During my travels, I uncovered other liberations. I found, for example, that English was quietly becoming an Indian language. When I heard it in the bazaar, it sounded like a curious mixture of English and Hindi. They called it 'Hinglish'. It was all the rage among the young, whose minds, I felt, were confident and decolonized. Advertising slogans claimed 'Life ho toh aisi' and 'Dil mange more'. My newspaper boy assured me, 'Aaj busy hoon, kal bill milega, definitely.' The Bania's assistant warned me about the vamp in our neighbourhood: 'Careful, sir-ji, voh dangerous hai!' The anchor on Zee News' evening bulletin offered a mix of three English and four Hindi words: 'Aaj Middle East mein peace ho gai!' Linguistic purists were horrified at this slang, but I loved it and began to pepper my English with 'acchas', 'chalos' and 'yaars'. It was a breathable idiom, loose like a sari, not buttoned up in a suit and tie. Indian English had been set free, turning into a hip party, full of babble and tomfoolery—everyone was welcome, provided you wanted to have fun.

We had, of course, been mixing English words with our mother tongues for a hundred years. But it had been an aspirational idiom earlier—a sign of upward mobility in the emerging middle classes. Hinglish (and its regional variants) was now the 'cool' and liberating way of speaking in upper-middle-class drawing rooms. It made me wonder what language Indians would be speaking a hundred years from now. Hinglish? The English language, too, had grown out of an Anglo–Saxon mixture in the bazaar during the fourteenth century, when the upper classes spoke French and the educated clergy spoke Latin. But then Shakespeare came along a hundred years later. Borrowing freely from everywhere, he made English into a great language. Would Hinglish have to wait for a Shakespeare?

Salman Rushdie had begun to set Indian English free by 'chutnefying' the language, but this was not Hinglish. He had come a decade too soon; Hinglish had yet to become ubiquitous.

I wasn't too worried about being deracinated—the old, colonial disease that had so troubled Edward Said. I now believed that a person could be multirooted, like the banyan tree. Languages tend to evolve naturally, and one shouldn't get too anxious. The mumukshu libertarian in me certainly did not want the state to interfere, telling us what to speak. It's true that I still felt embarrassed speaking English in a country where only a tiny minority understood it. I spoke Hindi or Punjabi in the bazaar to shopkeepers, taxi drivers and to those who helped around the house. But they were the 'supporting cast' of my life. Although English was becoming an Indian language, it still defined a caste.

My essay, based on my three-month odyssey, appeared as a cover story titled 'A Million Reformers' in *Business World.* To see one's work in print is a great kick for any writer. The word *thymos* in Ancient Greek also means a desire for recognition. All human beings want to be somebody, not a nobody, and I was no different. The article made an impact, and I was suddenly in demand. It had slotted me in a niche, however. If I had carried a calling card, it would have read 'Cheerleader for the Reforms'. But I felt that I had a bigger story to tell. Should I write a novel? No, I didn't have the imagination of Tolstoy. What about a memoir? That was too personal, and you needed to be somebody before anyone would want to read you. What about a collection of short stories? No, again. It was beyond my competence—only a Chekov could pull off such a delicious dish. Since the essay had worked, I settled on the long narrative form. I had found a voice and a prose style using the first person, which allowed my mind to meander. It was a malleable style, letting me blend memoir, observation, speculation and opinion.

I began excitedly to work on *India Unbound,* my first book of non-fiction. But it was slow going; I wasted too much time. I used to promise myself each night, 'I shall write a thousand words tomorrow.' The next morning, walking from my bedroom to my study, I would get waylaid by the newspapers and dawdle over them over cups of tea. On some days, my overbearing neighbour would corner me, insisting on a walk in the Lodi Gardens. There was a smiling do-gooder who made me join her morning yoga class—'it's good for you.' There were other time-wasters:

emails, phone calls, social media. Before I realized it, the morning was gone. There were other promises to keep: an approaching deadline for a magazine article; someone's manuscript sitting on the shelf, waiting for a foreword; a television debate in the evening. There was always something that put me on someone else's agenda. By the evening, I would get the awful feeling that my book had not moved an inch.

So I set a routine. I promised myself that I would go directly to my study at 6 a.m. and write till noon. No newspapers, no morning walks, no yoga—none of the things that sensible people did. On my desk, I placed other prohibitions: no email, no messages, no social media, no phone calls (unless the house was on fire). I got a secretary to answer the phone and emails, do bank work, pay utility bills; I was not to be disturbed till after lunch. At noon, after writing for six hours, I would go for a swim at the Delhi Gymkhana Club next door and follow it with a relaxed lunch with Bunu. After that, I would actually lie down for an hour, often reading the newspaper. Only after 2.30 p.m. did I meet my secretary and attend to the affairs of the world. Early evening was social time, when I met people. I would persuade them to join me for a walk in the Lodi Gardens. Around 6.30 or 7 p.m., it was the time to relax: I would walk across to the India International Centre or the India Habitat Centre, where there was always a movie or a concert or a book talk. Finally, dinner around eight or so, then a bit of reading or TV, and I would be asleep by ten. I have been doing this for twenty-five years.

There is irony here. Writing is about spontaneity, imagination and freedom—the opposite of a rigid discipline. Yet, to make writing possible, one needs a life of habit, self-control and order. When I quit the salaryman's life, I was seeking freedom from the nine-to-five, deadening, grubby routine. Yet, I ended up replacing it with another rigid order. Habit provides the momentum that keeps me going now. Had the would-be writer waited for inspiration, he would still be standing at a street corner, waiting. A writer doesn't become a champion when his book comes out and fame begins. He becomes a champion in the lonely dailiness of his work. As someone addicted to moksha, I learnt that liberation dwells in discipline.

There were other problems in writing *India Unbound.* The first-person narrator tended to become self-indulgent and a bore. The difficulty was the big fat ego. While rereading the first draft, I found it narcissistic and self-absorbed. So I took a red pencil, brutally slashing the offending passages. I rewrote them, downplaying my own importance. I also wrote slowly, correcting as I went along while envying writers who polish off a book in a year. Sometimes, I agonized over a paragraph for an hour. The fifth draft was clearer, surer. I used to hope that writing would become easier with time, but it hasn't. It's every bit as hard as it was in the beginning. The act of writing is not romantic—it is hard work, perspiration, like any other job.

It took me four years to write *India Unbound,* but in the end I pulled it off. Penguin reported good early sales. It also got good reviews. It was the first book to predict the rise of India. India, too, would oblige over the next decade—not only by rising but surpassing even my own expectations. Soon, I acquired an agent in New York. Two top publishers fancied the book enough to begin a quiet bidding war. Thus, one afternoon, I found myself in Manhattan, in the luxurious Park Avenue apartment of the legendary, black-bearded Sonny Mehta, publisher of Alfred A. Knopf. By his side was his charming editor Robin Desser. I was in heaven, being wooed by a literary icon, who had published Nobel laureates and Pulitzer Prize winners.

Knopf bought my book with a fat advance that shocked me. Bunu was thrilled—she had already made up her mind that she was a starving writer's wife. Robin suggested a few important improvements in the book. When it came out, Knopf sent me on a three-week tour of American cities to promote the book. I enjoyed being made much of—staying in grand hotels, picked up in limousines, interviewed by local TV stations and newspapers. Then came the rave reviews in the *New York Times, Washington Post, Wall Street Journal* and other papers. They referred to it as 'literary non-fiction', which pleased me no end. It was just the beginning. *India Unbound* went on to be published in many languages, many countries, and was even filmed by the BBC. Fame and fortune were at my feet.

But I had much to learn about speaking in public. In the middle of my first book talk at the Asia Society in Manhattan, I began to read from my book. I thought this was what you did. When I looked up, the audience was asleep. Lesson #1: always look the audience in the eye. The greatest actor will fail if he tries to read from his book. Lesson #2: you need to pause, hesitate to hold an audience. Take a moment of impressive silence as you are searching for the right word. The naturalness of an impromptu narration captivates people. Lesson #3: appear modest, show a sense of your limitations. Lesson #4: always rehearse before getting on the stage.

Interviewers and audiences had a standard question: 'How did you begin to write?' I didn't have any formal training, I had to confess. But I felt that each course at Harvard had been a test in writing clearly, each term paper a lesson in composing clear, vigorous sentences. Thus, writing, for me, began as a way of tidying up my thinking.

'Did any book help you to write?' someone asked.

Yes, Strunk and White's *Elements of Style*. It taught me to write simply—as I speak, in an informal, relaxed way. 'Use the active voice,' it instructs. I have been active-voicing ever since. The book came with history. I told them how Miss Allen had handed me a torn copy of the book on my last day of high school. She, in turn, had been presented with it by her grandmother when she graduated from high school.

My mother was enjoying my literary success even more than I was. She couldn't stop talking about it, showing everyone reviews and photos. My parents visited us often, now that we lived only a half day's journey away by train. They had settled in the ashram at Beas after my father's retirement. He was helping to build a hospital there as a voluntary worker. She had been reluctant to leave her social circle, her status behind in Chandigarh. In the end, she had agreed, but only after my father promised to let her take all her mod cons to the ashram.

During one of her visits, she was concerned. Why was I was working 'like a maniac'? She wanted me to relax. 'Do you enjoy writing?' she asked. I wasn't sure. I only knew that I was drawn like a magnet each morning at six to my desk. My fingers would begin tapping the keys of my computer and words begin appearing on the screen. This would go on for the whole morning. I wouldn't even be aware that I existed, till, suddenly, I would look at the clock and utter, 'O my God, it's noon!' So how could I answer if I was enjoying myself? I wasn't even there. She gave me a weird look.

It was a novel experience to be living near the family. Both my brothers were settled in Delhi. So were numerous cousins of various shapes and sizes. Meera, too, was back. My parents had persuaded her to return from California. She was living in a 'what-if' trap. Each day, she looked back at the past, thinking of the paths not taken, not knowing whom to blame for her 'wasted life'. Sometimes, just carrying on is an achievement. Meera's unfulfilled life continued to cast a shadow on my happiness, reminding me of Tolstoy's opening line in *Anna Karenina*: 'All happy families are alike; each unhappy family is unhappy in its own way.' We were a normal family in other respects, neither too close nor too distant. Family problems don't have easy answers; one needs maturity to cope with them. My mother, as always, worried about everyone: How was I living without a monthly salary? Would my middle brother, 'America-returned' Manni, succeed in becoming an entrepreneur? Would Tutu, my youngest brother, cope after a failed marriage? A mother's love is like nothing else—it follows no rules, daring the world, not letting anything come in its way.

Our children were more blasé at my literary success. Kim Kanishka had graduated from the University of Chicago and was working in an advertising firm in New York. He eventually moved to Singapore in a global role. Puru, in his final year at Vassar College, was showing a flair for writing. We encouraged him to become a writer. After graduation, he set himself up in a small apartment in Greenwich Village in New York to write a novel. After a year, he found the experience too strange—all his friends were at work, doing things in the big world, while he was at home alone, sitting at his desk, staring at a blank sheet of paper. Admitting defeat, he joined an insurance company but quickly found that it wasn't the life he wanted. He made quick amends.

Passionate about the visual arts and interior design, he and his partner started a furniture company, whose products were based on their original designs. They shifted to India, setting up a factory near Delhi. Like any start-up, the business had its ups and downs, but it was hugely successful in the end. They worked hard, built a nice international brand: DeMuro Das. Eventually, they got a smart showroom in Manhattan and were covered regularly in design magazines and newspapers. They were beneficiaries of globalization, their entrepreneurial success reinforcing my conviction about the virtues of free trade.

Life, they say, begins and ends with family. It may well be true. They also say that family is everything, which is untrue. Yes, family is important, but too many people in Asia obsess over their children, living their lives through them, leaving the children trapped in family restraints. We were luckier. Our children had grown up relaxed—so laid-back, in fact, that Puru forgot to tell us that he was gay. He dropped this information casually while mentioning over dinner that he may not have enough half-sleeve shirts. 'I happen to prefer the same sex, but if you prefer the opposite, well, it's your life'—this was his attitude. We took his admission on his terms, and he appreciated our easy-going reaction. But we never spoke of it in public because homosexuality was still a criminal offence. This was until 12.35 p.m. on Thursday, 18 September 2018, when the Supreme Court decriminalized it. A great burden was lifted for Puru, for us, and for millions of Indians who had lived under a tyrannical colonial law for 157 years.

After five years of writing op-eds for the *Times of India*, I was invited to do a 750-word column on Sundays. A newspaper column is a short essay, a form of writing that owes its birth to Michel de Montaigne, a French official who temporarily retired in the 1570s and set up a room in his house, where he began to write his observations on life. He called them *essais*. Writing these 750 words was easy for me, oddly enough, because of Procter & Gamble's legendary one-page memo. (You weren't allowed to write more than a page at P&G. If it was longer, it was returned, unread.) It had been humbling for a Harvard graduate, CEO of the Indian subsidiary, an author of plays and a novel, to be sent to a P&G class to learn to write. I discovered that writing a memo is an art. There is an inherent conflict between the reader and writer. The writer of a memo wants to build a case slowly, leading to a conclusion. The busy reader wants the conclusion upfront. Brevity is a virtue. A memo is not a detective story; so a good first sentence has to tell the reader why she should be interested in what the writer has to say. And the last sentence has to offer her compelling reasons to believe the writer's conclusion.

What drove me to write my columns was a moral vision of a good society. The crushing weight of the Licence Raj had made me a libertarian. But my readers had been brainwashed for forty years in central planning and collective, statist solutions. Whereas I was suspicious of state power, they believed in a paternalistic 'mai–baap' state. To persuade them, I had to be open-minded, write colloquially. A newspaper column is persuasive when the writer is self-critical, aware of his limitations, and adopts an easy, modest manner. But it has to be authentic. It cannot be a pose. The problem is that when you have strong convictions, you tend to be assertive, not humble. You also spend so much time alone that your lump of ego begins to weigh a tonne. I could have done with a lesson in self-forgetting from Kamble.

Instead, I learnt it from my corner store. Although plastic was becoming increasingly common, my friendly grocer still wrapped her packages in newsprint. One evening, on the way home from the Lodi Gardens, I remembered I had to pick up a pack of dried fruits. She wrapped it in page 8 of the previous week's *Times of India*. Walking home, I found my column staring at me. And I thought it had been carved in stone when I wrote it. Its short shelf life was a shock and a lesson in humility.

All things considered, it had been a risky decision to quit my job at the peak. It could have gone all wrong. Luckily, I made a soft landing, managing to come out of my midlife crisis in one piece. It's easier to create a new self than to mend a broken one. When I returned to India, I could have gone anywhere, just as India could have gone anywhere. We had parallel lives—just as I had got unshackled from my job, so had India been liberated from the Licence Raj. Both of us began to fashion new selves. It was the age of possibilities. I got caught in the excitement of a nation on the make. Since politicians were unwilling to sell the free-market reforms, the job fell on me. I found a sense of purpose. I had once thought that my earlier life in business had been wasted. But those 'wasted years' had given me experience of real life, which went on to become the raw material for a writer. I had lived a double life for twenty-five years. That quarter century of writing on weekends had given me the confidence and skill to embark on a new full-time writing career.

This period of my life was filled with hope. Sometimes I may have lost confidence, but there always existed a quiet optimism. Hope is different from optimism. Hope says that something will turn out well. Optimism is the sense of certainty that the path I am on is the right one. I felt that certitude. Since I was fashioning a new self, I would ask myself: Shouldn't it be the kind of self I had always wanted? Since I had renounced the transactional gods of corporate life, many burdens had lifted. I also aspired to become a better human being. I wanted my new self to be lighter, playful, and I wanted to live life as though it were a low-stakes game. I had always wanted to be free as a bird. The shell, however, had to break before the bird could fly.

It was when I switched careers that the shell broke finally. I was ready now to be guided by laghima. Lightness is a child's core competence, not an adult's. But there is a child hidden in every adult, and success lies in finding it. Would I be able to recover the child of Lyallpur who used to be running, smacking kids older than him, getting into all sorts of trouble in the Company Bagh? Would I now redeem my mother's ambition and become a 'dancing star'? Nietzsche insists that one must have chaos in the heart to give birth to such a star. Well, I had seen enough chaos in my life to have earned the right to be that star. But whether or not I would succeed was still an open question.

17

Fathers and Sons and Gods

'Few sons are like their fathers,
many are worse, only a few are better.'

—Homer, *Odyssey*

'Are you afraid of dying?' I asked my father. He thought for a few seconds, then replied. No, he was not because he knew where he was going, and it was to his real home. Besides, the Guru would be there to help him across. All his life, he had been readying for this moment.

I was sitting beside my father, feeling awkward and self-conscious as he lay dying in Moolchand Hospital in Delhi, felled by prostate cancer. There was an indefinable ache, a desperate yearning to close the chasm between a living son and a dying father. At three that morning, Meera had phoned to say his condition was worsening. She had been doing night duty, sleeping on the attendant's cot in the same room. I changed, put on my shoes, and drove to the hospital with Bunu and my mother. We were calm, expecting bad news. The doctor said the problem lay in the swelling in his brain. He had given up hope. As we walked into his room, the screen was glowing, the graph beeping as the monitor tracked his pulse and his breathing. He lay motionless. IV tubes were attached to his body, the fluids going in rhythmically. The breathing machine rasped on. I couldn't tell if he was still alive.

A few hours later I found myself alone with my father, looking at his familiar face. His dark eyes were closed; his small, emaciated body was still. It seemed to have shrunk. I called out to him, but there was no reply. I thought of all the things I wanted to say to him. Why is it impossible for a son to express what's on his mind to his father? There was always silence when we met, a long quiet. Yet, he had shaped me, ever so subtly, reminding me about 'making a life' each time my mother had badgered me about 'making a living'. He was the soft one, leaving my mother to do the hard job of raising us. He had never tried to live his life through me, allowing me plenty of room to be my own man. Once he had told my mother he wanted me to be better than he was. An odd thing to say for a man who was a giant in my eyes. And now the giant was dying.

My father had always been a distant figure. I never had emotional access to him. The same applies to me, I suppose. I, too, have failed my sons in this regard. The best gift a father can give to his children is to give them more of his time and his heart. I wish we had taken long walks together, chatting about this and that, without making a point. I might have repeated it with my sons. A son can never know his father properly because he is born after his father. The father has already experienced so much by the time the son grows up. They say 'like father, like son', but I don't know if it's true. I am quite unlike my father, and my sons are quite unlike me. In my case, our resemblance breaks off sharply on the religious question. The things which he was totally certain about were the existence of God, the soul and the law of karma—the very things about which I was unsure.

The nurse interrupted my thoughts. As soon as she came in, my father opened his eyes and gave a faint smile. It was the smile he had given two days ago to the Guru, who had come unexpectedly to sit beside him for more than an hour. For an instant, I felt as though the man before me was not my old father but a young man who had a son like me. The nurse turned on the overhead light, although it was daylight outside. I was looking now at a small, dying man. This was when he talked and told me that death was nothing to him, that he'd been waiting to go to his real home. The nurse told me gently it was time to let my father rest.

I got up to leave. At the door, I turned around and looked at him for the last time. I thought I was looking at a different face—of a man who had devoted his professional life to bring water to semi-arid Punjab. In his early years, he had worked ceaselessly, building canals to irrigate a dry land. He helped construct the Bhakra Dam after Independence, which erased droughts and famines in the region forever. Men like him set the stage for the 'green revolution', which would go on to feed a billion Indians, transforming a 'basket case' of the 1960s into a major exporter of food today. In the mid-'50, he helped negotiate a water treaty with Pakistan, dividing the waters of the Indus and the rivers of Punjab without a war.

Happily, my father died unaware of the tragic irony that followed his triumphs. Populist politicians in Punjab embarked on a race to the bottom, promising free water and electricity in exchange for votes, destroying thereby the state's finances. To top it, farmers were guaranteed a generous support price for their crop. With nothing to lose, they began to overuse water—cultivating water-guzzling paddy, absolutely the wrong crop in a semi-arid land! This has resulted in dangerously depleting aquifers below, reducing water supply for the future. The farmers' children became addicted to drugs or wanted desperately to leave home. As if this wasn't enough, environmental activists turned against big dams like Bhakra, undermining my father's lifework. Some call it 'the curse of water'—not unlike 'the curse of oil' in the Middle East. Others refer to it as the price of success, i.e., there is no free lunch. My father's story appears to me, however, to resemble a Greek tragedy—a tragic hero going from triumph to inevitable doom.

Death is an old story, but it is new each time to the person dying and to those left behind. My father died later that day, 30 March 1998. Looking at his dead face, I experienced the mystery of life. I had admired him all my life, even though we had differed on the big questions. I had never engaged him on the subject of God's existence. Perhaps, it was a fear of causing him pain. He was aware, deep in his heart, of my loss of belief. My letters from Harvard must have given me away. I had once written to my parents that I could not answer 'Who made me?' because I could not reply to the next question, 'Who made God?' So, I had junked the first-cause argument for God's existence. My mother blamed Harvard for my arrogant scepticism. Was I really arrogant? Was I like Icarus in Greek mythology, who sought to fly on artificial wings of feathers joined by wax? His father had warned him that the sun's heat would melt his wings. But the reckless son, heady with excitement, spurning his father's wisdom, flew too high, lost his wings and crashed into the sea.

Existentialists had taught me that life has no inherent meaning—its only meaning is what I give it. The universe doesn't care what sort of life I lead; only I care. So life is not about finding myself or God, but creating myself. Since there is no God-given purpose, only I can give it purpose. The universe exists only because I do. God is a dream of humans, says Unamuno, and humanity's prayers are to make sure He doesn't wake up. I believe it is a human being that makes the truth great; it is not the truth that makes humans great. I wanted to talk about these things with my father but couldn't, for fear of hurting him. Even though he had never pushed his spirituality down my throat, I felt guilty for thinking these thoughts, as though I was letting the side down. Now that he was gone, a burden had lifted. I felt free. I'm ashamed to admit it, but it felt like another sort of moksha. I was no longer ashamed of being an agnostic. I could now live without pretence, admitting openly that a belief in God and a disbelief in God were both examples of wishful thinking.

The day before my father died, the nurse had been leafing absently through that morning's *Times of India*. I don't know what came over me. Instead of asking her how he had spent the night, I prodded her to turn to the edit page of the newspaper. It was a Sunday, and I knew it carried my Sunday column. She looked confused, then turned to the page. She found my column with my picture beaming next to it. She was impressed and gave me a big smile. I was relieved. She had recognized me. I was no longer a 'nobody'. It was pathetic: I was worried about being a 'somebody' instead of being concerned about my dying father. There is no end to human vanity.

The nurse's copy of the *Times of India* had a banner headline, announcing that Atal Bihari Vajpayee had become India's prime minister. It was his second term in a bizarre sequence of coalition politics: he had served first for thirteen days in 1996; then for thirteen months from March 1998; and finally, a full term from 1999 to 2004. He led the right-wing nationalist Bhartiya Janata Party in a coalition government. But he was a moderate—he had condemned the destruction of Babri Masjid in Ayodhya in 1992 by Hindu extremists. He did not advance the

core Hindu nationalist agenda to the disappointment of the hardliners.
Vajpayee was also a sensitive, philosophical poet, and it felt nice to have
Plato's 'philosopher–king' at the top. His great achievement was to
continue the path of economic reform, albeit in a slow, stealthy manner.
His government ushered in the telecom revolution, opened up the power
and insurance sectors, launched ambitious road projects and privatized
many unviable state companies.

With his compassion, his poetic flourishes and good humour,
Vajpayee was a popular prime minister. A dark cloud, however, hangs
over his rule. It is difficult to speak of the murder of innocent people, but
it is also impossible to remain silent. Two years earlier, on the morning
of 27 February 2002, a train had arrived at the Godhra railway station in
Gujarat filled with Hindu pilgrims returning from Ayodhya. An argument
erupted on the platform between passengers and hawkers; soon it turned
violent. Suddenly, four coaches of the Sabarmati Express were burning,
and fifty-nine Hindus trapped inside died in the fire. It led to three days
of Hindu–Muslim clashes and sporadic episodes of violence for a whole
year. The death toll was 1044 Muslims and 254 Hindus, according to
official sources. Narendra Modi's state government was accused of failing
to control the violence, and Opposition parties demanded the chief
minister's dismissal.

My worst fears of Partition returned to haunt me as I watched the
scenes of horror night after night on television. There were no moderate
voices, only shrill, harsh ones. I couldn't get Ayan out of my head. What
had gone wrong? Secularists blamed BJP's electoral strategy of polarizing
the Hindus to win votes. Hindu nationalists blamed the Congress party's
strategy of appealing to Muslim vote banks. Unfortunately, there was no
Mahatma Gandhi in 2002 to keep the peace. In 1947, Gandhi had trudged
successfully through the Bengal countryside, a one-man peacekeeping
force, and Bengal had remained relatively peaceful, unlike my Punjab.
The only words that consoled me was an odd statement by a European
tourist on primetime TV. In an impromptu interview on a street corner in
Mumbai, she said that in a country of a billion people, of strong religious
emotion, it was remarkable that there was so little violence in India.

Ever since Partition, India had experienced sporadic incidents of
communal violence. The only other one I recall was in Delhi in 1984,
when one of our company's employees, a Sikh boy, had got roughed up.

It had happened right after Indira Gandhi's murder by her Sikh bodyguards. In the following days, there were riots all over Delhi, in which Hindus had taken revenge and 3000 Sikhs had died. Rajiv Gandhi justified it infamously by saying, 'When a big tree falls, the earth shakes.' I was equally disappointed with Vajpayee. He had preached the virtues of tolerance but had failed to condemn the massacre of innocent citizens in 2002. I later learnt that Vajpayee had planned to sack Modi at the BJP's national executive meeting in Goa. But Modi surprised him at the meeting, offering to resign. There were cries of 'No, no!' heard around the room. Arun Shourie, his minister, rose to explain why the prime minister had taken the decision. But his voice was drowned out by the crowd. Vajpayee remained silent, humiliated.

I asked myself: Where had the excellent idea of secularism failed us? Why couldn't it stem the tide of intolerance? Hinduism was, after all, a way of life, not a way of belief. It recognized the truth of all religions, which was the basis of its tolerance. It had 330 million tolerant gods, none of them could afford to feel jealous. India's Muslims also were among the most moderate in the world. Hindus were too diverse, too individualistic to accept the monolithic, parochial ideology of Hindutva. So, what went wrong? Was it because many vocal secularists had once been Marxist, who had contempt for all believers? They saw only the dark side of religion, its intolerance, forgetting that religion had given meaning to humanity since the dawn of civilization. Because secularists spoke a language alien to that spoken by the vast majority of Indians, they were only able to condemn communal violence, not stop it.

Meanwhile, prosperity had begun to spread visibly across the country, and it helped to divert my mind from the communal poison. Even slow, frustratingly slow, reforms were adding up, and they had added up to make India the world's second fastest-growing economy, after China. There were still too many obstacles in the way of producers, however. Licence Raj may have gone but 'Inspector Raj' was alive and well. The midnight knock of the inspector was an ever-present source of fear and corruption. A farmer could not hope to get a clear title to his land without bribing a revenue official. It took 10–15 years routinely to get justice in the courts; millions of undertrials languished in jail because justice was too slow. One in four teachers in a government primary school was absent, and one in two was not teaching. A cycle rickshaw puller or a street vendor had to part with a portion of his daily earnings in bribes to the police. A quarter of members of Parliament had criminal charges against them. It was bizarre—here was a country with a booming economy, but people despaired over the delivery of basic public services. It was a tale of private success and public failure.

Instead of celebrating the economic rise of my country—telling my sceptical friends, 'I told you so'—I was glum, filled with melancholy. I spoke to my mother. She told me not to despair. I was in the Vanaprastha, the third, 'forest-dwelling' stage of life. 'Third-stage melancholy' was not uncommon. I wondered if the great Sanskrit epic the Mahabharata held any answers. I was aware that the epic was obsessed with questions of dharma, of right and wrong, and I wondered if India's foundational text might help me to recover a meaningful ideal of civic virtue. My friends reacted strangely to my Mahabharata project. One accused me of escaping to religion. Another, a grey eminence from the Indira Gandhi regime, reproached me for turning saffron, becoming a votary of the Hindu Right. Neither could accept my project for what it was: a project of self-cultivation. A third, trying to be helpful, suggested I read the other epic, the Ramayana, instead. I quickly dismissed his idea. Although the Ramayana was a superior literary work, I had found it tiresome—the story of an ideal king, his ideal wife, an ideal brother, ideal subjects; even the villain was ideal. I preferred the Mahabharata—it was more real, about our imperfect lives, about good people acting badly.

I was toying with the idea of moving briefly to Banaras, the home of classical Hindu learning, when I ran into Raman (the poet A.K. Ramanujan) in Lodi Gardens on a spring evening in 2002. His stray remark about finding 'eternity in Regenstein' set me thinking. He was referring to the University of Chicago's library, with its unmatched collection of pre-modern Indian texts. Even more, to the university's galaxy of Sanskrit scholars—Wendy Doniger, Sheldon Pollock (both students of my Harvard guru, Daniel Ingalls) and many others. They would teach me how to interrogate an ancient text. Although the pundits in Banaras might do a great job of transporting me into the past—to the 'wonder that was India'—what I really wanted was for the past to speak to me, to teach me how to live in the present. So I decided it was going to be Chicago. Since I still had to persuade Bunu, I came up with a ruse: I packaged our two-year stint as an 'academic holiday', where she would be able to audit lectures in Renaissance painting, Chinese ceramics and do many other fun things. She was sceptical but agreed in the end. My mother, however, thought Chicago a peculiar choice. The city of gangsters seemed an odd place for a forest dweller in the third stage of life.

So I found myself in a classroom in windy Chicago in the winter of 2002, an improbable student—a husband, a father of two grown men and a taxpayer with considerably less hair than his classmates. It was biting cold outside, but Wendy Doniger consoled me: 'No such thing as being cold, only being underdressed.' On my arrival, Sanskrit scholars wanted to know what I wished to learn. 'How to live,' I replied. They looked at each other, amused, and came up with a reading list that included four classical texts. Each one pertained to one of the *purusharthas*, the four aims of the classical Hindu life. Ancient Indians were sensible, I felt, pursuing multiple ends, not a single, all-engulfing one. The four ends had to do with livelihood (*artha*), virtue (dharma), desire and pleasure (kama) and liberation from human bondage (moksha). There had been a nice balance in antiquity when Indian civilization was not as other-worldly as it became later in medieval times.

'What about the Mahabharata?' I asked. They smiled and placed it at the end of the list, claiming it would be icing on the cake. The four texts on their list, they assured me, led to the Mahabharata, and the epic would synthesize it all in a grand finale, true to its heady boast: 'What is here is found elsewhere / What is not here is nowhere.' If I followed their prescription, they said with a smile, I would become a cultivated man. Put thus, it sounded as though I was going to finishing school, with echoes of my father advising me to 'make a life'. Thus I began a new phase in my life. At first, the mighty academics did not take me seriously—in their eyes I was a businessman. But they confessed later that they had seen a childlike curiosity in me, an enthusiasm that was infectious. Soon they resigned themselves to having me around, calling me a 'perpetual undergraduate'.

By the end of the year, I had become dangerously addicted to the Mahabharata and fell hopelessly behind in the rest of my reading. One morning, I was feeling exhilarated. Reading the opening lines about the beginning of the war, I couldn't contain myself. I ran excitedly up the 271 steps to the tower of the Rockefeller Chapel. At the top, looking at the sky, I imagined the magical bow slip from great Arjuna's hands. In the brutal magnificence of the battle formation at Kurukshetra, the great warrior was refusing to fight. His debonair charioteer, the blue god Krishna, rising to the occasion, was trying to persuade him to follow his warrior's dharma. This would go on for 700 verses to become the 'song celestial', the Bhagavad Gita.

The epic is not only a moving tale, witty and ironic, revelling in moral dilemmas, but it is also about the way we deceive ourselves; about how we are false to others; how we oppress fellow human beings; and how we are deeply unjust in our day-to-day existence. But is this moral blindness an intractable human condition? Or can we change it? I sought answers in the epic's elusive concept of dharma. 'Dharma' is a frustrating word. It can mean many things—duty, law, justice, virtue, religion. But it mostly means doing the right thing. It provided the underlying norms of society, creating obligations for citizens and rulers, and bringing a degree of coherence to everyday life. I was struck by a single quality: it did not seek moral perfection—there were no ten commandments. It was pragmatic, closer to our experience as ordinary human beings in a hazy, uncertain world, quite unlike the narrow, rigid positions that defined the debates on American television in those post-9/11 days.

I would lunch sometimes at the Faculty Club, relaxing afterwards over coffee and the *New York Times*. To my surprise, I found that I was judging the stories in the paper—the actions of rulers, CEOs and policymakers— through the lens of dharma. It was bizarre: How could an ancient Indian concept offer insights into events in contemporary America? But it was not so strange as I thought about it. The notion of dharma was alive and well in the Indian imagination. An uneducated villager knew in her bones that dharma was the moral imperative of the cosmic law holding the social order together. To our founding fathers, nation building had been a moral project, and they had placed *dharmachakra*, 'the wheel of dharma', at the centre of the nation's flag. The great scholar P.V. Kane, recipient of the nation's highest honour, the Bharat Ratna, had called India's constitution a 'dharma text'. Not surprising, then, that my regular *Times of India* columns also began to change imperceptibly at this time, shifting focus from economic to governance issues.

I began to believe that some nations possessed a code word, which, like a key, unlocked their secrets. That word was 'liberty' for America. It was 'dharma' for India. Some of the best and oddest things in these nations only made sense through their code words. Americans carried guns on the streets in the name of liberty; Indians justified their unjust caste system through dharma.

By the middle of my second year in Chicago, I had read the major texts on my list. I finished reading *Arthashastra*, a text about economics and politics to understand the material goal of artha; *Kamasutra* had been the obvious choice to learn how to cope with desire and cultivate pleasure; *Manusmriti*, the law book by Manu, had introduced me to the formidable goal of dharma; although the Upanishads introduced me to the final aim of moksha, it was Adi Shankara's commentary on the *Brahma Sutra* that elaborated it from an Advaita Vedanta perspective. Meanwhile, a new book, *The Difficulty of Being Good*, began to take shape in my head. I was not following the standard formula—first do the research, then write the book. Reading the ancient texts in Regenstein was such an attractive life that I feared I might get hooked and spend the rest of my life doing research. So I adopted a new mantra: I must write 250 words a day. Some learn by making copious notes, I learn by writing, by interpreting daily what I am reading; it has the added benefit of knowing where I am headed in my book.

We returned home from Chicago in May 2004 to find a new government in power. It had been a shocking defeat for Vajpayee. His five-year rule had been a period of stability, good governance and vigorous reform. A massive number of jobs had been created. All the polls had predicted a comfortable victory for Vajpayee, and no one could explain his defeat. The Congress claimed that it had succeeded because of support from the rural poor and the low castes who had not benefitted from the reforms. Secular voices attributed the loss to communal violence in Gujarat. The BJP, Vajpayee's party, blamed it on its coalition partners, who had lost key southern states. Although Vajpayee did not get re-elected, I felt he had set the stage for high growth and prosperity in the following decade.

The stock market crashed soon after the new government came to power. Leftists in the Congress-led coalition announced a 'Common Minimum Programme', a veiled signal of the end of reforms, particularly privatization. The market, however, recovered a few days later, when Sonia Gandhi appointed Manmohan Singh, architect of the 1991 liberalization, to be prime minister. I was thrilled. There was still lots to be done, and I had high expectations of this second generation of reforms. My optimism, however, was tempered. I had a niggling fear that free, competitive markets were not in the Congress party's DNA; the Congress was always ready to make a false trade-off between growth and equity. Rahul Gandhi was already making worrisome noises about shifting emphasis from 'jobless growth' to welfare programmes. I worried that Manmohan Singh was too mild and self-effacing, and might not have the guts to stand up and say, 'For heaven's sake, let's create wealth first, before we distribute it.'

I tried to settle down to work after our sojourn in Chicago, but the new book refused to move. I missed my father. I couldn't shake off a feeling of gloomy emptiness. Meera and my mother were alone now, still living at the ashram in Beas. One night, at 10 p.m., I hopped on to the Frontier Mail to visit them. Soon after dawn the next morning, after crossing the Beas River, I got off the train. The old village station was the same as before. There was a sleepy tonga waiting outside. I woke up the driver, threw my bag on to the tonga, and we were on our way.

Just before we reached the ashram, I saw a lush green field fresh from the monsoon rain, greener than any I'd ever seen. I jumped out of the tonga. Memories filled my heart as I ran to touch the 'green, green grass of home', as the song goes. Soon, I was home, embracing my mother and sister, with tears in our eyes. They meant to give me news of the family, but memories of my father kept intruding. In the evening, we went for a walk that was filled with nostalgia. Passing by an empty field, we reached the ground where my eleven-year-old brother had won fame by thumping the cricket ball into the Guru's satsang. No one had minded the ball's intrusion except our humourless neighbour. When we reached the old guest house, I smiled at the familiar room on the first floor. It was from here that yours truly, aged twelve, had masterminded Operation Slippery Bananas, confirming to the ashram security my mother's label of 'Troublemaker', which I had acquired at age four. Soon we reached the banks of the Beas, from where I remembered throwing my dead father's ashes into the river.

After dinner, we sat under the stars. I was overcome by the grandeur of the universe, feeling fortunate I was alive. Many experience this emotion from time to time, wondering why we are here. Where did we come from? My father's response had been God. I had grown accepting one truth—my father's belief in the transcendental—but had discovered another: the empiricist view that knowledge is based on evidence. A man of few words, my father had rarely spoken about his spiritual path, believing, like Lao Tsu, that those who know don't speak and those who speak don't know. Spiritual truth couldn't be put into words, he felt, it had to be experienced.

My mother seemed to grieve less for my dead father and more for her living daughter. She was still struggling to understand what had cut short the life of a great talent. She couldn't accept the thought of mental illness or that the cause might be genetic. I explained to her calmly that her own sister, her sister's son and her brother—they had all been victims of mental illness. But she wouldn't hear of it. The stigma of madness was too much.

'How can you be so calm?' she chided me. 'You're just like your father.'

Sons do grow up to be their fathers. But likeness isn't only a matter of the genes. It is also about cultivating the qualities of the heart. My father's qualities were heroic. He had lived a worldly life but had been a renouncer at heart. I may not have agreed with him, but I admired the power of his convictions. My mother wished I hadn't lost my faith. I couldn't accept religion after Partition's tragedy and, more recently, after the communal violence against Sikhs in Delhi and against Muslims in Gujarat. However beneficial it may be to an individual, religion had an enormous capacity for violence.

'Your father's was not religion; it was spirituality,' she said quietly.

After my father's death, I experienced the winds of liberation. I could now talk openly about my convictions. I wanted to tell my mother that there wasn't any reliable evidence for God or for the soul or for rebirth. When we die, it is over. The only way we live on is through what we pass on to our children, through our genes. But I chose to remain silent—I knew it would disturb her. I did tell her, however, that my consciousness was real. The voices had convinced me of it. I did not know what consciousness was, but I didn't think it was made up of matter, as materialists assumed. Neither was it transcendental, as my father believed. My dilemma was that I could not explain how I was double. How was I able to experience myself as subject and object at the same time? The *Yoga Sutra* says that the mind has the ability to reflect on both the seen and the seer, but I couldn't grasp how it could do so.

Both my father and I were agreed that my 'self' was something I had constructed via my consciousness, not something out there. But I couldn't take his leap of faith. He believed that my 'self' had to be got rid of if I were to discover my real self, which is atman, the soul. I worried that if I lost my constructed self (no matter how illusory), I would lose my humanity. My father had the same problem with desire. He explained that if I satisfied one desire, a new one would take its place. It's an endless thirst, never dying. His answer was to stop desiring. This is how one gained mastery over oneself. He held up *vairagya*, detachment, as a goal of life. Again, I couldn't bring myself to agree. If I stopped desiring, I would no longer be human. Even the Upanishad says, 'man is made of desire' (the Brihadaranyaka Upanishad, 4.4.5.). The spiritual aim of his moksha was ultimately to conquer desire, vairagya. I felt it was an impossible goal. The best one could do was to strike a balance between overindulgence and complete repression of one's desires.

As to the meaning of life, I believe it has none. For the rest of it, I go along with modern science. Fantastic as it seems, I believe the universe was created spontaneously from the Big Bang. No one knows how it happened. When I returned from Beas, my mind was at peace, and before long I got into the swing of writing *The Difficulty of Being Good.* There was an inviting familiarity about my study, which pulled me each morning from my bedroom at the first light of day. Bunu called it 'my cave', although it resembled a library, housing rows and rows, shelves and shelves of books collected over the years from my college days. I have actually read most of the books! The only thing new was a computer. I had written *India Unbound* on long ruled sheets of yellow paper. Calligraphy had been important to me then. The computer, however, offered too many practical benefits, and one morning at the end of the millennium, the calligraphy ink pens on my desk became obsolete.

Working with the Mahabharata reinforced a profound sense of continuity with the past. All human beings need a permanent address—local roots, identity and a link with the past. A writer needs it even more because he aspires to speak of universal truths about human beings. Once upon a time, so many used to envy me and my business-class, jet-setting lifestyle in a multinational company. They didn't realize the price I paid for it. I could discuss breezily the latest plays on Broadway or critique the latest Booker Prize winner at a cocktail party. But I was becoming more and more superficial and inauthentic. The globalized cosmopolitan is at odds with the universal. The more a person belongs to his time and place, the more he belongs to all times and places. The universal is in one's backyard.

Since I was writing about moral dilemmas in my new book, I had to be careful not to preach. Every writer is a moral agent. Writers tell stories, evoke our moral imagination, educate our capacity for moral judgement. The right voice in a story gets over the problem of moralizing. From Cervantes's *Don Quixote*, I learnt to speak in a language that one speaks to oneself when one is alone. Luckily, I had found this voice in *India Unbound*, and it carried effortlessly into my new book. Each of us has a distinctive voice, I think; when you find it, you become authentic. It's not worth copying someone else's voice, which is like living someone else's life. When you discover your voice, it becomes a potent weapon. It doesn't mean the reader will be attracted to it, because taste is an individual preference, subjective and intangible. Just hope someone wants to hear it, pay attention to it. You can't look for a voice; it just appears. If you write enough words, I believe, it presents itself one day. It then evolves without your realizing it.

Along with computers came email around this time. On the advice of the *Times of India*, I began to plonk my email address at the end of my fortnightly column. Thus I began to receive letters from readers. Their fury sometimes surprised me. One outraged reader wrote that two of his articles had been rejected by the newspaper. 'Why did the *Times* reject my work, and publish a fourth-rate writer like Gurcharan Das?' I took his letter to the editor. Trying to sound sympathetic, he said, 'You're not fourth-rate—you are third-rate, at least.' He gave me an impish smile and sent me off.

Another provocation came from a reader in Mumbai. In elegant calligraphy, he wrote inelegantly, 'You disgusting pig, yes, you, Gurcharan Pig. Unfortunately I subscribe to the *Times of India*, because of which, week after week, I am forced to read the pigshit you keep defecating— glorifying globalisation, free markets, reforms, bullshit, blah blah. Everyone knows that the only beneficiaries of globalisation are America and Multinationals. They cheat, exploit the rest of the world.' My reader went on to give the example of a computer he had purchased that did not contain the software to run the DVD-ROM. He had complained to the dealer but to no avail. He ended his letter characteristically, 'What do you, free market Bastard, have to say?' My advice to the reader was to clean his mouth with or without a multinational toothpaste. Next, rewrite a straightforward business letter, deleting the expletives referring to animals, their excreta and those that raised doubts about my paternity. This might sacrifice his natural style, but it might save the global capitalist system.

A reader from Nagpur complained that I was creating an unhealthy division in his family. 'We always read the Sunday paper together as a family under a tree in our courtyard. We also drink tea leisurely and there is harmony in our home. Until we read your column. Then we begin to argue and our peace is shattered. My wife always takes my son's side. My son and I are drifting apart, thanks to you.' After all this, I quietly stopped mentioning my email address at the end of my columns.

When schools reopened after the summer break, I got a phone call from the principal of one of the city's premier schools asking me to address her students. 'Oh, good,' I said. 'I shall speak on dharma and the moral dilemmas in the Mahabharata.' She grew defensive, pleading with me not to do so. There were important, secular persons on her governing board, and she didn't want to be accused of teaching religion. I was flabbergasted. Something was clearly wrong. 'Surely the Mahabharata is a literary epic,' I said, 'and dharma is about right and wrong. Where does religion come in?' She withdrew her invitation politely, leaving me wondering. If Italian children could proudly read Dante's *Divine Comedy* in school, and the English could read Milton's *Paradise Lost*—both had many mentions of God in them—why couldn't Indian children read the Mahabharata? I despaired over the unhappy truth that young Indians were growing up without knowing how to use their rich past. We were, thus, abdicating our traditions to the narrow, closed minds of fanatical Hindu nationalists. I blamed our secularists as well—they were equally fundamentalist in their antipathy to tradition.

I was travelling fairly regularly now, speaking at literary festivals and other gatherings. On one of these trips I found myself in Shillong, Assam, speaking on dharma to a conclave of Roman Catholic bishops. From there, I flew to Chennai to speak to students at the Indian Institute of Technology. I had a few hours to kill after the talk and decided to visit the Madras Museum in Egmore. While I was admiring a Chola sculpture from the eleventh century, which had been created in the once-great city of Tanjore, a middle-aged, barefoot woman in a south Indian sari stood behind me. I made way for her. Without self-consciousness, she came forward and placed a vermillion mark on the Shiva Nataraja. I was appalled. Didn't she realize this was a museum, not a temple?

Soon, I felt contrite for judging her. We lived in two different worlds. Mine was secular; hers was sacred. Both of us stood before the bronze statue with different expectations. For me, it was a 900-year-old object of beauty; for her, it was God. Mine was aesthetic pleasure; hers was divine *darshana*. She didn't see what I saw—a brilliant work in bronze by an early Chola artist. I admired the weightless joy of the dancer, so skilfully captured by the sculptor. I moved along, going past other sculptures, getting irritated when they were dusty, or ill lit or poorly spaced. But just as quickly, I felt embarrassed with my petty concerns, my niggling mind.

I looked for her after a while. She was still there, absorbed by her light-footed, tireless, prancing God, whose dance actually brings the universe into being. Without missing a beat, and in the fullness of time, he dances out of existence. There was a luxuriant richness in her sacred world, I felt, compared to the poverty of my weary, feeble and secular existence. To her, the drum in Shiva's right hand, with its drumbeat, announced a momentous event. The flame in his left hand told her that the universe was about to be created. His lower right hand bestowed upon her freedom from fear. His raised left arm was a symbol of her release. For someone carrying out such a momentous mission, her God looked cool, athletic and debonair.

Although my mystic father did not worship Shiva, he shared the richness of her sacred life. My modern, secular, English-speaking life, in comparison, seemed empty. I would never know the depth, the opulence of their world. My secular friends were quick to brand her superstitious, illiterate and casteist. But she was probably more tolerant, accepting of diversity, because she was capable of seeing God everywhere. She thus had something to teach both the secularists of the Congress party and the Hindu nationalists of the BJP. They might even learn the real meaning of secularism from her.

In my world of museums, concert halls and bookstores, there was plenty of search for beauty but no place for the holy. When Nietzsche said 'God is dead', he meant that modern, secular individuals like me had lost the possibility of faith. The meaninglessness of a non-believer's life had brought us to an absurd situation. Sartre and Camus had offered consolation—'Man creates his own meaning,' they had said, but that is easier said than done. That woman's life, on the other hand, held the possibility of fullness and wholeness of being.

I turned to look once again at the statue of Shiva Nataraja. He was still unperturbed, absorbed in the serious business of creating and destroying the universe. There was something new, however. Under his raised left leg was a marigold flower! I decided the next time the world gets too much for me, I would visit a museum. If I'm not careful, I too might experience eternity.

This chapter of my life has been about fathers and sons and gods. My father's death casts a shadow, but it was also a liberation. I was freed to speak about my beliefs. Every son has a duty to become his own man, which he fulfils when he takes a different path from his father's. Both of us were mumukshus—he was a searcher for a grand, spiritual moksha; I was after a more modest one—a human, non-transcendental freedom in this world. He wished to be liberated from desire, which he felt was the real culprit behind suffering. But I enjoyed my desires—and the happiness they brought, even if temporary. He felt I was aiming too low. But I feel that desire is at the root of being human. My father claimed there was no end to desiring: if I was poor, I would want to be rich; if I became rich, I would desire respectability and turn to charity. Desire was endless. In that case, I told him, even the desire for moksha was a desire.

Certainly, desires do change. Meanwhile, I must confess that I have had lots of fun enjoying the desires and pleasures of the world. What is wrong with that? What is wrong, he said, is the tiresome and endless striving, not getting anywhere. His moksha was a destination where one would finally attain peace, eternal bliss, free from ceaseless change. There would be no more suffering between the fleeting moments of happiness. But I wonder if his conception of moksha may be a tad boring—long stretches of nothing happening, a chill of loneliness with all activity ceasing, no consciousness, none of the good life. I think I would still prefer the brief, intense pleasures of the day, with sparks of joy, friendship and good humour. Even if it meant spells of pain, suffering and third-stage melancholy in between.

The drama of fathers, gods and sons was happening amid unprecedented prosperity during this period. Communal violence also seemed to be a part of the mix. It was all distressing, always reminding me of Ayan. The barefoot lady in the museum helped me to understand that the problem may well lie in the way we defined secularism. The English-speaking elite, like myself, had embraced unthinkingly the Western ideal of secularism, which meant the separation of religion and state. However, the lady in the museum, who saw God everywhere, may actually have a secular temper more suited to a country overflowing with religion. She was more likely to respect all religions. This was her lesson for me. We needed to adopt her mantra of secularism: respect all religions.

The best thing my father gave me were three words, 'Make a life.' Each time he uttered them, I would soar high and break into song. He gave me the courage to shed the bondage of wage slavery, of whimsical bosses, of a nine-to-five routine. With it, I achieved another sort of freedom. I hoped it would make me a better person—less self-absorbed, more caring—and bring a life of harmony, free of the noise and chaos of the world. I hoped the intellectual fulfilment would end the ceaseless, futile striving that had dogged my business life. But it wasn't working out that way. Although I was putting my heart into my writing, I found new, alien desires springing up. I began to expect premium treatment at literary festivals, top billing in papers. I wanted the anchor of a panel discussion on TV to come to me before the others. I wanted my book to be displayed ahead of those by other authors. In climbing new ladders of success, I was becoming a slave to another bondage. This was not the moksha I had dreamt of.

18

The Road to Freedom

'I was coming to that troubled twilight time, a time of regrets that resemble hopes, of hopes that resemble regrets, when youth is past but old age has not yet come.'

—Ivan Turgenev

By a strange twist of fate, I found myself standing bewildered on the stage before an angry crowd of 37,000 protestors in Cairo's Tahrir Square. The mob was baying for the blood of their disgraced leader, Hosni Mubarak. The speakers, one after another, were inciting the crowd. 'You have three minutes,' the guy in charge was saying. 'Speak slowly.' Pointing to the Arab woman standing next to me, he said, 'Give her a chance to translate.'

'What do I say?' I pleaded.

'Oh? Don't you have a speech?

I shook my head.

'We got the wrong guy,' he said in Arabic. Shrugging, he turned to me. 'Well, you'd better wing it.'

I was in Cairo on 8 April 2011 to attend a conference organized by the democracy movement of the Arab Spring. Earlier that morning, I had presented the 'Indian model' for Egypt's future at the Shepherd Hotel. Someone, it seems, had read *India Unbound*, which was why I had been invited and given a ticket to history in the making. They had to cut the conference short because a spontaneous protest had erupted next door at Tahrir Square. Having nothing better to do, I joined a bunch of journalists at the conference, and we wandered off to the Square. I couldn't understand a word they were saying. Before I knew it, I was being shoved and pushed in the maddening crowd and lifted on to the stage amid the confusion.

'I bring greetings from Al Hind, the land of Gandhi,' I improvised. The crowd broke into applause. Clearly, I'd made a good start. The translator gave me an encouraging look. She resembled Miss Allen, although she was lighter. I didn't know what to say next. But I think the resemblance triggered off something Miss Allen had once said about democracy. So, I repeated her words: 'Democracy is about people like you and me, deciding to set up a government. We rule ourselves, not ruled by the high and mighty. You will say, but we don't know how to rule. I will say, it is better to have people who don't know than to have people who know and are corrupt.' I was now getting into the rhythm and began to speak about the rule of law. It was a mistake. The Egyptians lost interest and grew restive. They were far more concerned with hanging their generals than in learning about the pillars of democracy. My three minutes were up.

At three o'clock the next morning, I woke up to the sound of gunfire. They must be bursting firecrackers, I thought. There was a knock. It was my host in pyjamas, whispering that the army had moved into Tahrir Square. I should be prepared to flee as my 'three minutes of fame' had been posted on YouTube. Filled with fear, I changed quickly, picked up my laptop and passport, and waited. I must have fallen asleep on the armchair, because the next moment it was seven o'clock and I was still alive. A thick cloud of smoke could be seen from my window hovering over Tahrir Square. I switched on the TV and turned to Al Jazeera. Yes, the army had come. They had been looking for soldiers and had found two officers hiding in the adjoining mosque. After capturing the officers, they had left quickly. I was still filled with fear. So I cut short my visit, hopping on the first flight home. When our plane entered Indian airspace I breathed easily, feeling a new respect for my relatively stable country.

The previous morning in Cairo, young Egyptian journalists had asked three questions after my presentation. How did you keep the generals out of power? How did you become one of the fastest-growing economies (and an outsourcer of IT services to the world)? And how did you achieve social harmony in the world's most diverse country? In particular, how did India manage to have such a moderate Muslim population? I'm not sure how well I answered their questions. But they made me think. The questions pointed to the three attributes of a successful nation—democracy, prosperity and social harmony. They forced me to relook at India.

The first question was their way of asking how India had remained democratic over last sixty-five years. I felt it was something of a miracle. We were lucky. India had been founded by saints—our 'liberators with clean hands', as André Malraux put it. Even the army held them in awe. More than anyone, Jawaharlal Nehru deserves credit for embedding democracy and the rule of law into the national fabric—an exceptional achievement among postcolonial societies. You don't have to look far—Pakistan, next door, is 'an army with a country'.

The answer to the economic question was market-based reforms. After four sad decades of lost opportunities, India finally got its act together in 1991. Since then, every government had reformed in a slow, stealthy manner, and even slow reforms had added up to make India one of the world's fastest-growing economies. As a result, around 400 million people had crossed the poverty line, and there was a rapidly growing middle class. If India continued to grow in the next three decades at the same pace as it had in the last two, we could look forward to a country where the quality of life would improve for the vast majority.

The third question of the Egyptians reflected the Arab Spring's fear of radical Islam. They explained to me that 12 per cent of Egyptians were Christian and didn't feel secure. At the same time, 13 per cent of Indians were Muslim, and they did feel secure. How did this happen? I didn't have a good answer, but it made me think. I realized that the threat to India is not from without, from Pakistan or China, but from within. It would only take a few thousand insecure Muslim youths to join hands with global Islamic terror outfits to produce chaos and quickly undo the vast gains made by the nation.

We had a good scorecard. But why was I unhappy? I couldn't be sure. It may be the pervasive failures in governance, the same reason that had sent me on a quest for dharma almost a decade ago. India's was a sweet and sour tale, I decided; the nation had risen from below, despite the state. We were a bottom-up success, quite unlike the top-down success of East Asian countries that had been steered by the state. Not only I, but the ordinary Indian was feeling discontented. Indeed, at that time we had our own version of the Arab Spring, an anti-corruption movement led by Anna Hazare, who had mounted a massive protest against corruption in the Congress party.

My worst fears about the Congress-led government had proved correct. The reforms had come to a halt, despite Manmohan Singh being at the top. Everyone knew that Sonia Gandhi was the real centre of power. Like her mother-in-law, she was forever ready to make a false trade-off between growth and equity, and launch the next vote-winning welfare scheme. It was a disheartening time for me as I waited anxiously, week after week, to write my next column about the next reform, which never came. I was being naive, believing that the Congress party had changed, but the leopard doesn't change its spots. It was, after all, the same party that had snatched our economic freedom via the Licence Raj, sacrificing the hopes of two generations. Milton Friedman's words rang in my head: 'A society that puts equality before liberty will get neither. A society that puts freedom before equality will get a high degree of both.'

Ironically, the decade after 2003 had turned out to be India's best in economic terms. The economy had grown 7.5 per cent a year, while population growth had slowed down. So, per capita, India had performed like an Asian Tiger. The government's best achievement was a welfare programme—offering 100 days guaranteed employment to the rural poor; its worst was to waive loans to farmers, which meant punishing the honest, who had dutifully repaid their loans. Such an immoral way to win the 2009 election! Almost as bad was the Food Security Act—it guaranteed almost free rice and wheat to 67 per cent of the people. You could have justified this step for the extremely poor (around 20 per cent), and that too during an emergency. It would surely wreck the nation's finances. As the years went by, corruption scandals erupted in the government, decision-making was paralysed, investors lost confidence, inflation rose.

I became deeply pessimistic about Indian politics in the second term of the Congress-led coalition. Like most people, I was disgusted with the Congress party's corruption but equally suspicious of the Bhartiya Janata Party's Hindu nationalism, especially after the Gujarat riots. Behind my pessimism lay a nagging sense of guilt. Had I personally taken the easy road in life, offering armchair commentary on politics and policies? Shouldn't I jump into politics and do some of the heavy-lifting work of changing policies? At the university, I had learnt from Aristotle that civic action was the high road to virtue. Ancient Greeks called the person who did not engage in politics *idiotis* (origin of 'idiot'). My former boss's words also haunted me. By not joining politics, he had said, I would be following the path of sheep, and this meant being ruled by wolves.

'Should I go into politics?' I asked Bunu.

'No,' she said vehemently.

She was not the right person to ask. She was reserved by nature and had always preferred the quiet, private life. She was embarrassed, in fact, that I was already too public, constantly under the glare of TV cameras and the press.

'Ask a friend,' she suggested.

It was then that the penny dropped. I had no friends. I had lots of acquaintances, but I didn't make friends easily. I'd never known the pleasure of relaxing in the company of men.

'Of course, you do.' She tried to console me. 'You have a few friends, but they are spread all over the world.'

In contrast, she had three or four real friends with whom she spoke at least once a day. She could phone them, even at three in the morning, just to say that she was feeling low. They knew each other's faults but still loved each other, and they could talk for hours without saying anything. As for me, I was more concerned with ideas than people. What interested me about a person was the meaning of his life, what it said about the human condition. If I met a businessman, I wanted to probe the link between business and economic prosperity of society. In the case of a politician, I would probe what power did to a person. If I met someone 'great', it was the essence of greatness that interested me; if he was a saint, it was the character of saintliness. In all these cases, there were characteristics which expressed not so much an individual personality as what it said about the world. I lacked the desire to get involved with the particularity of another person, with the quirkiness of his or her personality. Bunu knew this, but she found it odd and also sad. I lacked something, she said, and I would never be fully human as a result. Without knowing the joys of friendship, I would never live a truly fulfilling life. She was right, and the truth of what she said did shake me up. But it was too late to change.

One day, without the benefit of friendly advice, I decided to take the plunge into politics. The problem was which party to join. I wished good old Swatantra still existed. Anna Hazare's movement had brought a fresh new party, the Aam Aadmi Party, but I didn't feel enthusiastic about it. It was too quick to promise free electricity, free this and free that. I wanted a party that would focus on the long-term reform of institutions. There was none. Amartya Sen had suggested reviving the old Swatantra Party, but it didn't seem practical. India already had too many parties. Only the two leading national parties had any chance of getting elected. Moreover, a pro-market candidate stood no chance at the polls—the 'invisible hand' of Adam Smith was, in fact, invisible to the voter. Even intellectuals found it hard to grasp how the self-interest of millions in the marketplace could lead to the success of the whole society. Thus, a candidate who promised free rice or electricity would always win.

Another thought came to my mind: yes, the existing parties may be flawed, but if I joined one I might be able to subvert them from within, push them in the right direction. I decided to give it a try and meet their leaders. My friend Suman Dubey set up a meeting with Sonia Gandhi, and my sister-in-law, Bina, set up a meeting with L.K. Advani, head of the BJP. Both encounters were disasters.

I arrived at 10 Janpath filled with hope and enthusiasm. Mr George, Sonia Gandhi's secretary, warned me that meetings with the grand lady lasted strictly twenty minutes. I should get up as soon as she did. Gandhi opened the conversation with a smile and a question. Pointing to a story in that morning's paper on the coffee table, she asked what conceivable difference would opening the insurance sector to foreign investors make to a poor farmer? Wasn't the country wasting time over such frivolous things when we should be worrying about the farmer's family going hungry at night? I answered her excitedly, explaining how crop insurance would help farmers; how competition from overseas insurance companies would make Indian companies more efficient. I went on and on, till I realized that I was speaking to the air. She had lost interest but was too polite to say so. Since I found her silence unnerving, I kept talking about the other reforms that needed to be done. It felt very odd talking to oneself.

The meeting with Advani was equally useless. Although he was aware of my writings, he asked me about my personal ideology. How did I define myself? I told him I had been a socialist at the university. 'Well, everyone is a socialist then!' he smiled. Working under the Licence Raj had, however, turned me into a laissez-faire libertarian. Ever since, I had vigorously defended the 1991 liberalization and begun to believe in a minimalist state.

'Ah, a market wallah!' he exclaimed.

But two decades later, I realized that I had been wrong. I told Advani that after encountering horrific failures in governance, I had understood that the state was crucial for the success of markets and of democracy. Hence, I no longer thought of the state as a second-order phenomenon. I was now a classical liberal. I had also joined the board of the Centre of Civil Society, a classical-liberal think tank devoted to education reforms.

'But you still have deep faith in the market?'

'Yes, because I have a deep suspicion of state power.' I still preferred market outcomes to bureaucratic ones. India still had to right the pendulum after forty years of socialism.

'Is socialism such a bad thing?' he asked.

'Socialism is the most moral of human beliefs,' I said. 'Who could be against the equality of all human beings? But how to get there is the problem. Socialism inevitably turns into statism, a command economy with state ownership of businesses, extortionate tax rates and a loss of freedom.'

Both of us agreed that if socialism was translated into high-quality education and health care, no one would object, but unfortunately, India had failed in this regard.

Advani asked about my views on Hindutva. I told him I was comfortable being a Hindu and, like a good Hindu, respected all religions. I was not a Hindu supremacist, nor a Hindu nationalist. I did not approve of Muslim bashing. The BJP's role in the 2002 Gujarat riots was deplorable. He smiled sadly, congratulating me on my frankness and clarity. We chatted politely. It was clear that he had little use for me. Both Sonia Gandhi and he had calculated that I had no chance at the polls. I was not unlike other English-educated professionals who had been edged out of mass politics by the 1970s. Far worthier persons than me had failed. Manmohan Singh, Arun Jaitley and Nandan Nilekani—all had failed to win an election. (Shashi Tharoor was the exception that proved the rule.)

I was disappointed but not surprised to be out for a duck as a wannabe politician. Bunu consoled me, saying it was probably for the best. Nor was my heart truly in politics. The politicians I knew were thinking only of the next election, whereas I was thinking of the next generation. I would never be able to master the art of lying. Besides, there were too many criminals in Indian politics, and I didn't want to be a member of that club. If you committed a small crime, you went to jail; if you committed a big crime, you went into politics.

The dramatic experience at Tahrir Square was not wasted, however. I wrote about it in a long essay, which became *India Grows at Night*, ranked by *Financial Times* as one of the best books of 2013. I wasn't happy with the title and wanted 'India Grows at Night When the Government Sleeps'. But my publishers nixed it, thinking it too long, too insulting. The book recounts the story of 'bottom-up success'. It begins as a tale of two cities, Gurgaon and Faridabad, both on Delhi's outskirts. Faridabad had all the advantages—an active municipality, fertile agriculture, a railway line to Delhi and a host of industries. Gurgaon was wilderness—a sleepy village with rocky soil, from where even the goats ran away. But twenty-five years later, Gurgaon had become 'Millennium City', a symbol of rising India, with 32 million square feet of commercial space. Home to the world's largest corporations, it got fabled apartment complexes with swimming pools, spas and saunas, dozens of skyscrapers, twenty-six shopping malls, seven golf courses and countless showrooms of world-famous luxury brands. Faridabad was still mired in red tape.

How did this happen? Gurgaon's disadvantage turned out to be an advantage. It was ignored by the state. Not having a municipality meant less red tape, less corruption, fewer bureaucrats to block things. Gurgaon was the work of a visionary builder, Kushal Pal (KP) Singh. Seeing the miracle, people asked: Why do we need a government at all (with corrupt politicians and unresponsive bureaucrats)? They shrugged and said, 'India grows at night when the government sleeps.' The tale of two cities was a story in miniature of a new India where prosperity was spreading despite the state.

This tale of private success and public failure also had a downside. Gurgaon's laissez-faire model lacked basic public services—unreliable sewage system or water supply, erratic supply of electricity, few decent roads, no public transport. All these were privately provided until the state government finally woke up. The moral of my tale was that instead of celebrating India's heroic rise from below, despite the state, we had to reform the state. India had to learn to grow during the day. Neither the Faridabad nor the Gurgaon model was the correct one.

* * *

I was now in that phase of life from where youth seems long gone and middle age seems to be passing quickly by. I was at the top of my game as a writer, pushing ahead with brute ambition in the glare of TV cameras and sycophantic buzz. I was respected—on the boards of companies and non-profit organizations. Young writers wanted blurbs—those quippy phrases on book covers—and their books began piling on my shelf. On rare days when the writing had gone really well, I would be like a bird singing after a storm—sometimes, I would actually jump out of my chair and begin to dance. Yes, actually twirl, try and do a pirouette like a ballerina. Who knows, maybe I was redeeming my mother's endearment, 'dancing star', which she had pinned on me when I was three. The writing life felt sublime. But its joys were private and secret, felt only by the writer. To an outsider, I appeared to be mostly staring at the amaltas tree outside my window.

As I think of these ecstatic moments, I feel I owed my good fortune to having a sense of purpose. And it was a mighty purpose in my eyes. I am not sure how I had found it; but then, one doesn't *find* one's purpose, one *creates* it. It was also a milestone on my moksha journey. I had achieved a degree of autonomy as a writer after quitting the corporate life. I was no longer directed by a boss or a board. My life and my decisions depended on me and my choices. I was at the centre of my universe.

I may have glimpsed the perfect life, but I must confess that it was not a continuous state of being. The days of the 'dancing star' were erratic and infrequent. Most of the time, I was a creature of routine. I was dead to the moment, busy making plans or being super productive. By the time I finished one book, I couldn't wait to begin the next one. I may have freed myself from the bondage of the business life, but there were new burdens in a writer's life, and they quickly replaced the old ones. It was not just deadlines for articles or commitments for new books. There were new demands of vanity. I wanted to be invited to literary festivals, to be interviewed on television, to give speeches related to the subjects of my books. Yes, I found I was leading, once again, a double life. There was a private life of writing, solitary and lonely. The other was a busy public life of interviews, panel discussions, travel, appointments and time schedules.

How we fill our moments is how we spend our days; and how we fill our days is how we live our lives. It's good to have a purpose, and I was lucky to have one. But it is not good to be forever in a trance of busyness. On most days I seemed to barely exist. In the mornings, I would be thinking about what I had to do in the evening. In the evenings, I was preoccupied with what was coming the next day or the next week. I was diligently thinking ahead, planning for the future. Meanwhile, life seemed to be flowing past while I was absent.

Being busy is also a decision. Real freedom, I think, needs less striving. The good life needs one to be relaxed and at ease with the world. But I feared that if I stopped being productive, I would appear worthless in my own eyes. More questions arose. How could a writer stop being busy? How could he write a book and not care if anyone read it? Promoting a book was also a duty that one owed to the publisher. The wise ask us to live in the present, treat today as though it is our last. But this is easier said than done. The present remains elusive. The Gita advises that if I act without desire, *nishkama karma*, without caring who gets the credit, my life would be authentic. It's a wonderful, unselfish thought. Kamble could achieve this, but it was beyond me. My ego, I found, would not shrink that far. Alas, there was a serious shortage of the good life.

And so, I asked myself, is the lofty life of a writer another trap of ambition and endless striving? Before I could answer the question I got distracted by my ten-year-old granddaughter, Maya, who was visiting us from Singapore. She had been out that morning in Khan Market and announced that the Belgian chocolate shake at Big Chill was 'amazing'. Her eyes then fell on a teenager's book lying on my desk; it was written by a friend. I presented it to her. Leafing through it, she uttered, 'Awesome.' To her, everything was either 'awesome' or 'amazing'. In my day, a standard 'delicious' to describe a milk shake and a 'thank you' on receiving a book would have been fine.

I tend to reserve 'amazing' for the wonder I feel at seeing the night sky, with its billions of stars. I am 'amazed' that a one-and-a-half-kilogram mass of jelly that I could hold in my palm—my brain—could contemplate the meaning of infinity and question my place in the cosmos. What I find 'awesome' is that I am conscious that I was conscious. In that mass of jelly, there had somehow arisen consciousness, and it was telling me that I was alive in a cosmos of mostly inanimate objects. Especially awe-inspiring to me is the fact that my brain is made up of atoms formed billions of years ago. These atoms now formed the mass of jelly with which I could ponder over stars in the universe as well as my own consciousness, which was conscious of itself.

My granddaughter and I seemed to be speaking different languages. I blamed the Americans. She must have picked it up at her school, the American School of Singapore. We seemed to be playing different games as well. I was going for a stately cover drive in English cricket; she was going straight for a home run in American baseball. The following day, Maya gave me a hug before setting off with Bunu for Khan Market. 'You are awesome!' I declared, surprising myself. I am a joiner when it comes to my grandchildren. Kim Kanishka and Mitali had given us two. The other was her seven-year-old brother, Kabir, whose obsession in life was football. Since consciousness had been on my mind, I recounted to them the old story of the two birds perched on a tree—one eating the fruit, the other watching. It was an uncanny repeat of my father's act when I was their age. I told Maya that the two birds were symbols of the two voices inside each of us, that we talk to ourselves. The bird who had enjoyed the chocolate shake at Big Chill was the eating bird; the one who had found it 'amazing' was the witness. My father, I told them, used to call the second one 'godly bird'.

'You mean, there's God inside me?' asked Maya sceptically.

'My father certainly thought so.' She gave me a look. I reminded her to be sure to tell me when she ran into God.

'You're awesome, Dada!'

After Maya and Kabir flew back to Singapore, I returned to the nagging shadows in my life. Seeing me moping around, Bunu tried to cheer me up. 'Lighten up,' she said. 'Smile.' She reminded me that it was I who had once taught her the philosophy of laghima.

Yes, I could do with a bit of laghima. My writing life was even busier than my business life—it was silly. Writing should be play, more laughter. If I wasn't careful, this busyness might turn my writing into propaganda. I was taking life too seriously. Lightness and weightiness are an attitude of the mind. They are choices. Heaviness, of course, has a positive side; it has made me responsible. I keep my commitments. But it has also brought new oppressions of vanity, and they are not pleasant to behold. It was time to loosen up, shake off the gravity and recover the lightness I still experienced on rare days. The question, however, was how to shed that burden and make the rare days of a dancing star more frequent and normal.

Two incidents occurred in the following months that confirmed my diagnosis, upsetting my self-centred world. A week after my grandchildren left, I found myself at the Jaipur Literature Festival. It was India's most prestigious literary event, and I was chuffed to be invited to speak about my book *India Grows at Night*. While mingling among the literary greats from around the world, I learnt that they might have to cancel my session. A more 'popular' writer had agreed to come at the last minute and taken my slot. I was angry. 'How could they do it to me?' I thundered. I went to raise hell with the organizers. I was ranting and raving, telling them how important I was. My books had made an impact. Didn't they realize I was essential to the world? What I wrote mattered to the universe. Just as I was making a total fool of myself, a young man surfaced from behind. Quietly, he offered what my granddaughter would have called an 'amazing' proposition.

'I am a big fan of your books,' he said. 'And you're welcome to have my slot. Because of an emergency in the family, I have to return home. Many of my friends are here, and they have come to listen to you. They'll be disappointed if you don't speak.'

I was stunned. Deeply moved by the young man's sacrifice, I protested, making polite noises. 'No, no, I couldn't! But I was secretly pleased. The organizers were also relieved. They had one less disgruntled, narcissistic author to deal with. They were also puzzled because there was never a move to cancel my session. It must have been a rumour that I had heard. When I returned to the hotel, I felt ashamed, comparing my disgraceful behavior to the stranger's generosity. The following evening, I was introduced to my bête noire, the man who had supposedly stolen my slot. It was at a grand dinner thrown by Penguin. I was narrating to him the touching tale of the young man's renunciation when the bête noire's eye caught the attention of an attractive female face in the crowd. He stopped my story instantly and asked me if I knew the woman's identity. I shook my head. Without an 'excuse me', he walked away in her direction, leaving me in mid-sentence.

When I became an author I believed, naively, that I would also become a better human being. Art is supposed to encourage empathy. Writers need empathy to create characters—they have to learn to put themselves in the shoes of others. Homer chose to sing the deeds of his Trojan enemy Hector while praising, in the same breath, the glory of Achilles, the hero on his own side. But this act of identification, I realize now, is an instrument of the writer's craft and imagination. It does not lead to your behaving well with your neighbour. This is why writers are not necessarily good people. Oddly enough, I find that businesspeople are nicer. To succeed, they have to care for their employees and their customers. Writers only need to care for themselves.

The following week I was back in Delhi. I was feeling low after the events in Jaipur when an invitation arrived asking me to participate in a conversation with the Dalai Lama. I had long admired the spiritual leader, and the invite quickly lifted my spirits. Bunu, too, was excited and decided to come along. Donald J. wrote to say that he was also attending the same conference. We travelled together to the Himalayan Buddhist retreat of Dharamshala. On the journey up, we reminisced about old times. I told him about the 'Donald J. Effect'—how our walks along the Charles River in the 1980s had left a deep impression on me, reinforcing, in particular, my consultative style of management.

I caught him by surprise when I asked, 'Isn't the Buddhist monk's life pretty bleak?' Too much obsession with suffering, crushing of desire, etc. Doesn't it kill all the fun? No pleasure left. He became defensive. He felt I had misunderstood the Buddha. The problem lay in the mistranslation of *dukkha* as 'suffering'. By dukkha, Buddha had meant to refer to the idea that life was unsatisfactory—too much craving, vanity, people clinging to their egos. You were healthy one day, sick another. Nothing was permanent. Of course, there were moments of happiness, but nothing good seemed to last. Donald J. wondered why I wasn't equally disillusioned with the human condition.

Of course I was, but I merely nodded in agreement and let him continue. The Buddhist solution, he reiterated, was to recognize that my 'self' was a construct of the mind and to stop clinging to it. One had to get rid of the ego, the 'self', to develop a cultivated state of mind.

'I don't want to get rid of my 'self',' I told him bluntly. It would amount to getting rid of my humanity. But I agreed with almost everything else he had said. I would settle with diminishing my ego, not getting rid of it.

The Dalai Lama was utterly charming, in a playful mood, making jokes left and right. Instead of a serious holy man in maroon robes, he seemed to be my model of light living. What had brought us together was the Dalai Lama's desire to learn more about gross national happiness (GNH), the official measure of prosperity of the Buddhist kingdom of Bhutan. I was invited because someone had read *India Unbound* and thought I might offer a liberal Indian's perspective on GNH. In his opening remarks, the Dalai Lama confessed that he was a socialist, but he was also interested in how markets might enhance human choice, freedom and happiness. The Dalai Lama, his eyes twinkling, asked many questions and chuckled ironically when someone mentioned the term 'compassionate capitalism'.

I got an opportunity to speak to the Dalai Lama privately for a few minutes afterwards. I told him that I was a writer but the whole 'busyness' of my life was getting me down. I was still ambitious—on fire all the time—but I felt I was losing it when it came to living a happy, joyful life. He grinned and said, 'If a successful writer cannot be happy, then who can?' I told him that each day I seemed to create problems for myself and for others with my ego. I wondered if I should do something different in life.

'Should I become a monk or something?' I asked, surprising myself. I don't know where it came from, especially after I had referred to the 'bleakness' of a monk's life on the way up.

'Bad idea!' the Dalai Lama replied.

Instead of giving up my dream occupation, he suggested I spend time each day doing nothing. Just sit, relax, enjoy observing whatever thoughts came into my head. Just observe, without judging. Since I was an intellectual, it would be more difficult to do so. My mind had become too complicated, 'stuffed with too much stuff'. Doing nothing would help me to let things go a bit. Besides, I had nothing to lose—there was no such thing as a future (which was also a construct of the mind). I was confused; I didn't know quite what to make of his words. He seemed to be suggesting some sort of meditation. But I had already tried meditating without getting anywhere.

'Just remember, there is nowhere to get to. Nothing happens next; it is all here and now,' he said.

Thus, the sixth decade of my life came to an end. It confirmed my ideal of moksha was not to abandon the world but to make my world more habitable. Unlike religious and spiritual moksha, whose aspiration was for absolute freedom, my ideal was a limited one. When it came to my public life, I shifted from a laissez-faire, libertarian position of the previous decade to the more old-fashioned, classical-liberal position, which was more at home with ambiguities. I now believed strongly in an effective, liberal state. I am suspicious both of the Left and the Right, because they are both prone to statist solutions which undermine human liberty. Left-wing liberals abused me for being a 'neoliberal' and criticized me for not caring about inequalities created by the market. That was unfair, I felt, because I believed that the best way to lift the poor was through good education, health care and a social-safety net. Beyond that, I preferred to focus on jobs and labour-intensive growth, not on giveaways by the state.

But labels can be simplistic. There is much to admire in the conservative virtues of thrift, hard work and a desire to preserve what is good in the past. Equally commendable is the compassion of the left liberal—the consistent championing of the underdog. Human beings desire both liberty and equality. Both are good things, but I place liberty higher, unlike Left liberals. Perhaps, it is the result of the scars left behind by the Licence Raj. Or it is my moksha instinct. I want my life to depend on myself as much as possible, not on others. Unfettered, both liberty and equality are problematic. Absolute liberty for the wolves is death for the lambs. Absolute equality kills the human need to excel. The Soviet Union's collapse has taught us that the human ego will not shrink that far. Closer to home, I've learnt that it's dangerous to put dreamers in power. Nehru wanted the equality of socialism, but what we got was an oppressive statism that killed our spirits. Around the same time, Jinnah wanted a state based on Islam, and what Pakistan got was a haven for Islamic terrorism. Had Jinnah not been so insistent, the subcontinent might have remained united. Both nations would have been spared the absurd tragedy of Partition and the never-ending Kashmir problem.

Like Isaiah Berlin, I have learnt to be wary of romantics and saints. It is better to have modest persons in power. Sadly, India lost Lal Bahadur Shastri too soon. He was the most modest of men and full of robust common sense. One should not seek perfection in politics or in personal life. Hence, my ideal image of moksha is not a horse without a harness but a 'horse easy in its harness', as Robert Frost put it.

I am suspicious of all ideologies. I worry about the recent rise of right-wing nationalism in India and in the world. For most of free India's history, however, the Left has held sway. Although the Left has played a laudable role in reminding us of the poor, it has also been wrong so consistently.

It still backs government monopolies instead of competitive markets. It protects organized labour (8 per cent of labour) at the expense of 92 per cent unorganized workers. Until the 1990s, it opposed computers in offices and banned English in primary schools. Its foreign policy during the Cold War landed us on the losing side of history. It was silent during the Emergency, when the entire Opposition was in jail. It did not condemn the Chinese invasion of India in 1962. And going further back, it sided with the British during the Quit India movement!

In the private sphere, my sixtieth decade had brought me success as a writer. Ironically, though, it was the writing career that was letting me down. I was becoming enslaved by new strivings. The sense of life's absurdity was beginning to surface again. Instead of shedding masks, I had put on new ones. It was a bit of a shock for me to discover that writers and artists were no better than others as human beings. As these new burdens piled up, I was back at square one, feeling, yet again, a bit like Sisyphus staring at the rock that had slid down the mountain. I began to think of the futile task of pushing the rock up the mountain.

The Dalai Lama, like Donald J. before him, might have nudged me towards something I could believe in. I did not become Buddhist, but I accepted its analysis of the transitory nature of human identity. Since I was aware of the stream of thoughts in my head, I wondered if his advice to be 'idle'—to observe, not judge my thoughts—could somehow help me to get rid of the nastier emotions that continued to bring so much day-to-day grief. Would I ever be free of the big fat ego? If the answer was 'yes', then it might lead to another sort of moksha, a modest, non-transcendental one, achievable in this life.

19

Another Sort of Freedom

'It is the mind alone that creates
bondage and liberation.'

—Amritabindu Upanishad

One spring evening in mid-February 2013, Bunu and I found ourselves among the glamorous, artsy crowd of Delhi. Escorting us past her garden's blooming dahlias, our hostess lamented the short spring season. Saying this, she leaned over, exposing her bosom through her low-cut blouse, which matched her chiffon sari. Although no beauty, she had an arresting face with thick black eyelashes, and I stared admiringly. Paying no heed to the impression she had made, she led us into the drawing room. Putting an arm around Bunu, she said, 'Come, come, my dear, I have something to show you.' And the two set off towards the kitchen.

I looked around but didn't recognize anyone. Meeting strangers at a party is awkward, particularly when the hostess has not introduced you or slotted you into a comfortable compartment. It is easier to break the ice when you know that someone is someone's aunt, or a teacher or golfer. I tried to make a clever remark to the person standing next to me, but the conversation did not flow. I wandered off to look at the host's formidable collection of paintings on the surrounding walls—a Ramkumar in pastel shades, a meditative Gaitonde, energetic horses of Husain, and others.

I wondered what motivates a collector to collect. Is it a desire to surround oneself with beauty? Or a hard-headed calculation of the return on investment? Or maybe a wish to build a reputation as a cultured person? I wasn't aware of my host's motives, but I had been driven to build the P&G collection in Bombay for the first reason. It had backfired because most employees did not find beauty in abstract art—they would have preferred decorative pictures.-

As I was completing my round, I spotted an attractive, vaguely familiar face. She was sitting alone on a sofa, her hands folded in her lap. For a second, I was confused, thinking it was a figure on a canvas. Women have always been an enigma to me. I walked up to her, harbouring thoughts not befitting a man of my age. She surprised me, announcing my name impulsively. Seeing the puzzled look on my face, she added, 'Who doesn't know you? Night after night on TV, you are famous.' I was flattered. 'I bet you don't recognize me, though?' Before I could reply, she burst out, 'Alisha!'

'My first love!' I exclaimed.

I was embarrassed at my impulsive response and didn't know what to say. We stood in uncomfortable silence until a waiter came to our rescue. 'What will you have?' I asked her. Both of us ordered fresh lime sodas. As we waited for our drinks, distressing memories of her in school, and later in Bombay, came racing back. Alisha had changed—no longer angular, her face and body had filled up. In a plain cotton sari, she blended easily into this artsy crowd. Her sleeveless blouse drew attention to her neck and shoulders. She had aged well and was still lovely to look at. The simple 'cotton look' spoke of a friendlier, mellower disposition.

'So, how have you been? What are you doing?' I asked.

She opened her hands in her lap and then looked up. 'I wish I had something to do—if only to escape from myself.'

'Can one ever escape from oneself?'

There were many things I wanted to say, but I managed only to ask how she happened to be there that evening. Her husband, I learnt, was an old friend of our elusive host.

'And here I am, waiting for my husband. I seem only to be waiting these days.'

The waiter returned with a bucket of ice, soda, sugar syrup, a container of salt and two glasses containing fresh lime juice. Alisha added sugar, salt and ice to her drink. I drank mine plain. The mention of her husband made me mildly jealous, but she did not speak about him again, even though I gave her several opportunities. It was difficult to believe that this disenchanted woman was the same person that had brought me to my knees, not once but twice. She seemed to have lived with disappointments, but they had left her as desirable as ever. I wish I had been able to reciprocate some of her confidences that evening, but I was too overwhelmed, confused.

Soon, the others arrived. First her husband, then Bunu, and finally, our host. There were the usual introductions and small talk. It was clear to both Alisha and me that we were attracted to each other, and matters could easily have gone further. After some time, Bunu and I moved on to join other groups. At the end of the evening, Alisha and I went our separate ways. Although we did run into each other from time to time after that—and each time with mutual delight—we observed the *Kamasutra*'s sensible advice. It is natural, says the *Kamasutra*, for a man to be attracted to a beautiful woman. It is equally natural for a woman to be attracted to a handsome man. 'But after some consideration, the matter goes no further.'

Although matters did not go any further, I realized how much I had missed Alisha and our life of shared sensual pleasure in Bombay. In my busyness as a writer, I had almost banished desire from my life. The party had the unintended consequence of pushing me to explore the beguiling realm of *kama*, of 'desire and pleasure', in my next book. Desire, of course, had troubled me, especially when I was younger. But with age some of the torment of youth had gone. While working on my dharma book, I had stumbled upon an intriguing line in the Mahabharata: 'Desire is the essence of life,' it said. I hadn't thought much about it then, but I was ready now to find out, to explore the entire realm of kama. There were many questions. How did ancient Indians think about the domain of sensual intoxication? How did a deeply religious land of renouncers abound with erotic sculptures, love poetry and texts like the *Kamasutra*? And why had the Indian middle class turned prudish today?

I put these questions casually to Bob Goldman, the renowned Sanskrit scholar from the University of California, who was visiting Delhi with his wife, Sally. Instead of giving me answers, he had a thought: Why don't we create a kama reading group? What was that? A bunch of like-minded persons would read a text and meet once a week to discuss it. What a nice idea! Before I could wrap my head around it, Bob had translated his thought into action. I soon got an appointment letter for a fellowship from the University of California. And so, in September 2013, Bunu and I found ourselves in a magical Berkeley home situated amid a cluster of ancient redwood trees.

I was sceptical that anyone would want to read ancient and medieval Indian texts on desire. To my surprise, however, more than a dozen people showed up. We were a motley bunch that gathered on Monday afternoons, from 3 to 6 p.m., in Dwinelle Hall. Among them were Sanskrit scholars, an Indo–American novelist with an interest in tantra, a ninety-year-old expert in Jainism, a feminist and an aficionado of medieval Sufi poetry. Since the course was not for credit, curiosity and love of the subject had brought us together. And it was among these happy few that my biography of sense-intoxicating desire was born. I was at an age now when I was mostly reliving memories, some intimate, others wistful and still others so distressing that I was left sweating. I wished I had attempted this book earlier, when desire was more troublesome. Gradually, however, I concluded that an ageing writer with a life full of experience may be better equipped to do this than a young, vigorous warrior—much in the way that a recollection of love is more powerful than the original confused experience.

I quickly found a cosy corner in the library, where I made wondrous discoveries among Berkeley's rich archives. I was amazed at a verse in the Rig Veda, the first scripture of the Hindus, telling me that the cosmos was created from 'the seed of desire in the mind of the One'. But ironically, India's middle class today seemed to deny desire. The ancient Hindus had even elevated it to a goal of life, creating a handsome, charming god of love called Kama. How sexually liberating and creative the Gupta period must have been, giving birth to the extraordinary *Kamasutra*, beguiling Sanskrit love poetry and erotic statuary!

As my book began to take shape, I realized that the biography of desire needed a narrative. And so, I invented a new form, a mixture of fictional memoir and philosophical reflection. I created sensual characters and lived vicariously through them for the next four years. The search for beauty and pleasure ruled my life during this period, sending me to art galleries, music concerts and gay soirées. Bunu was surprised at the change, but I loved my new mask. *Kama: The Riddle of Desire* was launched to good reviews in 2018. The same year the Supreme Court in India also obliged with historic verdicts related to sexual freedom, overturning old colonial laws on homosexuality and adultery. Overall, it had been a heady ride, celebrating the freedom of kama—another significant milestone in my life's journey in search of moksha.

During this period, my friends and acquaintances didn't quite know what to make of me. Ever since 1995, when I became a full-time writer, they had pegged me as a libertarian economist, obsessed with liberal market reforms. *India Unbound* and my umpteen columns had reinforced that image. In 2008, they were perplexed when *The Difficulty of Being Good* came out. Where to slot me now—mythologist, classical scholar, moralist? And when the book on kama appeared ten years later, they were totally confused. Sexologist? Aesthete? Hedonist? Meanwhile, I faced a moral dilemma pertaining to my political identity. It was a conflict between two aspects of moksha which came to a head during the national election of 2014.

There is always a trade-off at the ballot box. Should I risk secularism and pluralism for the sake of prosperity, jobs and clean government? Revolted by the corruption and paralysis of the UPA-II Congress government, I was clutching at straws, willing to try anything. In the past, I had mostly voted for the Congress, albeit reluctantly. The other parties were regional. A start-up, Aam Aadmi Party, had risen out of the ashes of Anna Hazare's anti-corruption movement, but it wasn't yet a serious contender. In this unhappy situation rose Narendra Modi, of the right-wing Bhartiya Janata Party (BJP), and he caught everyone by surprise. His campaign speeches, with a single-minded focus on *vikas*— investment, jobs, skills and growth—were fresh. His slogan of 'minimum government, maximum governance' appealed to the liberal in me.

And yet, I felt nervous. Modi was supposed to be authoritarian, polarizing, and he carried the stain of the 2002 Hindu–Muslim riots in Gujarat. But there had been no further incidents for more than a decade, and I hoped he had turned a new leaf. It was a conflict in my mind between economic and religious freedom. I agonized for weeks and then decided to vote reluctantly for the BJP. I was among the first liberals to publicly endorse Modi in my columns in the *Times of India*. My friends on the Left thought I was either blind to evil or naive enough to be swept by the Modi wave. The ones on the Right were still suspicious of me and had been so ever since I had publicly rebuked Modi for the 2002 riots. In the end, Modi won the 2014 election decisively.

My hopes, however, faded with time. It began with the bizarre and botched up demonetization of the currency in 2016. In an attempt to control 'black money' in the untaxed cash economy, the government suddenly withdrew Rs 500 and Rs 1000 notes. Instead of trapping rich tax evaders, the measure hurt small businesses and the poor in a country where 90 per cent of the transactions were in cash. Hindu nationalism began to polarize the nation, making Muslims feel insecure. To the government's credit, it brought in significant reforms—for example, the Goods and Services Tax, which made India one market—and it ushered in a digital revolution that almost doubled the banking population. But the government failed to deliver the promised jobs.

Yet Modi remained hugely popular. The Congress party, under Rahul Gandhi, seemed to self-destruct, failing to offer the voter a coherent alternative. In 2019, the voters had no choice but to re-elect Modi. Sadly, I was the man in the middle, disappointed with both sides, with no one to vote for. I had grown up believing in Nehru's idea of a plural India—the opposite of a nineteenth-century European nation state based on a single religion, language and ethnicity. But Nehru's lot had failed to appreciate that India also had an ancient civilizational unity, whose values resonated with the masses. This failure helped to revive the Hindu nationalists, who claimed that Nehruvian pluralism was merely about appeasing the minorities and vote-bank politics. But unfortunately, while dreaming of a grand civilizational state, Hindu nationalists were, in fact, trying to create a narrow-minded, identity-based European nation state—a sort of Hindu Pakistan.

* * *

It was now the evening of my life, and I was still restless. I could feel mortality creeping as I descended into my seventh decade. I was still hearing life's music, but the *ardharaswara*, the bass note, rumbled echoes of discontent. Despite considerable worldly success in my two careers, my vessel was not full. I had created and recreated myself. I had seen this, done that. I had experienced both longings and satisfactions. I tried to console myself—restlessness may well be in the nature of the human condition, and we're not meant to be satisfied till we die.

During the Covid lockdown, I stumbled upon a quote by Seneca, which spoke to my nagging anxiety. 'The busy man,' he writes, 'is busy with everything except living.' I was puzzled initially. What did he mean by 'living'? If anyone had lived a life, it was he. A philosopher, a statesman, an orator and a tragedian, he had not only been Rome's leading intellectual in the mid-first century CE, but he had also virtually ruled the Roman world during Emperor Nero's early reign. A person who had achieved all this in one lifetime had to be 'busy'. So why was he complaining about life passing him by? My own life paled in comparison, but I could still identify with his lament. When I showed the quote to Bunu, she called us both spoiled brats, dismissing my problem as 'third-stage melancholy'. It was an expression she had picked up from my mother, and she filed my complaints under it. The third stage, Vanaprastha ashrama, of the classical Hindu life is the period after retirement, when an active person is naturally susceptible to the blues, she felt.

I continued to grow sceptical of achievement and ambition. Although I'd had my share of good days, it wasn't enough to call it a good life. On the good days, I would be absorbed totally in my writing, working for hours without feeling tired or hungry. But on ordinary days, I would be living a 'task' rather than living a life. I would be hustling, as though the only point of it all was to make it to the airport on time. I had lost the hair on my head because of 'to-do' lists. Writerly longings had replaced old corporate ambitions. While I may have inherited the willingness to hustle from my mother, I was mostly a product of the modern hurry-hurry of life. So, the question: How to reclaim human dignity in a culture of busyness? Seneca's friends, the Stoics, had suggested that one ought to live every day as though it were one's last. A great ambition, but I found it too difficult to live that wisely.

I also suffered from other infirmities. Some critics of my writing could be blunt, even insulting. I would flare up, raise my voice. Slowly, I got resigned to criticism, learning to shrug, saying to myself that it came with the territory. This would unhinge the critic, who didn't know what to say. The whole thing would be over in seconds. Another problem was that I would raise my voice when I got impatient. Bunu had to remind me of this failing at least once a week. There were other deficiencies as well, mostly owing to vanity—lusting after prestige, the need to be liked. I still took myself too seriously. All this undercut my aspiration for moksha and laghima.

The search for moksha drives many to religion. Not me—I am too addicted to reason, unable to take the leap of faith. I delight in the messiness of the natural world and don't seek a supernatural world of eternal beauty. And yet, I am comfortable with Hinduism, which makes room for an agnostic like me. I can be a *nastika*, a non-believer, and still be a respectable Hindu. Hinduism has a place for everyone: If you like ritual, there are marvellously intricate Vedic rites; the philosophically inclined can turn to the exciting mental experiments of the Upanishads; idol worshippers are offered a rich menu of 300 million gods, none of whom can afford to feel jealous. Hindus know that each of their gods is a symbol of one God. Hence, in one breath, they can utter, 'There are many gods and one God.' Lovers of a personal god, like my father, have devotional, Bhakti sects to choose from. The dissenting renouncer, in contrast, dissatisfied with the human condition, can become a hero in saffron robes. Hinduism is a big civilizational tent.

My mother was disappointed that I had squandered my father's rich spiritual inheritance, losing a golden opportunity to gain the ultimate prize of spiritual moksha. I was mad to throw away the treasured mantra that would have freed me from the cycle of birth and rebirth. I wanted to tell her that not only did I not believe in God, but I actually preferred a world that didn't need Him. I kept these thoughts to myself, however, out of respect for her beliefs. I wanted human beings to be free of religion's slavery. I had seen enough during Partition, when people were too willing to pick up a weapon and kill cheerfully in the name of their God. I wanted a world where human beings could stand tall before life's meaninglessness, without having to bow before a higher power. Nature was extraordinary, the universe wondrous. I had no need for the supernatural.

Having abandoned my father's spiritual path—and all religious paths—I was left to fend for myself. Madhav Sayana, writing in the fourteenth century about the atheistic Charvaks and their idea of moksha, says, 'Bondage is dependence upon others, while moksha is dependence on oneself.' Well, I too had decided to depend on myself. It was liberating, yes, but it was also lonely. When I looked at the big picture, I felt that nothing

I did would matter a thousand years from now. I was only a tiny speck in the infinite vastness of the universe, and what I did didn't count. And I would die one day. So, what was the point of writing books? To what end? The gap between aspirations and reality would sometimes get unbearable. Once again, the old feeling of my life's absurdity would return. I felt as though my trousers had fallen down while I was receiving a prize in public.

'When God is gone, how do you give meaning to your life?' my mother had once asked. I had failed to give her a satisfactory answer. But I had an inkling that meaning emerges from pursuing something bigger than yourself. I had experienced it as a spirit of lightness. It usually happens when I am deeply absorbed in my writing. It is as if I am not even there—the fingers just keep hitting the keys of my laptop and words keep appearing on the screen. Sachin Tendulkar described the same feeling when he was approaching his last double century. He said the cricket ball had become so big that the bat just had to hit the ball. The psychologist Mihaly Csikszentmihalyi calls it 'flow'. The problem with this feeling is that it is temporary. The big question was: Could I extend it to the rest of the day, to the rest of my life? Could self-forgetting become an enduring attitude of living lightly?

Such questions had emerged early. For instance, when I first encountered David Hume's *A Treatise of Human Nature* at Harvard. I became aware of the stream of thoughts in my head. The voices first appeared involuntarily, a decade later, when I was in my early thirties. They convinced me that I could only be sure of the existence of momentary thoughts, not of the thinker. Like Hume, I looked for an author but could not find him. Was I then merely a fictional composite of my momentary selves? If so, how was I able to negotiate from one thought to the next? What provided continuity between my individual moments, I concluded, were my memories, my desires and my beliefs. But these mental entities also depended on the temporary roles I was playing, the masks I was wearing. They could not convince me of my permanent existence.

All this led to growing scepticism about my permanent identity. I concluded that my I-ness was a fraud, a sort of fictional narrator that held the story of my life together. I have been much influenced by Donald J., and by Nagarjuna's Buddhist idea of *anatta*, no-self. When the 'I' got busted, I was hugely unnerved. I could not live without a concept of personhood. But I still needed to get on with my life. Of all the emotions

I possessed, the most overwhelming was a deep concern for my own survival. I still needed an author, an object of my self-concern. If it didn't exist, how would I be responsible for my actions? Not just in a courtroom but in my conscience. For all practical purposes, I needed a stable concept of a person.

As time went by, I gradually became resigned to the absence of a permanent 'I', which brought a subtle change in me. I felt a sense of freedom, in fact, knowing that I was not my thoughts, and I began to view my identity as useful fiction, a practical necessity, a minimal self. I became a little more detached, seeing through the many roles I was playing in my life. My day-to-day life, however, did not change. I did not suddenly become selfless or philanthropic. Self-concern still defined my attitude towards myself. But I felt less and less at the centre of the universe—I was just one among others. My minimal self, in other words, was able to extend the same concern a little more easily to others. As a result, I began to feel a continuum or sameness with other selves. I did not constantly hanker after premium treatment for myself.

It was this awakening that raised a hope. If my minimal self could more easily identify with the selves of others, could I become a more empathetic, more compassionate person? Could I overcome some of the worst egotistical defects in my character and liberate myself from bondages that had nagged me all my life? I had lived my life in the constant belief that my interests trumped everyone else's. And my behaviour had been consistently egocentric. There were exceptions from time to time—a few early moments of awakening! The obvious one being the pencil box incident in kindergarten. When Ayan was about to be wrongly punished for stealing the rich kid's pencil box, he had cried out, appealed to me. But I had remained silent. My feeling of shame was followed by profound concern for Ayan, which has never left me. A few months later, I experienced this in a different way in those violent days of Partition. On this occasion, I felt a wave of empathy for the handsome Muslim policeman on the railway platform just as he was stabbed to death by two Sikh boys. I bumped first into Ayan and then into Partition, both without warning, and they pulled me out of my egocentric self, at least for a while.

I was fortunate to grow up in a family where I was occasionally offered intimations of goodness. My memories of these moments—my father working selflessly night and day, constructing the Bhakra Dam; or later, when he was tirelessly building a hospital at the ashram in Beas. It is hard to discern motives that drive individuals. Good actions are often driven by narcissism, making us believe we are better than others. In my case, I cannot be entirely sure why I donated a good chunk of our savings to become a founder of Ashoka University. Was I impelled by the obvious love for the liberal arts or by vanity, or by some combination of the two? Self-love is built into the structure of our consciousness. Ashoka University went on to become an outstanding institution, an oasis of excellence amid mediocre state universities. I may not know if God exists, but I do know a good deed when I see one. What matters in the end are outcomes, not motives of the actors.

There were more modest altruistic initiatives I took up during the second decade of this century. One of them was to fight the New Delhi Municipal Corporation to let us convert an illegal garbage dump behind our home into a natural pocket park. After winning the battle against the petty bureaucracy, it took quite a while for residents to stop throwing their trash there. Eventually, they changed their habits when they saw shrubs and trees coming up in the same space. A second was a project called Bolo English, a smartphone app to make young people fluent in English. It was my cook's daughter who gave me the idea. She arrived one morning from a village in Uttarakhand desperate to learn English. We put her first in a summer school, then in coaching classes, all to no avail, until she discovered Hello English, an app on my phone. She got hooked to it immediately. While she thought she was playing a game, she was, in fact, learning English. Within two months, she had learnt to speak colloquial English confidently.

I was thrilled and suggested to the Centre for Civil Society (CCS) to run a project to teach children through their smartphones. The timing was right. Covid had struck, schools had closed. And so, during the terrible pandemic, tens of thousands of children learnt English sitting at home. Based on the learnings from this project, CCS has been working to embed Bolo English into the curricula of both government and private schools. For me, Bolo English is not just another philanthropic venture; it is a moral pursuit—to help bridge the tragic divide in a country where knowing English puts you in an elite caste, while the rest are condemned to outsider status in their own land.

There are other memories that have reinforced my hopes of becoming a better person. In some cases, I was the victim—for instance, when Alisha rejected my flowers, or when the high school vice principal denied me a place in the college prep section. Instead of making me feel humiliated, the absurd injustice of their actions pulled me out of my shell, and I was able to identify with universal principles of justice. Another memory is of discovering the poverty of India for the first time during my summer break in college. I promptly returned to Harvard in the fall and began taking economics courses, and it went on to become a lifelong obsession. I even switched careers later in life and ended in writing umpteen newspaper columns on development. All these were moments of awakening in a mostly self-centred existence. But they proved to me that I could alter my orientation from being self-directed to other-directed.

It was a significant moment when I became convinced of this. Not only was I persuaded that my I-ness was a bit of a hoax—a role that I had been conned into playing—but the separation between me and the other person was reduced. The feeling of connectedness is the best foundation for ethics. Science was also on my side. Neuroscientists had confirmed that the self was a fiction of the social brain, imprisoning one in its ego shell. The thought that my own identity was a fictional composite of momentary selves set me free. When you don't have a permanent identity, you don't have to impress anyone. Not having the constant current of an 'I' following you, not having to live an image of yourself, is liberating.

It was truly momentous! I had found a worthy, 'all-natural' moksha, without any supernatural additives. The door of the cage had opened. A wild spirit of freedom took hold of me. I felt triumphant in discovering a purely mundane, natural conception of moksha, very different from my father's supernatural one. When an idea takes hold of your imagination— no matter how wild—it is yours. There was no stopping me now. No one could do it, not even my spiritually inclined friends, who found my novel use of the word 'moksha' offensive.

As the days went by, however, I felt something was missing. It wasn't long before I realized that my conception of moksha was a negative freedom. It was liberation *from* something—i.e., from my big fat ego. What is the positive state, I asked myself, that my moksha was leading to? A clue appeared one Saturday afternoon at the National Museum in Delhi. It took the form of a gentle smile on a cool, serene face of a sixth-century

Mathura sculpture from the Gupta period. It expressed many things: a calm equanimity, a sense of lightness and peace, suggestive of someone who didn't need to strive any more. Although cool, her smile also spoke of a warm-hearted goodwill. Yes, this was a worthy destination.

The following week, I felt pulled back to that alluring smile. On my second visit, I was drawn, in particular, to the lightness of her being. Her smile reminded me of the best moments of my life, reassuring me that I was capable of weightlessness. As a three-year-old in Lyallpur, when I discovered I could run, I had experienced zero gravity. I would be scampering, laughing, smacking kids bigger than me (until I whacked a VIP's kid in the Company Bagh and a policeman had to be called). When I was sixteen, I felt the same lightness of spirit, twirling with Maria at the I-House in Washington, DC, flying without wings, my body floating like a star a billion light years away. And more recently, on days when my writing would go sublimely, I would be like a bird ready to fly after a storm. As I think of these ecstatic moments of lightness, I feel they were produced by self-forgetting. The guru had predicted it when he changed my name. His ideal was to take one's work seriously, not oneself seriously. If Kamble could do it, so could I! It was the familiar spirit of laghima that accompanied all-natural moksha.

I couldn't keep away from that Mathura statue. On a third visit, I meditated on the equipoise on her tranquil face. Long ago at the university, I had learnt from Aristotle that a human being had many capabilities. To fulfil them was the path to a flourishing life filled with eudaimonia. A similar ideal exists in the classical Hindu concept of the four purusharthas, aims of life, as I've already mentioned. These are, in a sense, human potentialities. Maybe fulfilling them had led to the equipoise on her tranquil face. She had realized her human potential, and I had found not only the recipe for a flourishing life but the positive freedom in an all-natural conception of moksha.

While doing research on kama at Berkeley, I had stumbled upon some advice from Anandavardhana, the ninth-century Sanskrit literary critic. He suggested that a good book ought to confine itself to one of the four purusharthas. All of a sudden, it hit me: I had been following his advice all along. I first wrote a book on the goal of artha, material well-being, in *India Unbound*. I then wrestled with the second aim of dharma, moral well-being, in *The Difficulty of Being Good*. And in *Kama: The Riddle of*

Desire, I tried to come to terms with the third purushartha, kama, sexual and emotional well-being. The ancients called these three ends *trivarga*, and I had got a trilogy. By cultivating the goals of life in my writing, I had been rehearsing unwittingly for the equipoise that emerges from fulfilling one's capabilities. So, when would the rehearsal be over and the performance begin?

The quest for meaning is an old yearning in human beings. Animals, birds and trees don't seem to care. They simply live. Only a human being feels absurd, never a mouse. This is because humans have a reflexive consciousness, which takes the form of the two Upanishadic birds inside the head—one is content to live from day to day; the other is nagging constantly, 'What's the meaning of your life?' I have finally concluded that life has no inherent meaning. The universe doesn't care either. Only I do. This was why I was driven to create an 'all-natural' conception of moksha—to give meaning to my life.

I try to live nowadays in the deliberate pursuit of this naturalistic moksha. But it isn't easy. For a start, it is difficult to diminish the ego, because human beings are genetically programmed for survival. Then, it takes time to get out of the habit of demanding premium treatment. I find self-forgetting helps. When I am absorbed in the flow of writing a book, self-forgetting becomes easier. It is also easier to identify with another. But a flash of empathy for another's suffering is not enough. You have to learn to act on it. Like Yudhishthira at the end of the Mahabharata. He refuses to step inside heaven without the dog. I have a long way to reach his level of compassion, but I have realized that a selfless act of goodness is brighter than all the stars; it is itself an act of happiness. All this has helped me to break the worst of my old ego-filled habits, and I feel I am on the right track.

Sometimes this strange journey of life gets too much, and I am ready to give up. Then I have to remind myself that I come from a land where the gods are playful, and they created the world for the fun of it. Divine play is *leela*, another nice Sanskrit word, which reminds us humans not to take ourselves too seriously. If the gods could create me in a spirit of play, shouldn't I be freer, laughing more, living lightly? It is certainly the right way to be, I tell myself, as I journey on to winning my final prize of laghima, self-effacing flow and equipoise.

20

At the End, I'll Laugh at Anything

'So, have a little fun.
Soon enough you'll be dead
and burning in Hell
with the rest of your family.'

—George Carlin

'Don't you think we're going a little too fast? We're early, you know,' Bunu said.

I was driving her to the Delhi Gymkhana Club. It was not what she said that rankled but her indulgent tone, as though she were speaking to a tiresome child. She had adopted it lately. I looked over and watched as she shooed away a stubborn fly fluttering near her arm. I was on the wrong side of my seventies now but didn't feel it. I certainly wasn't senile, even though she treated me as though I were. We were going to meet our friends at the Party Cottage in the club to celebrate someone's seventy-fifth birthday. But I had a chilling sensation that I would be meeting death. Both of us were so absorbed in our thoughts that we didn't notice when I forgot to take the turn on to Safdarjung Road. We drove on for some time on Tughlaq Road before we realized that we had gone too far.

'Are we lost?' she asked in the same forbearing tone.

'We must be.'

I am at that stage in life where all the fun seems to lie in the past. Even though I don't feel old, I am afraid of dying. Last week I stood in front of the bathroom mirror, trying to imagine what it would be like to be dead. Perhaps I ought to close my eyes to get a better idea. I looked deep inside me. Then I tried to delete myself from the picture. I wasn't particularly successful. So I made a cup of tea and went and sat out on the veranda. Watching yourself in the mirror is like talking to yourself—like the Upanishad's two birds. What kind of person did I want to see in the mirror? I began thinking wondering if I'd been a good person. What would it be like to live forever? I thought of Yayati in the Mahabharata. He had lived to the fullest, enjoying all of life's sensual pleasures for a thousand years. It was exhausting thinking of it. I would have grown bored, I decided. Well, maybe not a thousand years. How about 342 years? This was Elina Makropulos's age in Karel Čapek's play *The Makropulos Case*. Her unending life has become a state of cold boredom and indifference. 'In the end, it is the same,' she keeps saying of her joyless life as she yearns for death.

I have lived most of my life thinking I would live on forever. But going by Elina's experience, it might not be such a good idea. The thought of doddering about, doing the same thing for hundreds of years, doesn't quite hit the spot. An endless life might be meaningless, and death may not be so bad after all. No wonder some people say that immortality is a fate worse than death. At least Yayati was smart. He exchanged his old age for his son's youth and continued to enjoy life's pleasures for a millennium. None of my sons would have agreed to that arrangement—even though I named my youngest one Puru, after Yayati's dutiful son, who gave up his youth to his father. Death is meant to remind us of the value of life. If I lived for a thousand years (or even 342), I might not value it as much.

I still maintain the same routine of the past quarter century. Waking up around 5 a.m. and writing till noon. I begin writing with the first light of day. I am lucky—I've never had to ask myself, 'What shall I do today?' It's a question peculiar to our age. Through most of history, no one had to ask it. You did what your father did; you were a peasant or an artisan or a landlord. What you did was taken for granted. In our age, retirement is a problem, especially for a busy man. Writing is my life, and despite my age I haven't lost the zest for it.

I follow up my writing with a swim at the Gymkhana Club. The heated water is an unbelievable luxury in Delhi's winter, just what the back needs after a long morning of writing, sitting upright. As its pores open, my body yields to the sumptuous comfort of warm water, and I am happy to be alive. I sometimes joke around with the guys in the locker room after swimming. One day, I announced that I wasn't afraid of death—as long as it wasn't mine. For me, the worst part of being dead is that my friends will still be alive, having a good time at the club. They'll be drinking chai and eating samosas, and I won't be there. They'll be going to parties, watching movies on Netflix and having fun without me. After a few days they will forget me, as though I never existed.

Sometimes, though, our locker-room conversations get heavy. One of the gang was feeling low last month, speaking about the pointlessness of spending years and years acquiring knowledge, accumulating experience, trying to be good, struggling to make something of yourself. What is the point, he asked, if you were going to die at the end? It's like building a beautiful sandcastle below the tideline. His words must have hit hard because I went home and told Bunu. I always eat lunch with her at home. On some days I might prefer a sandwich, but she insists that I stick to a full Indian lunch, as it's our main meal. She isn't into philosophizing and talking about life's meaning, and she tries to change the subject. But I persist. If nothing of me survives after death, what is the point of all this striving and ambition? Isn't it absurd to find that what you thought was your life all along was an elaborately staged production, a performance before an empty theatre? A calm, modest life might bring more happiness than all the striving and restlessness in the pursuit of success.

Bunu thinks I am being dramatic. Besides, she says it is not a suitable subject to discuss over lunch. In the end, however, she relents and tries to console me with the thought that I may live on through my books. If someone in the future would pick up a copy of *The Difficulty of Being Good* and would be drawn to some idea in it, then I would live on in their thoughts. I look at her doubtfully, but I feel pleased inside, even grateful. She is relieved when Lapsi, the street dog we have adopted, begins to bark, and I get distracted. At least, Lapsi doesn't worry about these things. Animals aren't aware that they will die one day. Humans get into these things because of our surplus brain capacity that created our reflexive consciousness. To cope with the fear of dying, humans invented religion. They began to believe in an immortal soul, making up stories of the afterlife. Then science came along, and it told us a different story about life and death—about how we evolved from animals. But many people still find it hard to stomach this and cling to the old, consoling ideas of life after death.

After lunch, I lie down for an hour or so, but I don't sleep. I read a newspaper or a book while I'm horizontal. Then I get up and deal with emails and the affairs of the world. One afternoon, however, I did something I hadn't done for quite a while. I fell into thinking about my mother. She had died fifteen years ago, and my memories of her were fading. After all, how long can one remain interested in a dead person? It's quite normal to forget someone after they die. A few days before she passed away, she had asked me what I thought happened when a person died.

'When you die, you just die,' I said. 'The body becomes a corpse.'

'But what happens to my soul?'

'If you mean consciousness, it too dies.'

'Do you really believe that nothing remains? All my thoughts, feelings, memories—they'll just vanish into nothingness?'

I nodded.

She became sad. 'No hope at all, then? It must be unbearable for you.'

Before I could answer she sighed, wishing I had been more like my father. He had welcomed his death. He viewed life as a prison of karmic action into which one was forced to be born and reborn in an endless cycle, and his purpose was to liberate himself, through meditation, from the karmic jail of birth and rebirth. This liberation was his moksha, and it freed him forever from being born again. Unlike him, I think rather badly of death because this may be the only life I would live. Death suddenly puts an end to all the good things I am experiencing—my pleasures, feelings, activities and hopes. Of course, it ends unhappiness too. But on balance, happiness seems to have outweighed misery in my life. Despite the restlessness and discontent, life has been worth living.

I now understand why my grandmother used to keep repeating, 'Shukar hai!' She truly understood the gift of life and could never stop thanking God for it. It gave her amazing clarity about her daily choices. I had once complained to her, 'Why couldn't I be taller?' She answered that some things are up to us, while others are not. 'You have only so many breaths to live. So focus on what you can change, and forget the rest.'

By five in the evening, I am ready for an evening walk in the Lodi Gardens. I am a sucker for company, especially of younger people. If anyone wants to meet me, I usually suggest an evening stroll. The paths in the gardens are passageways for talking, thinking or meditating. One day, however, an older man showed up at five. I looked up, and a stranger was staring at me—his eyebrows slipping down, bags under his eyes and sadness etched around his mouth. Except, this was no stranger. He was an old friend whom I hadn't seen for decades.

As we walked, he filled me in on his life. He had gone on to become a respected scientist, serving with distinction at top universities in America, and now lived there in a luxurious retirement home, not far from his children. Though we are contemporaries, he looks and behaves like a much older man. I remembered him as cheerful and lively, but now he was preoccupied with blood pressure, blood sugar and arthritis. He had acquired a lot of medical information and insisted on sharing it with me. I tried to change the subject, but he kept bringing the conversation back to his ailments.

After ten minutes in the park, he was breathing heavily, and I suggested we stop for a cup of tea at the India International Centre. But he did not drink tea or coffee. It wasn't because the doctor had advised him against it; he had foisted this prohibition on himself. So, we found a bench nearby, facing Sikandar Lodi's tomb. My friend had slipped quietly into the role of a senior citizen. Unlike me, who is always fighting old age, he was comfortable eating 'early-bird specials', taking Caribbean cruises and doing what the well-off elderly do in America.

'What's an early-bird special?' I asked.

He explained that it was early dinner at a low price to attract retired seniors in the evening—a ploy by restaurants to fill seats when they would otherwise be empty. I wondered whether he genuinely liked the early-bird special. Was he unthinkingly playing a role? He must have guessed what I was thinking. He told me he avoided silly ideas such as 'you're as young as you feel', which was a sure recipe to make a trim fifty-year-old flop down dead in his tracksuit.

Suddenly, he turned nostalgic on me, reminding me how we had first met in the summer of 1963 in Chandigarh, when I was deciding what to do with my life. I had rejected the academic world after graduating from Harvard and had found inspiration in the story of the mouse merchant.

'Imagine! Rejecting a prestigious academic life at Harvard and Oxford for an uncertain business career!' he said. 'But then, you were always a bit odd!'

Soon it was time for him to leave, and we walked back home. After he left, I decided that old age is worse than death. Death, at least, ended in nothingness. But old age continued as a travesty of life, with a frozen past and a dead future.

My visitor, however, had opened up the past, and I wondered what to do with it. When you get to be my age, you are always knocking into your past. There are things you remember and things you forget. Memory chooses what to bring into the present. Sometimes, these memories are sad, other times happy. Sometimes, these memories are of events that might not have happened at all. What matters in the end is not what happened but what you remember. And it might influence how you choose to live.

My visitor had called me 'odd'. Well, you would be a bit odd too if you had to live your life on the edge of the ridiculous. I was five when I first hit the wall of absurdity. A policeman's senseless murder on the railway platform in Jalandhar awakened me early to the madness of religious crowds during Partition. I suffered the same temporary insanity in kindergarten. Trying to help Ayan, I ended up hurting him. Again, at age thirteen, I was reminded of life's absurdity when my high school vice principal refused to let me into the college prep section because he saw a 'coloured boy getting too big for his boots'; America was preaching integration but practising segregation. When I started working, I faced full-blown lunacy during the Licence Raj. I was hauled up when the sales of Vicks VapoRub hit the roof during a flu epidemic and was treated like a criminal because we had produced more than our licence permitted. Absurd incidents such as these became raw material in my lifelong struggle for another sort of moksha.

I cannot imagine my life without a past. What if I died at twenty? Oh, no . . . then I wouldn't have met Bunu, nor had two lovely sons—I would have lost out on the delights of family life. What if I died at thirty? I would never have got to be CEO and missed out on the rough and tumble of the business life. If I died at fifty, I wouldn't have tasted success and fame as a writer. What about now? Is there anything more I desire? How about a Nobel Prize? A few years ago, I was bowled over when my Harvard roommate, Christopher Sims, won the Nobel Prize in economics. I wondered how it must feel, falling asleep at night, smiling and thinking,

'I won the Nobel, Mother!' Was this how Chris was feeling? Or are Nobel laureates like everyone else: ever ambitious, ever dissatisfied, hankering for more?

Of course, I don't deserve, nor seriously desire a Nobel. Certainly not when I am on the wrong side of my seventies, under a sentence of death. Life at seventy-five is just as absurd as it was at twenty-five, but at seventy-five one is more aware of the absurdities. The only authentic path is to be yourself. I'm the same person who was dubbed 'Nahin Kumar' by his kindergarten teacher, because I was always on the brink of trouble. My sales manager fired me on the first day at work because I asked too many questions. The seal of my all-natural moksha is that I have never been ashamed in front of myself, knowing that *only I could build the bridge to cross the river of my life.* Each of us faces pressures of expectations and conformity. People did try, without success, to force me to wear more conventional masks. They're still at it—now they want me to don the mask of a helpless senior citizen. But I refuse to do so.

When the curtain comes down on my life, I might discover that the performance was not entirely before an empty theatre. There may be a few stragglers in the audience filing out. One would exclaim, 'Lucky fellow,' as he steps on to the street. He would be right. Without a doubt, 'luck' played a key supporting role in the performance. I did not have to live with the sort of tragedy of a mother who has lost a child. My torments were more modest—when I was not loved in return, for example. My luck began at my birth. Had Bauji listened to the barber, my mother would not have married my father, and I wouldn't have learnt the difference between 'making a life' and 'making a living'—the two expressions that have defined my life. Had my father not been transferred to America when I was a teenager, I might not have gone to Harvard, where I learnt the art of making a life. Had I gone on to do a PhD in philosophy, I would neither have become a writer nor a CEO. These are some of the beguiling 'what ifs' of my life. You get the point: it is sobering to remember that the big decisions in your life were not yours to make.

Still, I am lucky to have lived when I have. Going by the headlines, you would think the world was going to hell in a handbasket, but that's not my experience. Famines, starvation and slavery are gone. People are better fed, clothed, housed and educated than ever in human history. A newborn can hope to live beyond eighty, and if it's a girl, she will have a life of far greater dignity. Clean water appears at the flick of a finger, and there are pills to erase deadly infections. Wars may not have vanished, but there's been relative peace since my birth during World War II. Knowledge, culture and entertainment are available in a shirt pocket. These are human accomplishments, and I feel fortunate to have witnessed them.

And my own life too has been quite the performance—a long-running one too. I began running in Lyallpur, and I've been running ever since. Yes, it's been exhausting! There were many twists in the tale—the most dramatic one in mid-life, when I stitched a new garment and put on a new mask, hoping it would fit me better. It did, the one-man show became truer. But if Nietzsche is to be to believed, 'all truth is crooked'. So are all lives. At the time of living, it's all zigs and zags. Only in retrospect do we straighten the narrative. While reliving my life, I looked for a pattern to help me make some sort of sense of my life. I looked in corners, I looked deep in the nooks of my memory. Eventually, I found it in a certain sort of freedom, an all-natural moksha. And now, it is time to free myself from words. It is time to act and complete the work in progress.

I may have entered the world crying, but I want to go out laughing. And now I'll laugh at anything. But I don't like laughing alone. Crying comes naturally to us. Laughing needs learning, acquiring the right attitude—the levity of laghima that Hanuman possessed, gambolling over the clouds above the Himalayas. My real hero, however, is Kamble. He lived a life of dignity, without a burden, taking his work but never himself seriously. Easy in his harness, he eased my transition from academic to business life. Music has also helped, although I haven't written about it. I often spend a quarter to half an hour listening to Bach in the midst of my day of busyness. It is an amazing, mysterious phenomenon, which, like laughter, comes closest to expressing the inexpressible.

Sometimes, though, there is sadness in my laughter. It isn't easy to do what India has done—become a free, vibrant nation, lifting 400 million people above the poverty line. My sadness, however, comes from its failure to become a middle-class country. I had dearly hoped in *India Unbound* that it would create an industrial revolution like our East Asian neighbours. But it has failed to do so, which has meant a failure to create middle-class jobs. Half the population is still toiling in the farms. With robotics and artificial intelligence on the horizon, it's going to be even more difficult in the future to create the jobs that machines will be able to do better than us. India's first forty out of the seventy-five years as a free country were a washout, in any case, under the Licence Raj. In the next thirty years, India did better. It has leapt, however, from a 'green' to a digital revolution, skipping the industrial revolution. What, then, of the hopes of the aspiring young? Are they forever condemned to a bleak life of low productivity?

Another sadness behind my sweet–sour laughter comes from the realization that my life is closing the curtains on a liberal age, which began at the end of World War II, in revulsion to the senseless violence of fascism, nationalism and dictatorship. The new hopeful age led to the spread of liberal democracies, globalization and welfarism. But that age seems to be coming to an end as the world is relapsing into illiberal nationalism, autocracy and fundamentalism. I have been an enthusiastic globalizer all my life, wondering sometimes why my love for my country has to stop at the borders. I regard all wars as civil wars, because we are human beings first and citizens of nations afterwards.

On a personal level, my entire existence has been a struggle to be free. I want to die, living, breathing the spirit of moksha in my own way, not owing allegiance to anyone—certainly not to rulers, heavenly or earthly. My worldly moksha is not some permanent state of enlightenment but a capacity to be free at this moment. I have an uneasy feeling, though, that my life's story is ending all too soon. There may not be enough time to fully implement my all-natural moksha and fulfil my destiny. It's not an easy path. I still tend to take myself far too seriously. I'm still too self-directed, finding it difficult to be other-directed. Empathy does not come naturally; it has to be cultivated. My 'goodwill' is still underdeveloped, and I'm too far behind in my aspiration for true compassion.

The urge to write a memoir is partially rooted in fear of death. I want to leave behind messages for my children and grandchildren, reminding them that I, too, was here. I, too, had the Belgian chocolate shake at Big Chill in Khan Market. I, too, found it 'amazing'! As I approach the finish line, I find myself asking once again, 'Is this really about me?' Is it a true account of a refugee kid from the dusty plains of Punjab? Is the life I am finishing the one I began? These questions freak me out. Once the panic is gone, I realize there is no real me. We are all constructed selves, hiding behind the masks we wear each day of our lives.

We live for a while, and then we die. It matters to us how we live our life in ways that it doesn't to animals. We want our lives to have meaning.

We also care about how we die. My idea of a happy death is to slip away gently, in the same way as I fall asleep. I want to die a natural death, without a doctor in sight. I want to go lightly, surrounded by beauty and good cheer, listening to the music of life with a smile on my face. When death smiles at me, I want to smile back. Socrates, too, was in good humour at his deathbed. Laghima is as much the art of dying as the art of living. Even though I know the answer, my famous last words will be: 'What's next?'

Acknowledgements

Writing a memoir demands reliving one's life, and reliving it, as I've said, is better than living it. While I was recreating mine, a number of generous souls came by to help me along the way. My happiest task is to express my gratitude. You are (in no particular order): Charlie Lee-Potter, David Housego, Oscar Pujol, Vineet Gill, Tarini Uppal, Milee Ashwarya, Tyler Richard, Mrinalini Patwardhan Mehra, Puru Das, Kim Das, Bob Goldman, Christopher Minkowski, Rebecca Gowers, Peter Akers, Phil Oldenburg, Jasbir Singh, Jane Anslev, Janaki Kathpalia, Montek Ahluwalia, Frank Trentman, Uma Waide, Jenni Watson, Joydeep Mukerji, Kunal Shroff, Prasenjit Basu and Camillo Formigatti. Thank you!

Scan QR code to access the
Penguin Random House India website